Shalom!

Ruth Gruber

AHEAD
OF
TIME

BOOKS BY RUTH GRUBER

Rescue: The Exodus of the Ethiopian Jews
Haven: The Unknown Story of 1,000 World War II Refugees
Raquela: A Woman of Israel
They Came to Stay
Felisa Rincón de Gautier: The Mayor of San Juan
Israel on the Seventh Day
Science and the New Nations
Puerto Rico: Island of Promise
Israel Today: Land of Many Nations
Israel Without Tears
Destination Palestine: The Story of the Haganah Ship
    Exodus 1947
I Went to the Soviet Arctic
Virginia Woolf: A Study

AHEAD OF TIME

MY EARLY YEARS AS A FOREIGN CORRESPONDENT

RUTH GRUBER

WYNWOOD® PRESS
New York, New York

Unless otherwise indicated, all photos are courtesy of the author.
This is a work of nonfiction, and for the sake of privacy, a number of names have been changed.

Library of Congress Cataloging-in-Publication Data

Gruber, Ruth, 1911–
    Ahead of time : my early years as a foreign correspondent / Ruth
Gruber.
      p.   cm.
    Includes index.
    ISBN 0-922066-64-7
    1. Gruber, Ruth, 1911–   . 2. Foreign correspondents—United
States—Biography. 3. Foreign correspondents—Europe—Biography.
4. Germany—History—1933–1945. 5. Soviet Union—
History—1925–1953. I. Title.
PN4874.G78A3   1991
070.4'332'092—dc20
[B]   90-22414
                                      CIP

Copyright © 1991 by Ruth Gruber
Published by WYNWOOD® Press
New York, New York
An Imprint of Gleneida Publishing Group
Printed in the United States of America
First Edition

For my children
Celia and David Michaels
my daughter, Barbara Seaman
and
my new daughter, Gail Dratch

Contents

Part One
BROOKLYN

1

1935

I paced the room. Had I been followed? Was the phone tapped? Was there a microphone hidden somewhere—in the ceiling perhaps, or behind the heavy German drapes?

It was nearly twilight. Outside the hotel window, the latticed steeples of the Cologne Cathedral—the Kölner Dom—stretched upward toward the summer sky.

Somewhere I had read that music drowned out a microphone, scrambled the voices. I switched on the radio. Beethoven's Violin Concerto filled the room.

I was mad to do what I was doing. Was any traveler safe from their surveillance? Surely they knew that I was a Jew.

From London I had written Johann, "I shall be arriving in Cologne on Tuesday. If you want to see me, come to the [Kölner Dom] Hotel at 5:30 in the afternoon."

That would give him the choice. If it were not safe for him to see me, he wouldn't come. If he had become a Nazi, then surely he wouldn't come. Still, I had to know.

Four years before, as Hitler was marching to power, we had met

*at the University of Cologne. Our friendship grew out of reading
Goethe and Rilke together, walking hand in hand through the great
German forests, impassioned discussions of German philosophers
and musicians. In that one year, on an exchange fellowship from
America, I had come as close as I could to German life, to the
Germany of Goethe's* Faust *and* The Sorrows of Werther.

*"Marry me," Johann had implored. "We, who come from two
religions, two cultures, two different civilizations, we will bring
strength to each other. We will bring strong, fresh blood to both our
races."*

*Races! The word had not yet become the hated word the Nazis
would make it. Sitting in the hotel room with its heavy German
furniture, I could still picture him on the platform of the railroad
station, seeing me off to America—the narrow, poetic face, the
shining black hair, and the dark eyes that seemed to have glints
and shadows of the Black Forest.*

*He spoke with urgency. "It's true, the Nazis are getting more
powerful every day, but there are also social democrats and communists and Prussian Junkers. And they're fighting each other.
We're not like them, you and I. We can have a beautiful life, and
together we can change what's happening here."*

*I knew he believed his own words, believed that two young stu-
dents could make a difference in this German world. I wanted to
believe it too.*

*"I can't make any decision until I go home," I said. "I must put
distance between us. Give me time."*

I had gone home to Brooklyn.

*A few months later my grandfather, Zayda Moishe-Avigdor Gru-
ber, who looked like Moses in my storybooks, died in his sleep. His
death shook me. On Saturdays and holidays, when I was four and
five, he had taken me by the hand to his little synagogue in Williamsburg and let me sit beside him. (Little girls could sit in the men's
section.) Solemnly, I drank in the prayers and the chanting, for I
was sitting next to my own Moses.*

I climbed the stairs of the tenement in which he had lived for forty years, since the day he had landed at Ellis Island from Odessa, where he and my grandmother had run a kosher inn. When I stopped at the stairwell on the second floor, his voice seemed to come to me: "You cannot marry this young man, no matter how fine, how noble you think he is. He is a Christian. This is your home. Here you belong. In America, among us. This is your fate."

I entered the spotless apartment. My grandfather lay like a dead monarch on the high white bed. I whispered to him, weeping, "Zayda, I heard you."

That afternoon I wrote to Johann. "It's like a fever that has broken. I know now it can never be."

He persisted. "You are wrong. We belong together. Give yourself more time. You will see that I am right."

In January 1933 Hitler came to power.

"He will not last," people said. "The man is ridiculous. In a few months he will be exposed and finished."

I was not so sanguine. Though I had fallen in love with Germany, I knew its dark side too. In that student year of 1932, despite the anguished warnings of the Jewish family I lived with, I had gone to a Hitler rally at the Messehalle, *the huge Exhibition Hall on the Rhine. I had clutched my American passport in my purse, my heart beating so loud I was afraid the storm troopers would hear it and grab me.*

Huge swastika banners waved in the packed hall; the stage was festooned with flags; brown uniforms with red swastika armbands were everywhere; anti-Semitic songs kept the crowd charged with shock waves of hatred.

Suddenly the audience screamed. Hitler was marching toward the podium, followed by stern-faced storm troopers. He waited on the stage until there was silence. Then he spoke, his voice hoarse, hysterical. He ranted against the Weimar Republic, against capitalists and communists, against America, against Jews. His audience shrieked with approval, their hysteria matching his. "Juda verecke [May the Jew croak]," he shouted. "Juda verecke." The crowd took up the cry. "Juda verecke. Juda verecke."

13

I left the Messehalle *unattacked but sick at heart. Germany had two faces. "Das Land der Dichter und Denker," the land of poets and thinkers, was also the land of* Lumpenproletariat *and screaming racists.*

Now, three years later, I walked restlessly to the tall window in the hotel room, drew aside the dark drapes and looked down at the city with its cluster of narrow medieval streets and its vertical electric signs, like Chinese banners, blinking the names of beer parlors and movies, and beyond the streets, the Rhine river on whose banks Johann and I had walked countless days and nights.

Would he be in brown uniform? Would he come?

Late afternoon shadows fell over the Cathedral. Down below I saw a group of storm troopers marching and singing. On the sidewalk, passersby waved at them.

Screams came from a nearby building. I saw two storm troopers pull an old man out of a house. His cries filled the air. But on the street there was silence.

2
October 1, 1911

I was born in a shtetl—a shtetl called Williamsburg—in Brooklyn.

At five and a half, I learned about birthing. Mama, short and stout, with thick, curly, prematurely gray hair, shrewd gray eyes, a determined chin, and wide hips, had given birth to four children in less than eight years. I was the youngest. Then, at twenty-nine, she discovered she was pregnant again. She was mortified. She was too old to have more children. What would the neighbors on Moore Street think? She told no one, not even my grandmother, Baba Rockower. Mama hid her shame beneath a huge blue woolen cape.

On a warm afternoon in May, she corralled her four children. "You," she said to my oldest brother, who was twelve and street-smart, "you take Harry and Betty and go to the movies. Here's a nickel for each of you." (For a nickel, two could see a movie.) Then she turned to me. "You're too small to go with them. You go in the bedroom and take a nap."

"And Dave," she ordered my father, "it's time. Run down to the corner drugstore and call Dr. Hyman. Don't call from our store. I don't want the customers to hear."

I tiptoed out of bed and watched from the bedroom door as Mama went to the kitchen, flung an oilcloth across the round table, hoisted her heavy body on a kitchen chair, and climbed onto the table. In minutes, I heard her drawing in sharp breaths that seemed to give her pain. Soon she cried out. There were other sounds I had never heard before. Then I saw her bend forward and lift a baby swathed in blood from between her legs.

At that moment Papa and the doctor ran up the stairs. While Dr. Hyman bent over the baby, Mama scolded them, "Where were you until now?"

Papa was contrite. "Three people were ahead of me at the telephone."

"You couldn't tell them it was an emergency!"

"Then they would have heard me, and you didn't want anybody to hear."

I fled back to bed and pulled the quilt over my eyes.

Mama was young and strong and had delivered her baby herself, yet custom demanded that she spend the next ten days in bed as a *kimpeturin*, a woman who had just given birth. Baba Rockower came every day to prepare her food and bring her the baby, wrapped in fresh white swaddling clothes. On the eighth day, my little brother, Irving, named Israel in Hebrew, was circumcised. It was his covenant with God.

Jewishness was my home, and God, sitting up in the sky, was my friend. Whenever I did anything wrong, I ran to the window and whispered, "Excuse me, God, excuse me, God, excuse me, God." He always excused me.

On Moore Street, I thought the whole world was Jewish. The butcher, the grocer, the dressmaker, the corsetiere who made my mother's corsets—everyone was Jewish.

Every day I sat on the street curb, watching and listening. Shabbily dressed hawkers shouted in Yiddish accents: "Old clothes, buy old clothes." "Fix your knives." "Sharpen your tools."

16

"*Gai schoyn* [Move along]." Men sat high up on their wagons, flogging their tired dray horses. I was too small to roller-skate, but my sister, Betty, two years older, dared to clutch the back of a wagon and screamed with delight as she was pulled up the bustling street.

Moore Street smelled of pickles in big barrels, of roasted chestnuts and sweet potatoes, of jelly apples and knishes and *haisse arbes* [chick-peas]. Each morning a man who looked like the giant in "Jack the Giant-killer," with sweat dampening his shirt, carried a huge mound of ice in iron claws from his ice wagon up the stairs to our flat over the liquor store that Papa owned. Then, looking down at me on the curb, he gave me a small chunk of ice to suck. "Take it, child," the giant said in Yiddish, and with his giant hands he patted me gently on the head.

On Saturday, the seventh day, Moore Street rested. The horses and carts did not clomp down the streets; the vendors stayed home; the iceman did not come. Only a few stores were open.

Early Saturday morning, Zayda Gruber came to the house to take me with him to *shul*. "Of all his fourteen grandchildren," Mama told me later, "you were his favorite, almost from the day you were born. I would put you out in the carriage to get fresh air, and he would come into the store, mad like anything. He would wave his finger at me like this." Mama shook her finger angrily. "He would yell at me, '*Nemm ihr arein* [Take her inside]. She slept out there long enough. You don't take enough care of her.' "

For Mama and Papa, Saturday was no day of rest. They locked the liquor store only on the High Holidays—Rosh Hashanah and Yom Kippur—and on the first day of Passover, when the whole family marched proudly to the synagogue. Papa, wrapped in his huge white prayer shawl, sat downstairs with the boys, while Mama, Betty, and I sat upstairs with the women. I sat solemnly, angry if the women chattered. I wished I were down in the big hall with Zayda, praying and swaying and singing in Hebrew, not one word of which I understood.

17

At lunchtime Mama served a big Shabbos meal of gefilte fish, chicken soup, boiled chicken, and applesauce. Then Betty and I walked the six blocks to visit Mama's parents, Baba and Zayda Rockower. They lived over their beer parlor in a corner house that stretched around Bushwick Avenue and Varet Street. Baba, taller than Mama, carried herself erect, always tightly corseted and elegant even in her housedress. Zayda, an engineer in Russia, portly, with a black sweeping mustache, had organized the David Rockower B'nai B'rith Lodge, which met in the meeting hall in their home. Seated on a throne, he presided over boisterous political meetings and pinochle games.

Betty and I were barely inside the kitchen when Baba Rockower made us sit at her round table and eat our favorite *rogalech*, little rolled cakes filled with raisins and nuts. Then, satisfied that we really couldn't put another morsel in our mouths, she said, "Now we go to the lunge." The lunge was a brown leather lounge in the parlor, where she took her daily nap. She handed me her steel hairbrush, stretched out on the couch, and while I stroked and brushed her long chestnut hair, she told us stories of her childhood in Russia.

She had come to America in her twenties and, needing to work, had never found time to go to night school to learn English properly. Her favorite advice to Betty and me was "You be good girls. You no talkit mit de boys. You kiss a boy, you get a baby."

After this weekly admonition, she read us articles from her Yiddish newspaper. Here I learned about Jewish *tzuris*—Jewish trouble—as distraught men and women wrote seeking advice from Dr. Klurman, whose name meant "the wise man." "Dear Doctor Klurman," one man wrote, "I left a wife and six children in Galicia. When I came to America, I was lonely, so I married another woman and now I have three more children. Please Dr. Klurman, what should I do about my wife and children in Galicia?" The questions intrigued me more than the answers.

Before dusk, Betty and I walked home, carrying bags of *rogalech*.

I felt snug and safe and loved in this small, all-encompassing Jewish world.

My Jewish world began enlarging when I entered P.S. 141, a girls' public school. Most of the teachers were young, second-generation Irish women. Teaching was their step up the American ladder, as being a priest or a cop or a politician was the route many of their brothers took. Black women were still on the bottom rung of the ladder. My first-grade teacher was an exception—a strikingly beautiful young black woman who taught our class of Jewish, Irish, Polish, and a few black girls to read and memorize poetry and to cherish books.

On a late spring afternoon I caught sight of her entering our flat over the store. Once again I hid behind the bedroom door as she climbed the stairs.

Mama answered the knock. "Yes?" she asked hesitantly.

I could hardly breathe.

"I am Ruth's teacher," she said.

"Her teacher!" Mama's voice trembled. "Did she do something wrong?"

"No, no. I just wanted to tell you to take good care of her. She loves books so much I'm sure that some day she's going to be a writer."

So she knows, I thought.

A girl's life in Brooklyn was different from a boy's. At three o'clock every day, my brothers went to Hebrew school to prepare for their Bar Mitzvahs. In a bare room with hard benches, their teacher, in a shabby black coat and a shabby black beard, taught them to read the Hebrew words but never taught them what the words meant. With a long stick, he whacked them over the knuckles if they misread a single letter. Mama was constantly bribing him with a bottle of wine from the store. "This is because you're such a good teacher," she lied bravely, "and please don't hit my boys."

Betty and I were jealous that only the boys went to Hebrew

school. "Girls don't need to go," Papa said. "Girls don't get Bar Mitzvah." Bat Mitzvahs for girls would come later. We insisted, and Mama backed us. So we attended Sunday school for awhile, but the teaching was superficial, the teachers inadequate, and we learned little except the Hebrew alphabet and songs we could sing at the Passover Seder.

Papa was our King Solomon, the wise patriarch to whom not only we but all our relatives and friends came for advice. Papa was six feet tall, handsome, with kind, gray-green eyes, a red mustache, and a gentle voice that he never seemed to raise. I loved him for his wisdom and his kindness, and I knew, even as a little girl coming in from the cold, when he bent down and took both my freezing hands in his and blew warm breath on them, that he loved me too.

Every month Papa sent money orders to the relatives in the shtetls in Poland and to others in communist Odessa. And every spring he would round us up: "Children, give me all the clothes you're not wearing any more. It's time to send a bundle to Europe." Even if I protested, "But I like this coat, Pop," he would say, "Send it. They need it more than you."

Mama and Papa respected each other's wisdom, yet it was hard to imagine two more unlikely people in love.

"I didn't want to marry Pop," Mama told me later. "I didn't even like him at first. I wanted my cousin Yidel Rockower. But my mother said, 'Marry Dave, he's a fine man. He'll be good to you.' My friends made fun of me. 'You gonna marry a greenhorn?' He was six years older than me. Once he took me to Coney Island; we went on the boat in 'The Old Mill.' It was dark inside, and he wanted to hold me and kiss me. I pushed him away. Then he wanted to give me a gold ring. My father said, 'You can't take it unless you're serious and you want to marry him.' My mother liked him more than I did."

"Did you fight your mother?" I asked. "Did you want to run away?"

Mama looked at me. "No, I listened to my mother, not like children today. Before the wedding ceremony—it was in the Capitol Hall on Manhattan Avenue and it was two o'clock in the morning because we invited so many guests—my mother was leading me to the *Chuppah* [the bridal canopy] and she whispered, *Tret im oiff de fiess, denn du vest sein dee balabusta* [Step on his feet, then you'll be the boss].' "

"But Mom, wasn't it awful to go to bed with a man you didn't like?"

"I was seventeen when I got married. I didn't know from anything. I didn't know what you do the first night. After the ceremony, my mother and my mother-in-law took me to the apartment Papa rented on Humboldt Street, and they said, 'Do whatever Dave tells you to do.' The first night we didn't do anything. They came and looked at the sheet and there was no blood. Then I began to fall in love with him."

Where Papa was quiet, Mama yelled. Where Papa mediated, she controlled. She forbade my brothers to read Horatio Alger books, the paperback stories of poor urchins who became millionaires. She had never read them but had somehow decided they were "dirty." The boys hid them under their bed covers and read them anyway.

Nearly everything Mama knew, she had taught herself. She had come to America as a five-year-old in 1893, twelve years after Czar Alexander of Russia was assassinated and the Cossacks began burning and looting and raping women in the shtetls. She was not allowed to finish elementary school, for her parents needed her to scrub the floors and wash the underwear of the immigrant boarders they took in to make ends meet.

But Mama was smart and sharp, and she taught us to hate idleness the way nature hates a vacuum. At dawn every day she chopped hundreds of pieces of herring and small, round slices of rye bread for the free lunch in the store. Afternoons she sewed dresses for Betty and me; mine were always too big, so they would fit next year. She taught me to sew fine lace around my panties and to crochet cotton lace on doilies for the armchairs. She cooked our meals in Jewish style with *schmaltz*, [chicken fat], and on Fridays the whole house smelled deliciously of the golden-braided challah baked and the almond zwieback she hid under the bed. She wanted to make sure we wouldn't find the cake before Shabbos. We always found it.

Summers she loaded huge baskets of food and shepherded all five of us and six or eight of the neighbors' children to Coney Island on the open-air trolley car.

"Are these all your children?" The conductor stared at us unbelievingly. Children paid half fare.

No longer ashamed of having a baby at the advanced age of twenty-nine, she said proudly, "Of course they're all my children," paid the fare, and promptly fell asleep until the trolley pulled into the station at Coney Island, with its wonderful smell of saltwater taffy and taffy kisses.

We were all sizes and shapes of children as we marched like a Fourth of July parade, carrying food and bathing suits, toward the beach and boardwalk. Mama paid our way into Taunton's Bathhouse, a shambles of wooden locker rooms lined up on a shaky wooden walkway over the sand.

On the beach Mama spread a blanket with the food and fruit while we raced into the water, swimming and splashing each other, coming out to play catch, then back into the ocean while Mama, in her black bathing suit, with its full skirt billowing around her generous hips and thighs, breaststroked through the waves. After feeding us, she stretched out on the sand and fell asleep. The beach at Coney Island and the trolley-car ride were the only times I saw her sleeping.

Late in the afternoon she gathered us together to go back to Taunton's. While the boys disappeared in the men's section, where, across a transom, we could hear them talking and laughing, Mama, followed by the gaggle of little girls she was chaperoning, opened the heavy doors of the steam room. She helped us pull off our wet bathing suits, rubbed our naked bodies with mineral oil, and, cupping her hands, slapped our backs with a drumbeat rhythm, insisting, "It's good for you. Breathe in the steam, that's good for you too."

The steam was so dense I could hardly see my own hand. But soon through the mist I could see little girls like me with no breasts, sitting on stone benches against the wall, and women like Mama with bosoms dangling like oversize pears or protruding like round honeydew melons, and loose stomachs drooping from childbearing.

I think I loved Mama most in that steam room, the caring, laughing, energetic Mama, slapping our backs and telling us it was good for us.

She always knew what was good for us. She had no use for doctors; she called one only if she thought we were near death. Once when she finally did call a doctor, she read the prescription, which, of course, she never filled. The only word she understood was glycerine. After that, she made us swallow a tablespoon of glycerine for anything from a sore throat to a bellyache.

On special occasions, especially on birthdays, Mama took us to Coney Island's Luna Park. On the carousel, we smaller children sat bravely, holding tight to the prancing horses, while our big brothers and sisters reached up from their steeds, trying to catch the brass ring.

Then on to the steeplechase, where, buckled tight, we held our breath as the car climbed the rickety tracks toward the sky, turned sharply, and with all of us screaming in terror, shot down to the ground again, our screams catching in our throats, until at last, still shaking, we were unbuckled.

"I wasn't a bit scared," we told each other and reluctantly left Coney Island. Mama slept all the way home on the open trolley. Back at the store, Papa had his arms open to embrace us.

In 1917 we woke up to find the big brothers of our friends suddenly in khaki uniform. Soon there were gold stars in some of the windows. The war ended with fireworks and bands playing and parades and girls hugging soldiers they didn't even know. The big brothers of our friends came home, some without arms or legs, and some in wheelchairs. In school we were told triumphantly, "We have won the war, the war to end all wars, the war for democracy."

Prohibition came in 1920. Papa, who would do nothing unpatriotic in this country he loved, closed the liquor store and turned to real estate to support the family. There was a depression in 1921; it was not a good time for real estate, but we lived frugally, and there was money to tide us over.

"Gussie," I heard Papa tell Mama, "it's time to move to a bigger place. The children are getting big. They need more room. We should move into a house of our own."

"What's wrong with where we are?" Mama protested. She hated changing anything that worked.

"A new house will cost us too much," she complained. "Besides, I don't want to move. From here, I can walk to my mother's house every day."

Papa insisted, "We'll find something not too expensive and not too far away."

"I won't know anybody there," she argued, but in the end, unhappy, she organized the move a mile away to the house on Harmon Street and Bushwick Avenue.

It was a turn-of-the-century, castlelike gray stone house with a front stoop, a black swinging gate, and a wrought-iron entrance door leading to the big kitchen-dining room where we did most of our living. In the back of the house there was a garden, a large yard, and a garage that had been a stable, with a steep ladder leading to a huge loft for the horse's hay. An architect had built the house for his own family with a small separate house for his office at the side. In this office, each of us had a desk, and here I began collecting books.

From our Jewish shtetl we had moved unknowingly into a German world. The baker on the corner of Evergreen Avenue was German; the grocer on Himrod Street was German; the beer parlors on Broadway a block away were owned by Germans; even the man who ran the candy store and sold ice-cream cones and my favorite food in the whole world, charlotte russe—even he was German.

In spring and summer and fall, the neighborhood boys played softball in the gutter with my brothers, and in the winter we built fat snowmen together. We knew their families had come from Germany; they knew we were Jews. We were friends, unaware of what was beginning to happen in Germany.

3

Goethe says that children rebel against their parents and return to their grandparents. My rebellion began in Bushwick High School against Mama and Papa, against orthodoxy, and against Brooklyn.

I had been skipped so often in elementary school (mostly because the classes were overcrowded), that I was not yet thirteen when I entered the sophomore grade in high school and came under the influence of Willis N. Huggins, a black history teacher who taught us the tragedy of black discrimination and inspired us to fight it.

Willis Huggins introduced African history into Bushwick High forty years before the civil rights movement.

"I want you to know," he told our class, a mist forming in his brown eyes, "I want you to know the tragedy of Negro men and women and children." (The word "Negro" was used then; "black" came later.)

"Imagine yourselves in an African village," he said. "You're happy young people living in straw huts with your parents and your brothers and your sisters. You're out hunting for food and Arabs capture you, or you're sleeping in your family hut and they tiptoe in and abduct you."

I shuddered. Papa had told me of pogroms he had seen in Russia, with Cossacks riding their horses into the shtetls, murdering Jewish men and women and children. Were the Arabs the Cossacks of Africa?

Mr. Huggins went on. "I want you to imagine how those young boys and girls felt when the Arabs tied them together with iron chains around their legs. They forced them to march for hundreds of miles to the coast. There they were herded like cattle onto slave ships, where many of them died. Those who reached America were sold to white slaveholders in the South."

American history became *his* history to me. He told us he was a follower of Marcus Garvey, the forty-year-old Jamaican Negro who had come to the United States in 1905, proclaiming himself "Provisional President" of Africa and "Leader of the Negro Peoples of the World." Now he was urging American Negroes to return to their African homeland.

"Some day I hope most of us *will* return to Africa," Mr. Huggins said, sharing his longings with us. "Then we will be truly liberated."

One morning he announced, "Try not to be absent from assembly tomorrow. I have a surprise for you."

I could not be absent, for I sat in the first violin section of the orchestra, and we played at every assembly. The next morning I took my seat in the orchestra pit. The students had not yet entered. I tuned my fiddle and looked up at the stage. I stopped tuning. There, next to Mr. MacDonald, our principal, and Mr. Huggins, sat the tallest, handsomest Negro I had ever seen. I recognized him from newspaper photographs advertising him as the mad, tyrannical ruler in Eugene O'Neill's *Emperor Jones*.

Was it possible? Paul Robeson had come to Bushwick High.

The auditorium doors opened. The orchestra burst into the lively "Soldier's March" from *Aïda*. Two by two, the students marched down the aisles. I kept glancing up from the music sheet to the stage, my heart thumping.

After the Pledge of Allegiance and "The Star-Spangled Banner," sung by Robeson as if it were a Verdi opera, Mr. Huggins introduced his friend, "the greatest singer in the world," who sang Negro spirituals, opera arias, musical comedy lyrics, and "Water Boy, Where Are You Hiding?" as we had never heard them sung before.

A few weeks later, Mr. Huggins stopped me after class. "I wonder if you would join me at the theatre for a matinee on Saturday. There's a play I would like you to see."

I felt my head whirring. A teacher taking a pupil to the theatre! Did he take other pupils? Did other teachers take their students too?

In the hallways, I had always seen him hurrying to our class with papers under his arms, never stopping to talk to the white teachers who gossiped and laughed together. Did he stay away from them, or did they avoid him? Later I learned that he was born in Selma, Alabama, in 1886 and had graduated from Columbia University in 1914, when Ivy League universities like Columbia, Harvard, and Yale were trying to prove with "scholarly evidence" that Negroes were an inferior race.

"I've never been to the theatre." I hesitated. "But . . . but I'd love to go."

His face crinkled into a sad smile. "I will pick you up at your home. I imagine your parents don't like you to travel on the train alone to Manhattan."

I expected trouble from Mama and Papa. I primed them carefully. "My history teacher is coming Saturday to take me to a play."

Mama stopped ladling out soup at the table. "How come?"

"He just asked me and I said yes."

"Why did he ask you?" Papa looked worried.

"I don't know, Pop. Just don't be surprised when you see him. He's a Negro."

28

"What did you say?" Mama's voice was rising. "A Negro?"

"That's right."

"You're not scared?" Papa asked.

"He's my teacher."

Papa pulled at his mustache. "It's good he's coming to pick you up, so we can meet him and make sure he's okay."

"Of course he's okay. He's the best teacher in the school."

All week they questioned me about him—"You sure you want to go? What will people say?"—until they reassured each other. In their temple of heroes, teachers were second only to rabbis. For them, teachers could do no wrong.

Saturday morning, Mama said, "Eat your lunch early. Otherwise you'll be hungry all afternoon, and you won't enjoy what you're seeing."

I gulped down some hot chicken soup when I heard the doorbell ring.

Mr. Huggins, in a black wool overcoat, stood at the iron grill door under the stoop, his black felt hat in his hand.

"Please come and meet my parents," I said, leading him through the hallway into the kitchen-dining room.

"It's very nice of you," Papa said, "to take Ruth to the theatre."

Mr. Huggins nodded. "We're going to see *All God's Chillun Got Wings* by Eugene O'Neill."

"Maybe you'd like a bowl of soup before you go?" Mama asked. "Or maybe a glass of tea and some zwieback?"

"Thank you. I wish I could, but we had better leave now. We don't want to be late."

Mama and Papa came with us to the door and then stood inside the front gate, watching their fourth child walk down the street with a black man. I was aware of eyes, of windows suddenly opening and neighbors peering out. I pressed my arms against my body and held my head high.

In the elevated train, people stared at the short young girl who looked even younger than thirteen, straphanging with a thirty-eight-year-old black man with a soft, broad nose and eyes filled with tragedy. I could hear people whispering, "Look at that young kid with a Negro." I cringed. He had heard them. He held up his hand, looked at it, and, in a voice that carried over the rumbling of the wheels, said, "There is not one single ounce of white blood in me."

It became a weekly ritual. Each Saturday we went to a different matinee, most of them plays about race discrimination. He was to fight the tragedy of that discrimination all his life.

In 1932 he became the sixth Negro in Fordham's history to earn a Ph.D., and in 1935, when Mussolini sent his armies into Ethiopia, he traveled to the League of Nations in Geneva to plead the cause of Ethiopian blacks who were being massacred by Italian whites. Appearing before world leaders, he predicted that if the Italian campaign destroyed Ethiopia, it would be "the beginning of a bigger and better Armageddon wherein the nations of the world will claw themselves in such a manner that the World War will look like a kindergarten."

Then something broke. On December 23, 1940, he was seen in Harlem at 11:15 A.M. On December 24, at 1:00 A.M., his overcoat was found on the George Washington Bridge with a suicide note for his wife.

On July 19, 1941, a body washed up in the Hudson. It was identified as the body of Dr. Willis Nathaniel Huggins.

No one ever revealed why he died.

4

The BMT train and the Williamsburg Bridge, flung over the East River, were my escape route from Brooklyn. Manhattan was my promised land. Here the writers lived, those who didn't flee to Paris. Novelists, poets, journalists—the people I admired most in the world—lived, I was sure, in attics in Greenwich Village, where they wrote their deathless works.

Each morning, now fifteen and a freshman at New York University, I climbed the steps to the elevated BMT at Kosciusko Street and sat at the window, watching the tenements flash by, until the train pulled into Marcy Avenue, the Brooklyn station that led to the Williamsburg Bridge.

I descended to the street, then climbed up another set of stairs to the bridge's narrow walkway. Manhattan rose from the river. The soaring stone buildings reflected themselves in the shimmering water, like two magical, identical cities, one real, the other upside down. I filled notebooks with anguished poems (fortunately never published) of how I was being squeezed at home like a sponge and would die if I didn't escape.

From the bridge I walked through streets crowded with the push-carts of Jewish vendors, streets with English noblemen's names—Delancey, Essex, Norfolk, Houston—then to the Bowery, where I stopped at my favorite secondhand bookstore. I reveled in the musty smell of the yellowing pages that often fell apart in my hands. Books. Old books. Secondhand books. If I could hold them, caress them, read them all—Dickens and Thackeray, Tolstoy and Turgenev—the door would open. The door to freedom. The door to being a writer.

It was still early in the morning as, clutching the paper bag of masterpieces that cost a nickel or a dime, I walked on to Washington Square Park, looking up at the university, a factorylike building of gray brick and glass. To me it was a palace.

The first day, my freshman English teacher, a large woman with mottled red cheeks, dressed in a wide skirt and plaid shirt, growled at us and printed on the blackboard: "My name is Mary Barnicle." Then, facing us and still growling, she said, "It is spelled with an *i*, not with an *a*. A barnacle with an *a* is a crustacean than sticks to the bottom of ships. I do not stick to the bottom of anything."

We giggled nervously until her reddish face burst into a smile.

It was a class in freshman composition, and we had to bring in a theme every week. She asked us to write about ourselves, search our own minds, define who we were and where we had come from.

One day she told me, "Miss Gruber, I like the way you write. I would like to send some of your essays to the *Atlantic Monthly*."

My themes to the *Atlantic Monthly*! Words I had written that might be in print. I counted the days and weeks, waiting to hear from the *Atlantic*, until she showed me the form letter rejecting them all.

"Go on writing," she consoled me. "Every writer can paper a bedroom with rejection slips."

A few months into the term, my German teacher, Professor

Adolf Meyer, six feet two, bespectacled and in his forties, invited me to a coffee shop near the university. I rode down the elevator beside him, scarcely reaching his chest, too excited to utter a word.

He too had tried to terrorize us on our first freshman day. "If any of you Jewish students think German is just like Jewish, and that you can pass this course doing no work, you're going to flunk. Yiddish is a language based on Middle High German, which took on words from a lot of European countries that the Jews migrated to. It's written in Hebrew letters. Knowing Yiddish can spoil your German. You better make up your minds right now to forget any Yiddish you know."

How could I forget Yiddish, the Yiddish I had learned from my grandmother? But soon I discovered, whenever I visited Baba Rockower, that my Yiddish words were taking on a German accent. Yiddish had not spoiled my German. German was driving Yiddish out of my head.

In the restaurant, Professor Meyer ordered coffee for two. "You seem to love German," he said.

How could I tell him I loved German because of the way he taught it and because I was falling crazily in love with him?

We began to meet regularly in a coffee shop near the school. I wore high-heeled shoes and dangling earrings, hoping they would make me look taller. I prayed he wouldn't know how young I was.

Professor Meyer taught German with such skill that by the second year I was able to take a job after school translating and typing letters for a German import-export firm.

Papa gave me a weekly allowance of two dollars, but I knew that I would have a better shot at independence if I had some money of my own. Mama was still trying to control my life. She had a roster of cardinal sins. Sleeping with a boy before you were married topped the list, followed by smoking cigarettes. Mama had no knowledge, nor did anyone else then, that cigarettes were dangerous; she just knew that nice girls don't smoke.

Ignoring a girl's need for privacy, Mama prowled through our dresser drawers. One day she discovered cigarette butts I had hidden the night before, intending to flush them down in the morning.

Mama pounced on me when I came home from school.

"You're smoking," she shouted.

I suddenly remembered the telltale butts.

"Don't you ever let me catch you smoking again. What kind of girl are you anyway? The next step you'll be a prostitute walking the street."

I had to escape.

Professor Meyer told me of a summer program at Mount Holyoke College. "It's a German program," he said. "For six weeks, you speak only German. I think you'd enjoy it."

"I'm going to summer school," I announced in the kitchen-dining room, where the family conferences took place.

"You're going to summer school!" Mama was instantly suspicious. "Did you flunk something?"

"No, Mom. It's a summer program where everything is in German."

"You don't know enough German? How come you already had a job 'cause you knew so much German?"

My brother Harry, who was studying medicine at Georgetown University in Washington, was home for a few days. He tried to stop the fight before it escalated. "Ruth, just where is this summer school?"

"Mount Holyoke."

"Where's that?" Mama demanded. "It sounds like a Christian hospital."

"It's in Massachusetts."

"That means you can't come home at night. I forbid it. You're too young to go away from home."

Papa, sitting at the head of the table, looked worried. "Do you have to go?" He never challenged Mama's decisions in front of us, even when he disagreed with them.

"What are you worried about?" I asked them. "I'm not going off to do something crazy. It's just a school to improve my German."

"But you know it already," Papa said.

"I want to know it better. I saved up money from my job. I'll pay for it myself."

Harry set down his cup of Mama's boiled coffee which his medical school cronies affectionately called "Gussie's bilgewater."

"You should let her go," he said. "It's a good idea to know a foreign language so well that you speak it like a native. Everybody should speak at least two languages."

"She knows—how many already?" Mama counted on her fingers. "German, Yiddish, English. French and Spanish she learned in high school. How much more does she need?"

"It'll help her later on in life," Harry persisted. "Besides, she'll get credit at NYU for it."

"Oh," Mama was suddenly interested. "She'll get credit! So how long is it? Only six weeks, and she saved up the money to go. What do you say, Dave? Should we let her go?"

Mama made the decisions, but she turned to Papa for approval. Papa nodded silently.

I looked at Harry with gratitude. What a noble doctor he will make, I thought.

Mama spent the next days sewing dresses I rarely wore (she still made them to fit the next year), helped me pack my bag, and even prevailed on my brother Bob, who had a convertible roadster with a rumble seat, to drive us up to Mount Holyoke so she could see where I was going to live.

"So this is what an out-of-town college looks like." Mama looked approvingly at Mount Holyoke's ivy-covered walls, garden walks, and great sheltering trees.

"Just drop me off here, Bob," I said, grabbing my bag. "Thanks for the ride, and both of you, have a good trip home."

"Not so fast," Mama said. "I want to meet whoever is in charge."

"It isn't necessary, Mom. Really."

"Don't tell me." She brushed past me and marched into the building, found the admissions office, and introduced herself to the woman in charge. I stood by, shrinking with embarrassment. "It's the first time my Ruthie is going away from home. So take good care of her."

"We will do our best." The woman smiled affably. I wondered if she had ever encountered anyone like Mama.

"Come on, Mom," Bob was impatient. "Leave her alone already. We have to drive all the way back to Brooklyn."

I walked back to the car with them and waved goodbye. Alone at last. Six weeks of freedom.

At noon in the oak-walled dining room, I met the other students. They were all instructors and professors in German, mostly from the South and the Middle West.

We ate and drank and studied and slept in German. English was *verboten*. Breakfast was a heavy German meal of eggs and bacon and fried potatoes. I carefully slipped the bacon to the side of the plate. In Harmon Street, Mama kept a kosher kitchen, and bacon never came into our house.

Classes began at nine, all in advanced German language and literature. We read Goethe and Schiller, plays by Lessing, and modern novels by von Kleist. We wrote German essays on what we were reading and took oral and written exams. Everyone seemed to pass with an *A*.

Each afternoon I would climb a hill on the wooded campus and shout German poetry to the wind. At night we sang German songs, popular songs, classical songs, even religious songs. Learning my name was Gruber, some of the elderly professors decided that I was a descendant of the Franz Gruber who had written "Stille Nacht, Heilige Nacht [Silent Night, Holy Night]." Nothing I could say—that I was Jewish, that my parents had come not from Germany or Austria but from Russia—would dissuade them. It was what they wanted to believe, what they were taking back to their colleges and universities. I could almost hear them back home in Michigan and Florida and Tennessee: "There was this young girl in the program—and she was descended from the great Franz Gruber."

Mount Holyoke opened an escape hatch out of Brooklyn. It was my first deliverance. I was ready for more.

5
Autumn 1928

I wanted to be a writer, but I needed to earn money if I was to be independent and to win freedom. I read a notice on the NYU bulletin board: "Typist wanted. Please call the Employment Office."

I hurried to the office on the ground floor and asked about the job.

"It's not an easy job," the employment officer warned me. "It's with a Hungarian nobleman. A baron. We've been sending him a new typist nearly every week, but after a few days he fires them. They're like revolving-door typists. Are you willing to try?"

"I'm willing."

"His name is Dr. Imre de Jósika-Herczeg. He's the president of some association of Hungarian emigrés and refugees. He lives right near here in Washington Square. Here's the address—28 West 10th Street. Give him this paper when you meet him."

I hurried to a quiet street shaded with tall trees and stopped in front of a three-story brownstone. A butler ushered me up a flight of heavily carpeted stairs to a dark living room where I sat nervously on the edge of a petit-point chair to await the baron.

He was a short, stocky man in his late fifties with silky, silver hair, a silver mustache, and a monocle hanging on his chest. He wore a dark suit with a striped vest trimmed in white cord and pearl-gray spats. He held himself stiff and upright, like an officer in the court of the Emperor Franz Josef, and he stared at me as if he wanted to probe my mind and terrify me at the same time.

"I am writing the history of Hungary," he said in a Hungarian accent. "I have had many writers, one more stupid than the other. Journalists. Editors. Incompetent, all of them. Now I have a new writer, a magazine editor. A lady. I want you to type her notes. I will return in one hour."

He handed me a batch of notes on a yellow foolscap pad and showed me up another flight of stairs to his bedroom-study. It had a double bed with a heavy bedspread matching the heavy drapes, a dresser, and a desk at one of the windows, with a typewriter on it.

I began typing the lady editor's rough notes describing the collapse of the Austro-Hungarian Empire after the Great War. Exactly one hour later, the baron returned, fixed the monocle over his eye and studied the pages.

"I pay one dollar an hour. Can you come back tomorrow?"

"I can come only in the afternoon. I have classes all morning."

"Afternoons are good for me."

One afternoon, after I had been typing his manuscript for about a month, he burst into the study. "Stop typing. This lady editor—she is stupid like all the others. I am going to use you as my writer."

"But . . . but . . . but, Baron," I started to say. I had never written anything except term papers and the themes Miss Barnicle had tried to get published.

He brooked no interruption. "I will dictate to you," he said. "You will come to my country home in Greenwich by train."

"But I have classes at the university."

"Then you will come in the time you have no classes, and you will come on Saturdays. I will pay you the same as before."

I knew two things about Greenwich, Connecticut—that it was famous for its millionaires and for its restrictive policy barring Jews from owning homes or property.

Early on Saturday morning I caught the train at Grand Central Station. A liveried chauffeur met me at the Greenwich station, opened the door of a black limousine, and drove through town onto the driveway of a mansion. A maid in starched uniform led me around the outside of the house to a small back room whose only furniture was a desk, a swivel chair, and a typewriter. But it was flooded with sunlight, and its window overlooked a vista of green lawn framed by great oak and maple trees.

The baron entered the back room looking like a country squire in white pants, a navy blue blazer with gold buttons, and white shoes.

"Let us go outside and walk," he said. "I will talk and then you will typewrite what I have told you."

For an hour or more I walked and scribbled in a school notebook as the baron described the agony of his beloved Hungary.

"Today we will talk about the terrible Treaty of Trianon which was concluded between the Allied Powers and Hungary. It was signed in November 1918 by Count Károlyi, that unintelligent, stupid, radical socialist dictator. Hungary was torn apart, given to other states by inferior, selfish, immature, stupid politicians. We lost ten million people with our beautiful forests, our silver and gold mines, our oil. Everything was stripped away from us. You hear?"

He turned his head to look at me for the first time and commanded, "Now you will go inside and typewrite."

The next day I went to the public library on DeKalb Avenue and brought home an armful of books on Hungary. I read about the Mongol invasion in the thirteenth century. The Turkish conquests in the fifteenth and sixteenth centuries. The union with Austria in

1867 that created the Austro-Hungarian Empire, where Germans and Magyars ruled a polyglot of subject peoples, including gypsies and Jews, until that fateful day of June 28, 1914, when a Serbian nationalist named Gavrilo Princip assassinated the Archduke Franz Ferdinand, the potential heir to the Austro-Hungarian throne, and destroyed the empire and world peace.

On my next visit to Greenwich, I felt a little more secure as we paced the quiet baronial park, its silence broken only by the birds singing in the trees and the baron's voice denouncing his three arch enemies—Count Károlyi, Béla Kun, and the Romanians.

I chased after him as his words became more hysterical until he grew tired, turned on his heels, and headed back to the house. "Enough for today. Now typewrite."

I let the blood spill out of the keys. I had learned that the bloodier my words, the happier the baron was. In white heat I wrote, "The blue Danube was no longer blue; it was flowing with the blood of six hundred innocent Hungarian people. Red Terror stalked the tragically truncated and wounded land. Hungary was bleeding."

A few days later the baron picked up where he had left off, even the note of hysteria.

"Béla Kun's Soviet Republic fell after one hundred thirty-three days. It was overthrown by the angry Hungarians and by hordes of Romanian troops. They marched in under the pretext that they were saving Hungary from Bolshevism. They invaded Hungary on the first day of August, 1919, for their own selfish purposes. It was rape. Rape. Romanian rape."

I visualized how I would describe beautiful Hungarian women being raped by hordes of Romanian barbarians. I would depict the rape like the pogroms Papa had told me about in Russia. Instead of drunken Cossacks breaking into the shtetls robbing, looting, screaming, massacring, I would substitute drunken Romanians. But I stopped short. The baron was not talking of women.

"The Romanians raped our libraries," his voice shook. "They raped our schools. They raped our institutions. They even tried to rape the great Royal Museum of Arts, but they were halted by General Bandholtz, the head of the United States military mission in Budapest."

Reluctantly I put the beautiful Hungarian women out of my mind.

The baron continued the saga.

"There was a counterrevolution. The Romanian troops were forced to leave Budapest, and the White Terror took over, killing those who had been sympathizers of Béla Kun and the Red Terror. Then in January of 1920, Hungary held its first election for a national assembly. The assembly elected Admiral Miklós Horthy, who had been commander-in-chief of the Austro-Hungarian fleet."

Horthy was high on the baron's short rostrum of heroes. They had both been part of the Magyar ruling class.

After several months we finished the section "Hungary After the War," and the job ended.

"Thank you," the baron said, writing the usual check for a dollar an hour. "You did a good job." It was the first time he had praised me. I was free to look for another job.

A few weeks later I received a telephone call from his valet. "The baron asks you to come to the house tonight at 8 P.M."

I was startled. "Tonight?"

"Yes. Be prompt. You know the baron is furious if anyone comes late."

I dressed carefully with a hat and veil, high heels, and white kid gloves.

"Where are you going?" Mama looked up from her sewing machine. "You just came from New York and already you're going back—and so dressed up?"

"It's the baron, Mama. He wants me to come to his house."

"What? You never worked for him at night."

"Maybe he's having a party, maybe it's a musical evening. He has a big grand piano. I'll tell you about it when I get home."

I took the BMT to New York, staring at the illuminated East River. I was as baffled as Mama. What could he really want? We had finished the segment. There was no more typing to be done.

Long before eight, I waited in the baron's living room while, one by one, five men and women entered. They sat on the petit-point chairs whispering, "What is this? After firing us, is he trying to hire us back?" They were the journalists and editors who had worked on the book.

The grandfather clock in the hallway struck eight. The baron swept in and announced brusquely, "I have brought you all back to my house to listen to the way I wanted this book to be written. I have invited the writer of one of the most important parts of the book to come tonight to read it to you herself."

He handed me the manuscript I had written. "Please begin."

I was aghast. These were *real* writers, *real* editors. The pages trembled in my hand.

I started reading. I began to delete some of the bloodiest sections, prepared to tell the baron, if he complained, that I was afraid the evening was getting too long and the people would walk out. He seemed not to notice. Occasionally, I caught a sardonic smile under the silver mustache.

When I finished, the writers and editors stood up. One of the men shook my hand. "Congratulations," he said mischievously. "You did it."

In the train, riding home to Brooklyn, I wondered how the baron could consider the writing of a teenager more valuable than that of experienced journalists and editors. Why was my writing more acceptable to him than theirs? Was it because I had written what he wanted to hear?

Six years later, the publishing arm of the American Hungarian Daily, Inc., published his book, *Hungary After a Thousand Years*. I turned to the section "Hungary After the War" and sighed with relief. Some far wiser and more experienced hand had blue-penciled my bloodiest creations. Still, much that I had written in that back room in Greenwich remained.

The baron's good friend, Count Albert Apponyi, wrote a laudatory preface: "I very much warmly recommend it to public attention." But none of the writers or editors or revolving-door typists were given credit. We were all ghosts.

6

No pregnant cat was safe on Harmon Street.

My brother Harry and some of his pre-medical school classmates snatched any cat with a protruding stomach. They shoved the cat, scratching and clawing and screeching, into a burlap bag, carried her at arm's length to our garage, and cautiously mounted the ladder to the former hayloft that was now Harry's laboratory.

Even the thought of what those future surgeons and radiologists and tuberculosis specialists were doing made me ill.

"How can you dissect a poor cat?" I demanded when I learned what they were carrying.

"We have to do it for anatomy," Harry tried to explain.

"Ugh. But you all seem to enjoy it."

"Who enjoys it? You know the first time I saw an operation and all that blood, I nearly fainted."

"So why are you becoming a doctor?"

He shrugged his shoulders. "Do I have any option?"

I knew Harry wanted to be an engineer. There was almost nothing in the house that he couldn't repair. But engineering schools were closed to most Jews. And Harry, who worried about Mama's and Papa's feelings, was fulfilling their dream. *My son, the doctor.* Despite the quotas, the *numerus clausus* in medical schools, he was admitted in 1928 to Georgetown Medical in Washington, D.C.

He bought a secondhand car for thirty-five dollars; its loose doors he glued together "with spit and adhesive tape."

"I'll miss you," I said, trying to smile as I waved him off to Washington.

In his second year he invited me to spend a week with him. While he was at classes, I sat in a small park near the Capitol building feeding squirrels and daydreaming that we would grow old together; he would be a bachelor and I an old maid, and we would live in an apartment where he could build whatever he wanted.

After four years at Georgetown, he won an internship at Kings County Hospital in Brooklyn, and then opened his office on the stoop floor of our house on Harmon Street. I was delighted. Harry had come home.

One day I answered our doorbell and found a man wiping his eyes.

"I want to tell you and your Mama," the man said in a German accent, "your brother Harry delivered my baby today. I took out my wallet to pay him, and he said, 'Put it away.' "

The man stopped. "You must excuse me for crying." He finally controlled himself. "Then your brother took out money from *his* wallet, put it on my table, and said, 'Buy milk for your wife and your baby.' That's not a doctor, that's a saint."

Harry could comfort the sick; he could weep with families when he told them that a son or a daughter was dying of TB, his specialty; he could win the admiration of his students in pathology. But personal happiness eluded him. Like many young doctors, he had fallen in love with one of the nurses at Kings County. Kitty was petite, funny, and Irish. He saw her secretly but never brought her home.

"Why don't you marry her?" I asked him.

"I can't. It would break Mama and Papa's heart."

"Instead you're breaking your own."

"I can't do it," he said. "It would kill them."

Bob, the firstborn, who had changed his name from Herman, was different. Handsome, dapper in the latest fashion, he told Papa he wanted to go to Syracuse University with some of his friends and become a lawyer. Papa put his foot down.

"I know those friends," Papa said. "If you go with them to Syracuse, you'll be running around all night with girls. If you want to study law in New York, I'll gladly pay for it. But you can't go out of town."

Instead, Bob answered a *New York Times* ad, applied for a menial job with the Upjohn Pharmaceutical Company, and worked his way up until he became chief of the New York office. Generously he gave all our college friends summer jobs, and when anyone complained that the Upjohn family-owned company hired no Jews, Upjohn's officials answered, "How can you say that? Look at Bob Gruber. Head of our biggest office—the whole New York area."

If it had not been for Bob, who, I think, never forgave himself for not staying home and studying law and who took college courses throughout his life, my brothers would have fulfilled the dream of a Jewish family: A doctor. A lawyer. A dentist. Irving, the youngest, whose birth I had witnessed, gentle and wise like Papa, became a dentist and then ran the Greater New York Dental Meeting, with some thirty thousand dentists flying in each year to attend the largest annual meeting of dentists in the world.

Betty and I were proud of our brothers and were forever bringing our friends home to meet them. Several fell in love with Bob, but he was too busy playing his own field to notice them. At the same time, he guarded us as rigorously as Mama did. When a boy in Betty's freshman class at NYU told her, "You've got gorgeous legs. I'd like to take you to the movies," she agreed to let him come to the house. Bob answered the doorbell, looked closely at the caller, and said, "You're not for my sister. Beat it."

I hoped Harry would forget his Irish nurse, Kitty, and fall in love with my friend Vivian Weiner. Vivian and I sat together in Miss Barnicle's English class, the two she predicted would become famous writers. We showed each other our amateur essays, our flawed short stories, our unpublishable poems, and dreamed of fulfilling her prophecy.

My sister Betty, one of the most beautiful young women at NYU, was my mentor, pulling me through science and math. Betty loved science; I found it incomprehensible. Betty loved new shoes; I hated them. So she broke my shoes in until they were stretched and comfortable. We cleaned each other's desks, knowing we could never throw out our own paper and notes.

Betty wanted the furniture in our bedroom to look modern; I had no interest in furniture. One evening we bought fifty-five-cent tickets at Gray's Drug Store to see *Earl Carroll's Vanities.*

"Look at that stage set," Betty whispered to me as we sat enthralled on the second balcony. "All black and silver."

The next day, while Mama was out marketing, Betty hurried to Broadway, bought a can of black enamel, and painted our vanity bench solid ebony. I glanced up from the pages of the book I was reading. "Looks beautiful. Just like last night on the stage."

Delighted with her new art form, Betty began attacking another chair with black paint when Mama came upstairs to check on us. Mama's scream could have been heard on Bushwick Avenue. "Are you crazy? What's got into you anyway?"

She grabbed the can out of Betty's hand. "Don't you ever let me catch you painting my furniture again. If you do, I'll . . . I'll break . . ." She stopped short. Mama's security lay in clinging like a tiger to what she knew and clutching what she had. She hated waste.

Yet she could be generous. If friends or relatives admired something in her china closet, she gave it to them. And she had a sense of what was fitting. Once she took me to hear Jascha Heifetz play, and while I was prepared to sit up in the second balcony as always, Mama said, "No. We'll buy first-row orchestra seats."

But the painting fiasco so frustrated Betty that for years no wall, no chair, no wooden bed or pipe was safe from her brush. Betty, the brilliant chemistry instructor at NYU, was a born-again house painter.

In the summer of 1929, Betty, eager as I was to get away from home, joined me for a six-week program at Harvard.

Harvard was still a men's college, but its summer school was open to women. Mama and Papa made no objections to our leaving Harmon Street. Mount Holyoke had shown them that summer schools were safe for a teenage girl. With the extra credit, I would graduate from NYU in three years—and that would save money.

We had a choice of traveling by train or bus or boat. There was no question. We would go by boat.

A few months earlier, the family had stood on the dock of the Cunard Line, waving Baba and Zayda Rockower off to Europe. They were making their first visit in nearly fifty years to Beremlya, the shtetl where Mama was born.

Mama was weeping.

"Why are you crying, Mom?" I asked.

"Who knows if I'll ever see them again? What if something happens on the water?"

"Nothing will happen. And Mama, you should be so proud of why they're going."

Zayda Rockower was carrying two thousand dollars—a fortune to me—to take to Beremlya so the little Jewish village could build a bathhouse and a *mikveh*, the ritual pool where women purified themselves before they slept with their husbands.

Some day, I thought, as I watched the ship slide gracefully out of the harbor, some day I will sail the Atlantic on an ocean liner.

Betty and I had bought tickets for a stateroom on the *Colonial Line*. Papa, with Mama sitting up front beside him, drove us in the Studebaker to the Hudson River dock.

"Be careful, girls," Mama turned around to warn us. "You don't know who is on these boats. Strange men . . ."

"We'll be careful." We kissed them quickly and skipped up the gangway. We dropped our small suitcases and my portable typewriter in our stateroom, and rushed out to watch the ship sail through the Narrows into the East River, then up Long Island Sound. A fairyland of lights lit up the waterfront on both sides of us until we headed into the Atlantic Ocean.

Far too excited to sleep, we spent the night on deck talking, walking, looking at the Big Dipper, reveling as the ship sliced through the waves and cascades of foam sprayed our faces and hair. In the middle of the night, the captain invited us up to the bridge to have coffee with him. Betty, who later became a skilled navigator on sailboats, was fascinated by his navigation charts. I was fascinated by the water.

The six weeks on the Harvard campus sped by all too swiftly. Mornings Betty audited a physics class, while I took a course in Shakespeare with Professor Albert Feuillerat, who analyzed each play through its language and taught us to love and understand not only the great dramas but the lesser-known ones too.

Afternoons we lay on the grass on the banks of the Charles River reading and watching boat races. Evenings we went to concerts on the campus. We grew closer than ever and made new friends.

Suzy Wasserman, plump and pretty, the daughter of a wealthy German-Jewish family, was taking a refresher course in chemistry. She had failed it at NYU. She searched for us one afternoon and dropped on the grass.

"I'm so glad I found you," she panted. "I just got my exam paper back. Out of a hundred questions, I got less than ten right. Finals are in three days, and I've got to pass. It'll be terrible if I go home and tell my parents I flunked chemistry again."

"Let me try to help you," Betty offered.

"It's heartbreaking," Betty confided to me after three full days of coaching. "She's very bright, but she's in a daze when it comes to chemistry."

Suzy failed the finals.

"I'm afraid to go home," she wept. "My parents will be furious."

"I'd flunk chemistry too," I tried to console her. "I'm an absolute illiterate in science."

"Would you tell that to my mother when we get back to New York?"

"If it'll do any good, of course."

A few days later, Suzy escorted me to her town house off Fifth Avenue.

"Suzy has told us about you," her mother greeted me in polite, highly cultivated tones. We were sitting in a living room as formal and heavily draped as the baron's. "It's too bad that she failed even the repeat summer course."

Suzy's pretty face seemed to crumple.

"Mrs. Wasserman," I said, "people good in one subject can be morons in another. Suzy and I are both hopeless in science, but we're pretty good in languages. Doesn't it count that in English she's so—?"

Her father, a Wall Street lawyer, dressed in a brown velvet smoking jacket, interrupted. "Everyone must know science. I will make certain Suzy takes chemistry again, until she passes."

A maid in a blue-and-white uniform appeared. "Dinner is served, Ma'am."

We descended to an oak-lined dining room below street level. A huge crystal chandelier hung over a table set with elegant matching dishes and crystal glasses. The maid carried a heavy silver tray of blood-rare roast beef around the table. I hoped I was using the right fork.

"You're not eating much, Suzy," Mrs. Wasserman said. "Is the beef rare enough for you, dear?"

"Yes, Mother. I'm just not very hungry." Suzy slumped in her chair.

"Did you have a good day today in school?" her father asked after a period of strained silence.

"Yes, Father."

"And how was your day?" he asked me.

"Fine," I said.

Soon after dinner I said goodbye and fled back to Brooklyn.

*   *   *

A few days later I met Suzy in the women's lounge. She was still downcast. "How about coming home with me?" I suggested, thinking my ebullient family might cheer her up. Better yet, she might even like one of my brothers and he might like her. "Everybody's home for dinner on Friday night," I said. "So you'll meet the whole gang."

"Don't you have to call your mother and ask her if you can bring a guest?"

"My mother's used to it."

"I better call home," Suzy dug into her purse for a nickel, "and get permission to stay away."

I began to have qualms. How would Suzy, coming from such wealth, feel in a house like ours? She had never set foot in Brooklyn.

"Sit right down," Mama greeted her in the big kitchen-dining room. Papa sat at the head of the table, Bob faced him at the foot, and the rest of us took our chairs. Suzy sat between Harry and me.

The magic of the Sabbath cast its spell over Harmon Street. In the china closet against the walls, the cut-glass crystal bowls sparkled like a thousand diamonds. On the big square table covered with a white lace tablecloth, two shining brass candlesticks stood like Old World towers guarding the two challahs, the golden-braided Sabbath bread Mama had baked. The whole dining room smelled of challah and chicken and lots of soap. I knew that even though we had a sleep-in housekeeper, Mama had been down on her hands and knees in the morning scrubbing the linoleum floor.

Dressed in a freshly starched housedress, Mama stood before the candles and the challah. All my life I had watched her cover her head with a white lace cloth and light the candles. But Suzy's presence made me see her differently, like a woman in a Rembrandt painting. She made a wide circle over the burning candles; then she covered her eyes and recited the benediction in Hebrew: *"Blessed art Thou, O Lord our God, King of the Universe, Who hast sanctified us by Thy commandments and instructed us to kindle the Sabbath lights."*

Her hands still over her eyes, she made a little speech to God in

Yiddish. "I beg you, take good care of my husband and my children, and let my children be honest and good and find favor by God and by man."

Papa stood up, king of the house, and we all stood up with him while he sang the *kiddush* prayer over the wine, joined by Bob and Harry and Irving. Then he poured red sacramental wine into his silver goblet—the only wine permitted during Prohibition—drank some, and poured the rest into our wine glasses. We recited the blessing, chanted "Amen," and drained the glasses.

Papa then blessed the challah, tore off pieces, and passed them around the table, Suzy whispered to me, "It's so beautiful, it's so—so Jewish."

The first obligatory course was gefilte fish. Everyone ate and talked. It was still summer, when our favorite topic was always the Dodgers at Ebbets Field, and you could tell from the laughter or gloom around the table whether the Dodgers had won.

The second course was Mama's chicken soup. "Eat," she commanded Suzy, "eat while it's good and hot."

"It's very good," Suzy said. "But I was so worried, Mrs. Gruber," she apologized, "coming here without letting you know."

Mama shrugged her shoulders. "It's nothing. All I had to do was put more water in the soup."

Mama now took a towel in each hand, opened the oven door, and pulled out a giant-size roasting pot filled with chickens, sweet potatoes, and carrots. She carried the pot to the table, set it down near Papa, and with a huge serving spoon, piled food on our plates.

The conversation never stopped. We interrupted each other, jumping from baseball to Charlie Chaplin and Greta Garbo and the latest escapades of our sexy Irish-American mayor, Jimmy Walker.

After the applesauce, the hot tea, and honey cake, Suzy whispered to me, "I've never been at a Friday night dinner like this. I think I understand something about you. You belong to each other. It's something I never felt before."

She walked to Mama and kissed her. "I hope you'll let me come again."

"Come as much as you like," Mama embraced her. "Remember, all I have to do is put more water in the soup."

"It's more than that," Suzy said, and added unpatronizingly, "I love it here. It's just like the peasants."

Mama laughed every time she told the story.

7

Late one October, Mannie Singer telephoned. "How about coming with me to the Palisades?" Mannie was a premed student at NYU.

"Sure," I said. "I haven't climbed those cliffs since high school."

I could see us scrambling over the rugged cliffs that rose up from the Hudson on the New Jersey side of the river, huge multicolored rocks with trees growing through their crevices.

Mannie continued. "I want you to help me find some albino frogs."

"Albino frogs!" I stopped myself from saying "Eekh." "What are you going to do with albino frogs?"

"It's a Mendelian experiment in genetics for my biology class. I'll mate the albinos with regular frogs, see which genes are dominant, and then write a paper on it."

I hesitated until I remembered that an ugly frog had once turned into a prince. "Okay, I'll go."

Early Sunday morning, Mannie appeared at Harmon Street lugging a canvas bag to put the frogs in.

We were both dressed for mountain climbing, with heavy shoes, wool pants, and warm sweaters. I was uncomfortable in my outfit, especially with the new hiking shoes; there had been no time for Betty to break them in. But Mannie looked like the outdoors man who blew cigarette smoke on the poster that read "I'd walk a mile for a Camel."

Camels were my cigarettes, too. I tossed a pack into my duffel bag, together with cheese sandwiches, fresh fruit, marshmallows, a lipstick, a powder compact, and other small items that I thought might turn out to be useful on a hunting expedition.

In the El going to Manhattan, Mannie gave me a spirited lecture on genetic mutations, most of which I didn't understand. At 42nd Street, we changed for the IRT north to Dyckman Street and waited for the ferry to take us across the Hudson.

The day was balmy. The sun made us peel off our sweaters. We stood at the rail of the ferry, letting New York fall away from us. On the New Jersey shore, we disembarked and began climbing the cliffs.

"We'll start around these rocks," Mannie said. My hiking shoes were squeezing my feet, but I paid no attention. I was too busy hunting white frogs.

"Here's one!" I shouted to Mannie, who was hunting nearby. Gingerly, I picked up the little white specimen. It wiggled in my fingers. Its short hind legs clawed the air. "It's no creature I want to stroke," I said. Mannie was leaning over me, inspecting my discovery.

"Just think what you're doing for science. Here, plunk it into this canvas bag."

I went back to the hunt.

"Another one," I called out. "Who knows? Maybe I'll find a slew of them. Mannie, what do you call a slew of frogs? There's a gaggle of geese," I chanted, beginning to enjoy the outing, "a pod of whales, a covey of doves, a pride of lions. But what do you call a slew of frogs—especially white ones soon to be ecstatic, mated for life in the cause of science?"

"Who knows what you call them?" Mannie laughed. "Just keep hunting. We're doing great."

We searched for about an hour, tossing half a dozen little white struggling creatures into the canvas bag. The day grew cloudy, the sky began to lower, and a cold wind blew through the Palisades.

Mannie rubbed his hands together. "I'm going to build us a fire and we can have lunch. Wait here while I find some twigs."

I started unpacking the food. Soon Mannie was back, empty-handed, his face burning red.

"Look at this." He turned to show me a huge rent in the crotch of his woolen pants. "I got caught in some twigs, and the next thing I knew I heard this awful ripping noise. I don't know how we'll get into the subway and back to the city."

"Go behind that tree," I said. "Take your pants off and hand them to me." I knew I could trust Mannie with his pants off.

"What'll you do?" he asked.

"Just hand them to me."

He slipped behind a tree, while I turned my head in the opposite direction, looking down at the Hudson.

"Here they are," he called out.

I opened my bag and fished inside. I came up with a needle and thread and a white handkerchief. I folded the ends of the handkerchief into a circle and with fancy embroidery stitches, patched the hole in his pants.

"Okay," I said. "You'll be respectable again."

Mannie stretched his arm in front of the tree, reaching for his pants, and a few minutes later came forward fully dressed.

"Who are you anyway? Betsy Ross?" He gave me a quick brotherly hug. "Let's make the fire."

While we ate the sandwiches and fruit and toasted the marshmallows, I took off my shoes. I could feel blisters forming.

"Get up," he said gently, and leaned down to help me. "You know I like you a lot."

He put his arms around me and kissed me on the lips. No one had ever kissed me this way before. I felt warm and wanted. I felt my body trembling with sensations I had never known. Even my thighs seemed to be tingling.

Mannie reached under my sweater and with his bare hand outlined my shoulders and my back. I yearned to be kissed some more. My heart pounded against his pounding heart.

"I think we'd better go home," I heard myself whisper.

"You're sure?"

"I'm sure."

I put my blistered feet back into the heavy shoes and held Mannie's hand as we descended the cliffs.

Mannie was a good friend, but I was not in love with him. In my German class, I had fallen in love with Joseph Ostro, a short, dark-haired, Russian-born student with a delicately molded Slavic face and large, melancholy eyes. He walked with the forward stoop of a scholar who spends hours poring over books. Even his skin, pale and white, looked as if the sun never shone on it. He wrote poetry and played the violin.

Each day Joseph waited for me after class, and in good weather he found us a bench in Washington Square Park. There he read me the poetry he had written. He began one of his poems, "You are light in my dark soul."

I showed the poem to Betty one night as we lay in bed.

"You're in love with him, aren't you?" she said.

I nodded. "It's so pure, so idealistic. He doesn't tell me he loves me. But I feel it. Look at this picture he gave me today."

I handed her a sepia-colored snapshot showing him in a rocker on a porch. He wore a white open-collared shirt, white bell-bottom pants, and white scuffs on his bare feet. His brown hair was combed carefully across his forehead. His chin leaned into the shoulder of his fiddle. His eyes, dark and haunted, looked up beneath heavy brows.

"He looks like a Russian Shelley or Keats," Betty said.

I took the photo from her and studied it. "Or straight out of a Dostoyevsky novel."

"What do you know about him?"

"Only that he was born in Russia and came to America a few years ago. I don't know if he has a family. I don't know if he lives alone. I don't know where he lives. Often, when he trails after me, it seems to me he's about to tell me something. But when I ask, 'Yes, Joseph?' he shakes his head and says nothing."

"It's just like you," Betty said, "to fall in love with someone dark and mysterious and probably neurotic. Why don't you fall in love with somebody normal?"

"I can't help it. Remember when that stockbroker, Gordon Sandrowitz, took me to dinner in the Waldorf Astoria. I lost all interest in him. He was a bore. I prefer the boys who take me to the Automat. They're usually more interesting than Gordon, and so are the people in the Automat. I want to know why they sit alone. Do they live in single rooms or cheap joints on the Bowery? What journey did they make, ending up at a table in the Automat? Why do they look so beaten by life?"

"How about Mannie?" Betty persisted. "The family would love him. He's good-looking, he's going to be a doctor, and he's Jewish."

"In love with Mannie?" I leaned back on the pillow. "My brave hunter of white frogs. I like him a lot. But he's a platonic friend. He's not Joseph."

One day after class Joseph led me to an empty bench near the Washington Square arch that framed the park.

"For you," he said, handing me a heavy package.

"What is it?"

"Open it and see."

I tore open the wrapping. Inside were two cloth-covered German volumes of Oswald Spengler's *Untergang des Abendlandes* [*The Decline of the West*]. On the frontispiece of the first volume, Joseph had written in black, jagged letters and in ungrammatical German, "Meiner lieben Freundin [To my dear friend], Ruth Gruber. New York den 29 Oktober 1929," and below it his name, "*Joseph Ostro,*" with the tail of the final *o* swooping across half the page.

"I can't accept these books," I protested.

"You must. These are my books, books I love. You must take them."

"But I can't. They're much too valuable."

"They are from my own library. If you refuse, you will hurt me deeply. I have special reasons for giving them to you. Reasons I cannot tell you."

At home I opened the first volume and at the same time turned on the radio for news.

"October twenty-ninth, 1929," I heard the announcer say in an ominous tone. "This day will go down in history." On Wall Street, the stock market had crashed.

I looked at Joseph's inscription on the flyleaf "den 29 Oktober 1929."

Was it prophetic that he had given me *The Decline of the West* on this day? Was October 29 the beginning of the end of Western civilization?

The next day a radio announcer reported, "More men have jumped out of the windows of the Eldorado, the newest art-deco building on Central Park West, than out of any other building in New York. They went to sleep last night thinking they were millionaires; they woke up to find they were paupers."

Soon my brother Bob's lawyer friends were hawking hot dogs in Ebbets Field, Harry's doctor friends were driving taxis, Betty's and my schoolteacher friends were selling trinkets in Macy's and the five-and-ten.

Fortunately Papa had never ventured into the stock market, but he had reverses in real estate when, overnight, apartments emptied in the two houses he owned on Flatbush's Lenox Road. People could no longer pay thirty-five dollars a month's rent for four rooms.

But we owned the gray stone house on Harmon Street; taxes were low, and we lived carefully. Bob was working at Upjohn, Harry was at medical school, Betty and I were at NYU, and Irving was at Boys High, the high school filled with bright Jewish boys. Our bevy of aunts and cousins and friends still came on Sunday afternoons.

Papa still brought home corned beef and pastrami and rye bread
and giant bottles of celery tonic. Mama still baked zwieback. After
all of us had demolished the food, Papa and our uncles would play
pinochle, and Mama and the aunts would gossip. And each night I
opened the heavy Spengler volumes and plowed through his theories of the so-called yellow race in the East taking over the West,
theories made more ominous by the stock market's collapse.

Each week Joseph brought me a new book, and each time he
waved aside my objections with the same words. "These are my
books, books I love. You must accept them." Goethe. Schiller.
Nietzsche. Schopenhauer. *Thousand and One Nights*. All classics
and all bound in cloth or red or green leather with gold lettering.
Pierre Loti in French. Omar Khayyam in English.

"Are you trying to mold my mind?" I tried to tease him one day
as we sat on a park bench.

He was too serious to be teased. "Books can mold minds," he
said. "Books can mold character and personality. Goethe and
Schiller can mold your mind; I can only be their messenger."

Children were playing near us; mothers wheeled their babies in
big black perambulators; students were sitting close together, holding hands.

"Please don't give me any more books, Joseph. I can't go on
accepting them. They're too precious."

"You must. You must," he cried. I had never heard his voice so
strange.

"You're depleting your whole library. Why?"

"In Russia if you have two pieces of bread, you give one away. I
bring you books, not bread."

"I feel you're giving away pieces of your own life. You must let
me return some to you."

A small smile lit up his pale face. "Just tell me which one of the
books you love the most."

"I will tell you. It is *Shir Hashirim*, the *Song of Songs Which Is
Solomon's*."

"It's mine too," he said, still smiling.

It was a large art book covered in off-white cloth, printed in Hebrew and English and illustrated by an artist named Zeew Raban.

"It has special meaning for me," he said. "It's an all-Jewish book. You know that in 1922, after the Great War, the League of Nations gave Britain a mandate to establish the National Home for the Jewish people in Palestine."

I nodded, wondering what relationship the *Song of Songs* had to a national home for the Jews.

Joseph went on. "This book was printed in Palestine just one year later. Look at the flyleaf when you get home. You'll see the publisher is called *Hasefer*, which means 'The Book' in Hebrew. We—you and I—we are the People of the Book, and who wrote more beautiful love poems in that Book than the wise king of the Jews?"

No longer did I struggle with Spengler's pessimism. Each night, before I went to sleep, I ran my hand gently over the illustrations of Solomon in his robes and the long-limbed, often naked woman he loved. I read and reread the words: "Let him kiss me with the kisses of his mouth, for thy love is better than wine. . . ."

Joseph never kissed me, as Solomon kissed his "black but comely" lover with the kisses of his mouth. Once in the park Joseph took my hand and held it. Blood seemed to surge from his hand through my body.

"Ruth," he whispered. "I love you."

"I love you too, Joseph."

I quoted from Solomon's love song: "My beloved is unto me as a bundle of myrrh, that lieth between my breasts. . . . Behold thou art fair, my love, behold thou art fair; thine eyes are as doves. . . . Behold thou art fair. . . ."

He held my hand even tighter. "I am to my beloved and my beloved is to me."

A few weeks later, Joseph disappeared. I waited for him in our German class, hoping he would turn up. I searched for him in the corridors of NYU and on the benches in Washington Square Park.

It was Professor Meyer who brought me the news. "I have just heard. Your friend Joseph Ostro is dead."

I screamed. "Joseph. Dead. My God, how did he die?"

"He took poison."

"But why? Why would he kill himself?"

"Depressed," Professor Meyer said. "He was a young man in a state of deep depression. You know how sad he was, most of the time."

"I know he was sad," I sobbed. "But sad people don't have to kill themselves."

"You better go home," Professor Meyer gripped my shoulder consolingly. "You don't look very good yourself."

I took the train to the entrance of the Williamsburg Bridge at Delancey Street. The Lower East Side was humming with push-carts and vendors shouting their wares. Other days I would have stopped to look at the pushcarts loaded with fresh fruit, at the barrels of pickles, at the ladies' dresses and men's three-piece suits hanging on poles, at velvet-lined trays of rings and earrings with fake stones. Today I scarcely saw them. I climbed up on the bridge and moved slowly on the walkway until I stood above the water. Water could always calm me. But not today.

Had I done something? Was I guilty in any way? He had held my hand, and I had not drawn it away. *"You are light in my dark soul."*

His soul was dark, like Raskolnikov's. But Dostoyevsky's hero had a streak of homicidal cruelty; Joseph was not cruel.

Why did he kill himself? What demons tortured him in that dark soul?

Maybe there is an urge in all of us, I thought, to destroy ourselves. How many times as a little girl had I said in frustration, "I wish I had never been born. I wish I was dead." Is death the ultimate answer to pain?

Tears were streaming down my cheeks. I felt helpless, powerless, confused. Could I have acted differently? Could I have done something, anything, to have prevented his taking his life?

Our love for German literature had bound us together. He had broken the bond. "Why?" I cried. "Why did you do it, Joseph?"

Ships sailed down the river shimmering in the sunlight. Trains chugged along the elevated tracks. Pigeons careened through the air and landed behind a barge dumping food overboard.

Skyscrapers mirrored themselves in the river, the skyscrapers of Manhattan scraping the sky. Life seemed to call to us.

You must have planned your suicide, I told him, the way architects planned these skyscrapers. Like a master plan. The way a Russian who shared books instead of bread would plan his life and his death.

Ruth Gruber at age two

Gruber's mother and father
in 1905

Grandma (Baba) and Grandpa (Zayda) Gruber
outside Ruth's Brooklyn home, welcoming her on
her return from Germany in 1932

Baba and Zayda Rockower
leaving for return trip to Europe
to build a Mikvah - the ritual
bath - in their shtetl, Beremlya,
in the Wolyn Gubernya, 1929

Gruber's eldest brother Bob in a
studio portrait, ca. 1936

Gruber's brother Harry as a
medical student in 1930

Gruber's sister Betty at NYU
graduation in 1929

Gruber's youngest brother Irving
at a formal dance in 1935

The Jewish ghetto in the Lower
East Side, New York City, in
the thirties, near the entrance
to Gruber's beloved
Williamsburg Bridge
(Photo by FPG International)

Joseph Ostro - who gave
Gruber his art books - at
New York University in 1928

8
1930

"Atta unsar thu in Himinam [Our Father Who Art in Heaven]" . . .

I strode through Washington Square Park memorizing the Lord's Prayer in Gothic. "Hallowed be thy name."

I was studying German philology with Professor Ernst Prokosch and trying to decide whether to apply for a master's degree in either English or German at NYU. Professor Prokosch solved the problem.

"Each year," he told me, "the German department at the University of Wisconsin gives a fellowship to one New York student. They select that student from one of the New York colleges—Columbia, Barnard, NYU, City College, Hunter, Adelphi—any one of them. I will recommend you for the fellowship this year."

Prokosch's name was magic in academia.

I tore open the letter that came from Wisconsin. "We congratulate you on being selected for the LaFrentz Fellowship in the graduate program of the German department. You will receive full tuition and a stipend of $600."

A whole year away from home!

I ran into the kitchen-dining room. Mama was baking strudel, Papa was reading his newspaper.

"I won it," I shouted. "I won it."

"Won what?" Mama asked.

"A fellowship. To Wisconsin. It means I can get my master's degree in German, and they pay for everything."

Papa put his paper down. "They must think you're pretty smart."

The family was so proud that no one uttered a word of protest when I told them I was going to hitchhike to Wisconsin. Nor were they worried. The streets and highways were safe. I could come home to Brooklyn at midnight, walk past a pitch-black alley, and know no fear. And on the roads, people of all ages were thumbing rides from New York to California.

A week before I planned to leave, Papa drove me in the Studebaker to his favorite service station to pick up a collection of Standard Oil road maps. I spread the maps on the dining table and, with the family approving, circled the places I wanted to see.

"Albany, first," I said. "After all, I should know the capital of our state. Then I'll go across the Hudson to Troy. Helen of Troy intrigues me. Then there are the Finger Lakes. I like that name." I circled Syracuse. Rochester. Buffalo. Niagara Falls, Detroit, Chicago, Milwaukee, and finally Madison. I was going to discover America.

"My daughter the explorer." Mama wiped her hands on her apron.

I sent my clothes and books off to Wisconsin, and in a tote bag, I packed a toothbrush, underwear, and the Standard Oil maps.

The August day dawned bright and hot when, dressed in brown oxfords, a navy skirt, and a white middy blouse, I kissed the family goodbye and took the subway north to Dyckman Street, the same route I had taken with Mannie Singer on our way to hunt frogs. I stood on the highway to thumb a ride.

Cars and trucks raced by and no one stopped. I kept waving my thumb in the air, pointing northward. The sun beat down. Long minutes passed.

At last a young couple with two blond children stopped their car.

"How far you going?" the driver asked. He was in overalls and a red plaid shirt.

"To Albany."

"That's our home. Get in."

I climbed in the back with the children, dropped my bag on the car floor, and leaned back in relief.

"You got family in Albany?" the father asked.

"No."

"You don't have friends or nothing up there?"

"Nope."

"What you gonna do in Albany?"

"Just looking around. I'm on my way to school in Wisconsin."

They shook their heads. "You gonna hitchhike the whole way?"

"I hope so."

They said little to each other after that. The children, a flaxen-haired little girl of eight and a boy of ten in overalls, wanted attention, so I taught them how to play "geography." "We begin with the letter a," I said. "Let's choose your town, Albany. Then you take the last letter—it's a y—and name a place that begins with y. Can you think of a town or a country that begins with y?"

"Yukon," the little girl called out.

"You caught on right away," I said.

They played the game so intently that I could look out the window and marvel at the majesty of the Hudson River. Road signs told us that we were passing towns that went back to Revolutionary days. It was late afternoon when we reached Albany.

"There's a nice clean boardinghouse downtown," the farmer said. "We'll drop you there."

I entered a white clapboard house with a wide verandah that might have been built in the nineteenth century. An elderly lady showed me to a low-ceilinged room with a cot and a dresser. "One dollar," she said. "Paid in advance."

On the street again, I found a diner, bought a nickel hamburger, and returned to the boardinghouse. I climbed into bed quickly. Not bad for the first day, I told myself, and fell asleep.

In the morning I explored the city. Albany was a sleepy-looking town with Victorian brownstones, brick houses, Gothic churches, and tree-shaded streets that ran up and down small hills. I caught a bus to the huge capitol building, a simulated French chateau overlooking the city. I would have liked to see the legislators sitting at desks making laws, but a guard told me the legislators were all home.

It was midafternoon and time to move on. With good luck I could reach Troy in an hour. I took a bus to the outskirts of Albany and stationed myself on the shoulder of the road.

Hours passed. I found a rock and sat on its jagged edges trying to decide what to do. A red ball of sun began to sink behind the hills. The sky became mauve-pink, then gray at twilight. I was about to go back to Albany when a truck rolled up.

"Which way you going?" the driver leaned out of his cab window. He was a large man with a reddish mustache and a kindly face. I felt a twinge of homesickness. He reminded me of Papa.

"Troy," I said.

"It's a little out of my way, but I'll take you there. It's getting late for you to be out alone on this road."

I tossed my bag up, climbed the steep step and settled in the cab beside him. He revved up the engine with powerful hands.

"Things are purty bad around here," he offered. "And gettin' worse every day. No jobs, no money, nuthin'. Where you from?"

"Brooklyn."

"No jobs there either, huh?"

I nodded.

"You lookin' for some kind of work?"

"No. I'm hitchhiking to school. Wisconsin U."

He turned to look at me in my schoolgirl middy blouse and navy skirt. "A little young, ain't you?"

I shrugged my shoulders. "I don't think so."

"Well, there's lots of folk in Troy rentin' out spare rooms. On'y way some of 'em keep the sheriff from takin' over their houses. You won't have no trouble findin' a place to sleep."

It was dark when he dropped me on a street that had several signs: "Boardinghouse: Rooms for Rent." I chose a white house that looked freshly painted. A heavily rouged woman in high heels answered the doorbell.

"I'd like to rent a room," I said.

She looked at me suspiciously. "For how long?"

"Just one night."

She hesitated. "What the hell, it's slow tonight. You can have a room for a dollar-fifty."

I handed her the money and followed her into an empty sitting room lined with silk-striped settees. A broad set of stairs with an ornately carved balustrade curved from inside the sitting room up to a hallway with doors on both sides. She opened one of the doors.

"Here you are. The bathroom's down the hall," she said and disappeared, her high heels clacking down the stairs.

I dropped my tote bag on the floor. The room was narrow, filled from wall to wall by a double bed with a gold-painted dragon's head with flaring nostrils jutting out of the headboard. There was no dresser. No closet. Just a nail on the wall to hang my clothes, and a nightstand with a porcelain pitcher of water set in a porcelain bowl.

I walked down the hall to the bathroom. A buxom young woman in a red satin bathrobe was standing at one of the two sinks.

"Hey kid," she said. "What you doing here?"

"Just spending the night."

"She sure is scrapin' the bottom, ain't she?" Her eyes went from my middy blouse to my oxfords. She shook her head. "New clientele," she muttered under her breath.

"What do you mean?" I asked.

"You work?"

"No. I'm on my way to school."

She threw her head back, roaring, "My God. Don't you know

what this is? It's a whorehouse. Business is so slow she'll take in anybody for a buck."

I bolted back to the room, grabbed my bag, loped down the curved stairs, and out of the house. I found another boardinghouse in the next block. The price was seventy-five cents a night, and the bed was clean. My heart was still racing when I finally fell asleep.

In the next days I learned several hitchhiking lessons. Get out on the road early in the morning. Find a place to sleep long before dark. Safest places are hostels run by the Salvation Army or the YMCA. Most of the rooms cost a dollar or a dollar-fifty a night. Hotels were two dollars, still cheaper than the New York City hotels that advertised in the *New York Times*—three-fifty for the Barbizon Plaza, five for the Essex House, and the Plaza, which overlooked Central Park, and where I dreamed that some day I would spend a night, charged eight dollars a room. Truck drivers were most likely to pick you up. Many of them, making long treks across the country, were lonely men. Some told me about their families, some wanted to know about my family, and some seemed happy not to talk, so I went to sleep in their cabs. I sent a trail of postcards home in the week it took to reach Madison, Wisconsin.

At the university, someone directed me to *Das Deutsche Haus*, the German House, where, since the German department had given me my fellowship, I was expected to live. The housemother, a tight-lipped woman, showed me to a bare room with a narrow bed, a dresser, and a closet.

I hurried out to register, impatient to begin classes and to see if any friends from NYU had arrived. Wisconsin had become the mecca for a host of New York students. I could hardly believe my luck when I was accepted for the poet William Ellery Leonard's seminar in modern English literature.

In the next months, I could almost feel my mind and body stretching. Reading. Writing papers. Browsing through Madison's bookshops and buying old books. Meeting old friends and new ones like Louis Zukofsky, the poet and critic, with whom I ate hot waffles crowned with vanilla ice cream and discussed the precise and unadorned prose that Zukofsky and others were making fashionable.

There was little time on weekdays to be alone. But Sundays were different. One winter Sunday afternoon, I walked along Lake Mendota, its icy shores fringed with lovely willow trees. I felt sad and lonely.

Had I separated from my family only to come to Wisconsin and find the umbilical cord could stretch a thousand miles? In Harmon Street, I had yearned for space, yearned to be alone when it was impossible to be alone. Now that I could be alone, I missed the warm glow of Friday nights with Mama lighting the candles and Papa saying *kiddush* over the wine, I missed the long talks with Betty, I missed sitting at my rolltop desk, I missed Brooklyn.

On the lake, I watched the skaters, arm in arm, wool scarves blowing in the wind, cutting figures on the ice. Iceboats were flying across the white frozen water. Somewhere off the campus students were hiking, skiing, tobogganing, or visiting the rich dairy farms that surrounded us.

I walked back to town. People were strolling down State Street; state legislators were in the bars and coffee shops talking of the bills they were introducing. Church bells were ringing, inviting Madisonians to vespers. I tried to find someone from New York to talk to. It was no accident that my friends were New Yorkers: most of the midwestern students had their own circles and cliques. Like expatriates, we holed up for comfort in each other's rooms. I often visited Suzy Wasserman, who had escaped from her parents and, reveling in her freedom, had decorated her studio apartment like a gypsy tearoom, with oriental cushions and dim lights. But that day, Suzy was not home.

I continued walking, wrapped in loneliness, until I ran into Joseph Rosa, an intense Hungarian whose accent was as thick as the baron's. Joseph, a graduate student in economics, invited me for coffee, the only luxury he could afford.

Beneath the somber look he studiously affected was a streak of mischief. While I sipped weak tea, he leaned across the table and whispered like a conspirator, "I am in love at one and the same time with two women. With you and someone I will never allow you to meet. Maybe I'm not Hungarian; maybe I'm an Arab who needs four wives to keep him happy." Cheered by his nonsense, I laughed.

But there was no laughter in *Das Deutsche Haus*. It was cold and dismal and was run like an army camp. Orders were pasted on the walls, and early curfew was a law never to be broken. I had not escaped from Brooklyn to be trapped by a rigid housemother who made me aware, with her angry stares, that I was the only Jewish student under her roof.

"I can't live there anymore," I told the head of the German department at the end of the first semester. "I can't stand the atmosphere. I'm going to find a room somewhere else."

His glasses framed his angry eyes. "You New Yorkers." I knew it was his polite way of saying "You Jews."

In a burst of rage that startled me, he went on, "You're all the same. You're always outsiders. You may be among the brightest, but you think you can make your own rules. You can't. You know what's going to happen personally to you? I predict, if you don't adjust to the world, you're going to wind up on a psychiatrist's couch."

I bolted out of his office. Suddenly the air seemed suffocatingly anti-Semitic. Would they pass me in German? Would they give me a master's degree if I dared to check out of *Das Deutsche Haus*? Whatever the consequences, I would not stay another night. I found a room with a friendly Norwegian family in town and settled in.

I was at my desk when my landlady, Mrs. Johanssen, knocked at my door. It was Easter vacation, and I was writing my master's thesis on Goethe's *Faust*.

"Iss letter come for you," Mrs. Johanssen said. She placed the mail on my desk and hurried out.

Carefully, I opened an impressive white linen envelope from the Institute of International Education. I had applied for a fellowship to Germany with letters of recommendation from Professor Prokosch and Professor Feuillerat, who had taught Shakespeare at Harvard.

"We are proud to tell you," the letter read, "that you have been selected for a one-year exchange fellowship to the University of Cologne. You will receive your tuition at the university, and $1,000 for your living expenses."

Did I really deserve this second fellowship? Maybe the German department would find out about it and flunk me. I pushed the doubts away and danced around the room.

Mrs. Johanssen burst in. "Iss something happen?"

"Good news! I'm going to Germany."

"Dat iss good news?" she asked.

"It's so good I'm not going to telephone my family. I'm going to go home to tell my parents in person."

"Dat iss a good daughter," she said. "Your Mama must be proud of you."

I hitchhiked east across the country and thanks to friendly truck drivers reached Albany in less than two days. Too restless to continue hitchhiking, I telephoned home from the railway station.

Martha, the sister of the corner baker on Harmon Street and another of the German housekeepers Mama kept hiring, answered the phone. "Your Mama and Papa vent out."

"Please ask them, if they can, to pick me up at six o'clock tonight at Grand Central."

Later I learned that driving to Manhattan, Mama kept repeating: "I tell you, Dave, she's pregnant. Why else would she come home in the middle of the year when she didn't even come home for Christmas vacation?"

"Gussie, just wait," he cautioned. "We'll find out soon enough."

"You're always on her side."

I saw them standing in the station. "Mama. Papa." I sped toward them, embracing them. "I'm going to Germany."

"What?" My mother shouted to Papa. "I wish she *was* pregnant."

"Everything is paid for. It'll all be free. A thousand dollars. It won't cost you a nickel."

The week at home was a disaster. Who ever heard of a girl going off alone to Germany, they asked each other. Papa paced the dining-room floor, his gray eyes hooded with worry.

"Ruthie, you're so young, just nineteen. I read terrible stories in the papers. They say this Adolf Hitler could take over Germany. What if it happens while you're there? Who knows what they could do to you?"

What was danger compared to another full year of independence?

"What can the Germans do to me?" I tried to sound casual. "I'll be away a year, that's all, and then I'll come back."

He continued to pace, shaking his head.

"Papa, you wouldn't be so upset, would you, if it was Bob or Harry or Irving? It's true, isn't it Pop? It's because I'm a girl."

"Well, girls *are* different. Girls have to be careful. Why can't you stay home like other girls? You don't have to learn how to cook or clean. You can always get help for that. It's more important you should have education. Everybody should have education. That's what's so wonderful in this country. Everybody can get all the education they want, and with education, you can get anywhere."

Then, probably hoping his story would soften me, he said, "I was so lucky in Russia. I was the oldest, so I was sent to school. I was the only one of my brothers who had an education. I loved school; I wanted to be a scholar. But then I had to leave and go out with my father selling lumber, and then working in their inn in Odessa. That was my education. Everything you do in life is part of education."

I saw my chance to strike hard. "That's what I want, Papa, just what you wanted in Russia. More education. Germany will help me with a career."

He stopped pacing. "I agree you should have a career. That's fine. With God's help, one of these days you'll meet a good man, you'll get married and have children. But you should have a career

too, because if your husband dies, God forbid, you have to have
something to fall back on. Be a teacher. Be a secretary."

"That's not what I want to be, Papa."

There was a long silence. He stroked his red mustache slowly. He
had made a success of his life in America, the immigrant twenty-
year-old who had traveled steerage, boxed in with a thousand other
immigrants, seasick most of the way and eating—when he could
eat—only herring and bread.

I never tired of pressing him to tell me the odyssey.

"I had to save for nearly a year to raise the fifteen dollars it cost
for the *Schiffskarte*, the steamship ticket. It was from Hamburg to
New York. Steerage. You couldn't bathe for two weeks, you
couldn't wash your clothes. The toilets were against the wall, a
couple of barrels with a board on top. The shipowners packed in as
many people as they could, like animals. They gave us water. But
food! Next to nothing. Many got sick; some died. Sometimes people
from first class would look down at us and throw us some food. But
who complained? Anything was better than what we came from."

It was 1901, the dawn of the twentieth century.

"And then," I asked, "what happened when you landed in America?"

"The first room I found was in a tenement. Every night I tied the
bottom of my pajamas with a rope, to keep the cockroaches from
crawling up my legs."

I shut my eyes in horror. He continued.

"Well, then I moved into Mama's place. They had three rooms,
all their five children slept in one bedroom, and on top of that they
took in boarders. I fell in love with Mama. She was pretty and she
was smart. She could speak English like a real American. I learned
how to sew sleeves in men's coats. I began working for two dollars
a week, then they raised me to ten, then twelve, and then fifteen
dollars a week."

Mama interrupted. "Six months a year they were on strike, three
months they worked, and three months they didn't have any work

at all. That's how he tried to make a living. So he gave up sewing sleeves in men's coats."

Papa nodded. "Then I got a seltzer route, also for fifteen dollars a week. I wanted to ask Mama to marry me, but I couldn't because I was saving every penny to bring my family to America."

"Your family back in Europe was very precious to you, wasn't it, Pop?"

I could see his Adam's apple move up and down. This was the hardest part for him to talk about. In Russia, his tall, bearded father, my own Moses, Zayda Gruber, had come home to his shtetl from a lumber-selling trip to find his house in mourning. His two little daughters were dead of dysentery. Then Baba Gruber, tiny, four feet eleven, nine years older than Zayda, gave birth to another girl and at last to a boy. And these babies too died of dysentery. Papa's birth in 1881 broke the terrible cycle. After Papa, four more sons were born, and all survived.

I waited until Papa regained his composure before I asked, "And then what happened?"

"It took me two years and I saved enough money to bring all six of them at one time to America. When I went to get them on Ellis Island, my father had some trouble with his eyes; they looked red. The Immigration people were ready to send the whole family to the side, maybe to send them all back to Russia, when I saw my mother.

" 'Mama,' I yelled. 'Mama! Mama!' The Immigration man saw it, and he waved his hand, 'Let them come in.' "

Now Papa was smiling. "In 1905, we got married. I wanted to buy Mama a pair of diamond earrings for three hundred dollars but she said, 'For what do I need diamond earrings? Better use the money to buy yourself a business.' "

"And you listened to her?"

"Don't I always? We bought Zayda Rockower's beer store at Fourteen Moore Street. We worked seven days a week, and in all the years we never sold a drink to anyone who looked drunk. We made it a wholesale and liquor store until Prohibition came. That's when I put up the sign: 'CLOSED UNTIL THE BAN IS OVER.' "

"Look how hard you worked, Papa," I said. "Don't you think I can work seven days a week too? I'm not afraid of hard work. You and Mama taught us that. Pop, don't you see, this will help me in anything I want to be later on."

"So what do you want to be?"

"A writer."

"Can you make a living that way?"

"Who knows? Famous writers like Sholom Aleichem, they make a good living. I have to try."

"Don't go, Ruthie. I'll give you anything you want. Only don't go."

"Papa, you left Russia when you knew it was the right thing for you to do—to go to America. This is the right thing for me, Papa, and it's the right time for me to go to Germany."

He cupped his face in his hands. "I see I can't stop you." He could convince all our relatives to accept his judgment. But not his daughter.

I felt his pain, but still I said, "I'm sorry, Pop. Nobody can stop me."

I had the fellowship—and a thousand dollars—in my pocket.

Part Two
GERMANY

9
Summer 1931

Back in Wisconsin, the university, reluctantly or not, forgave my escape from *Das Deutsche Haus*, accepted my thesis on Goethe's *Faust*, and gave me the master's degree in German and English.

"You won't have to hitchhike," Betty telephoned from Brooklyn. "Papa just bought a new Buick, and Bob and I are going to drive you home with all your gear."

"Come right away," I shouted into the phone. "Let's not even wait for graduation."

I walked for the last time along the willow-framed waters of Lake Mendota, remembering the Sundays of loneliness. I had drunk the wine of independence and found it bittersweet.

On the campus, I said goodbye to the faculty and friends, packed quickly, and hugged Mrs. Johanssen as Bob and Betty pulled up in the brand-new Buick. We tossed my bag and boxes of books into the trunk and took off.

The roads opened wide and empty before us. "You mustn't drive a new car fast," Betty warned me, while she and Bob took turns seeing how fast they could race it.

Two weeks later, the whole family came to the SS *Milwaukee* of the Hamburg-Amerika Line to see me off. Mama held my arm tightly as we wandered on the decks staring at the mahogany-walled lounges and dining rooms and the gilt-splattered ballrooms until we found the cabin I was to share with three others in tourist class.

"Not bad." My fourteen-year-old brother, Irving, in knicker-bockers, climbed the ladder and stretched out on my upper bunk. "If you don't fall out in case there's a hurricane."

I was on my way to a whole year in Germany, yet I knew the grief I was causing Mama and Papa. Mama was red-eyed. Papa's lips were drawn. My excitement was mixed with guilt.

"All visitors leave the ship," the loudspeaker proclaimed. The family hugged me for the last time. They stood on the dock toss-ing streams of colored ribbons at the ship, most of which fell into the bay.

Sirens blasted. Noisily, the ship's chains pulled up the anchor. I pressed against the rails. I had seen the face of anti-Semitism in Wisconsin's German department. What would it be like in Ger-many? Don't think about it now, I told myself. I threw my head back. The Atlantic Ocean stretched to the horizon, full of promise.

In the next days, I wandered through the Hamburg-American ship talking to everyone, the beer-barreled German men with three rolls on the back of their necks who ate steak and fried potatoes for breakfast, the prim and proper German women who wore long evening dresses to dinner every night, the American schoolteachers on a two-month summer vacation who swam in the pool, played Ping Pong in the game room and stretched out on deck chairs reading guidebooks or novels, the German officers who marched up and down the deck in spanking white uniforms as if they were on parade, and the German deckhands who came out after dark to smoke a cigarette and flirt.

Sitting at a desk in the ship's library, I wrote home:

"As soon as they learn I'm a student, the Americans want to talk books and literature, and the Germans, even the stewards who clean my room, want to talk philosophy and politics. These Germans seem so much more political than most of us. A lot of them have Adolf Hitler on their mind. The ones who hate him tell me he's a clown, like Charlie Chaplin with that silly little brush of a mustache on his lip; they're sure the good bürghers of Germany will never let him come to power. The ones who love him tell me he'll take over by 1932. My God, that's only next year! What a year this will be."

My favorite haunt was third class, the steerage of the thirties. Deep in the bowels of the ship, it was crowded and dark, though not as sardine-packed as the steerage on Papa's ship. I found it lively and interesting, for here were the students and the poor, the ones I felt closest to.

Up above, in tourist class, the social highlight of the journey was the costume ball. Some seasoned travelers had brought costumes from America. I tied a white paper banner with the words "Miss Milwaukee" in black crayon across my black evening dress, and won first prize.

In Paris, I took courses at the Sorbonne to improve my French, met friends from NYU at the American Express Office, and sat for hours at a sidewalk table of the Metropole Café, hoping I would see Ernest Hemingway and Gertrude Stein. I never did. But no matter. New people, new experiences, books—these were my passion. I traveled to London, then on to Holland, and finally reached Cologne.

In September 1931 I knocked on the door of an apartment building on Agrippina Ufer, a few blocks down the Rhine River from the University of Cologne.

"*Ich bin Ruth*," I announced.

The university, alerted from America that I was Jewish, had found a home for me with a Jewish family.

Frau Frieda Herz, small and round and friendly like my own mother, welcomed me like a daughter. Herr Otto Herz immediately assumed the stance of a German father. He was heavyset, paunchy, with huge blue eyes that seemed to have no lids. He was a successful broker on the grain exchange and ran his office in the front room of the sunlit apartment, the most desirable apartment in the four-story building that he owned.

Luisa, a delicate porcelain-skinned twenty-year-old, with large blue eyes like her father's, soon became my best friend. The Herzes, loving but stern, corrected my German accent and my American manners.

"My father," Luisa confided to me one night, "guards your virginity as closely as he guards mine."

My advisor at the university was a man in his thirties, Dr. Hugo Gabriel, who informed me the first day that his parents were Jewish but he was a Protestant. We arranged that I would take courses in three fields—*Germanistik* [German language and philosophy], *Anglistik* [modern English literature], and *Kunstgeschichte* [Art History]. My philosophy professor was the country's leading Nietzsche scholar, Ernst Bertram, who later became one of Hitler's chief ideologues. My English professor was Herbert Schöffler, who would later kill himself before he could be deported. It was in Professor Bertram's class that I met Johann.

He had stopped me one morning outside the lecture hall. "May I talk to you?" he asked in German.

"Certainly."

"My name is Johann," he said. "There are so few Americans at the University, only one or two perhaps. As for me, I have never met an American." His German was the *Hochdeutsch* of intellectuals, not *Kölsche Deutsch*, the dialect of Cologne.

"I am curious about America," he said. "Do you mind if we walk?"

We left the university and strolled along Agrippina Ufer toward the Rhine. The day was soft. People sat in cafés sipping beer.

Johann walked tall and straight, his stomach sucked in like an athlete's. His face was bony, his eyes dark and his black hair, brushed back, was brilliantine-shiny. Unlike the baggy, worn clothes of most of the students, his dark jacket and pants fit his body as if they were tailored for him.

We entered a sidewalk café and ordered coffee.

"How is it you speak German?" he asked. "I presume your family is German and you spoke it at home in America as a child."

"Not really. My family is not German; they came from Eastern Europe. And I learned German in college."

"In college—and you speak it so . . . ?"

"I fell in love with my German professor."

He smiled. It was a warm, attractive smile. I felt myself being drawn to him.

"I will tell you about myself," he said, "then you must tell me about yourself. I am an only child. My father is dead. My mother and I live alone. I am working hard to get my doctorate—maybe in the next two years—so that I can begin to support my mother. I want to be a writer, a poet, and a philosopher—like Professor Bertram."

"Is it true," I asked, "that Professor Bertram invites students to his home on Friday nights? But only young men?"

"Yes. I am one of them, and it's a great privilege. He's an inspiring teacher. We're so fortunate to come under his influence."

"Is he," I asked suddenly, "is he a Nazi?"

"Of course not," Johann bristled. "He wants to see Germany rebuild itself, become a great nation again. But a Nazi!" He said the word with contempt. "Never."

That night I lay on the narrow German bed, with its quilt filled with so much down that it looked a foot high, and wrote a tentative poem in my notebook: "Today I met/ a dark-haired student/ with a sculpted head."

A week later, we took chairs together, waiting for Professor Ernst Bertram to enter the lecture hall. Hundreds of students filled the room, joined by townsmen and women until the standing people made a human frame around the great hall.

Bertram opened a side door and, with a benign smile, walked to his table and chair. His hair fell loosely across his forehead; glasses rimmed his beaming, restless eyes.

He looked out across the adoring class, adjusted his glasses, and began. His voice soared, as he played Nietzsche's variation on the two souls that lived in Goethe's breast—day versus night, light versus darkness, good versus evil.

I sat enthralled, feeling Johann's presence beside me, as Bertram, like a guide in the forest of the German soul, led Nietzsche out of the darkness of suffering and bourgeois pettiness toward the luminescent holy Grail. It was not to find God, but to become the *Übermensch*, the Superman, who would one day become the hero of a new Germany. Through Nietzsche, Germany would rise beyond good and evil, "beyond itself," to new spiritual and heroic heights.

"Great men like Nietzsche," Bertram said, "create a spiritual climate, a spiritual substance that enters the universe and affects the strivings of all men."

I leaned forward, aware that Johann too was leaning forward, lest we lose a single word. Bertram talked of Nietzsche's birth and life, but not his death of syphilis in an insane asylum. The audience seemed to respond to each new thrust of learning. We were students, townsfolk, admirers, drawn together by the privilege of sitting at the feet of someone who, we sensed, was already part of twentieth-century German history. He was inspiring us to become pure and clean and noble. Johann and I walked out of his class, holding hands. I felt noble and clean and head over heels in love.

Just as I had done in Brooklyn, so in Cologne I began to bring students home. And just as Mama had welcomed my friends in Harmon Street, so Mama Herz welcomed them on Agrippina Ufer.

Sunday evenings were my favorite; informal family nights when we ate *Pfannekuchen*, potato pancakes with applesauce, or little kosher frankfurters with potato salad. One evening I brought Nathan Greenblatt, a scholarly-looking engineering student who clearly needed a decent meal. Mama Herz was happy to provide it.

Supper was a political battlefield.

"I tell you, Herr Herz," Nathan said, taking off his glasses and waving them in the air, "most of Germany isn't taking Hitler seriously enough. There'll be a reign of terror if he ever comes to power."

"Ridiculous," Papa Herz retorted. "Of course we know how dangerous he is, especially with all those *Lumpen* [ruffians] he has following him. But he has no political power."

"You're wrong, Herr Herz. He's doing everything according to the law. That's why they can't arrest him. He's building a powerful political machine and biding his time until he can get elected."

"I tell you he'll never get elected. The German people are too smart for that."

"He's changing his tactics, Herr Herz. At the beginning his followers were the poor, the unemployed, the dispossessed, the small-town people. Now he's reaching into the big cities, Berlin, Frankfurt, Cologne. He's going after the middle class and the upper class. Once he gets the bankers and the industrialists and the publishers, watch out, watch what he'll do with the Jews."

Papa Herz frowned. "So he'll go after the *Ostjuden* [the Eastern Jews who came largely from Poland and Russia]. They come to Germany with their big families and their rags and some of them give the German Jews a bad name."

I interrupted. "Herr Herz, you never asked me before. My parents are *Ostjuden*."

"From where?" He looked astonished.

"My mother was born in a shtetl called Beremlya in Wolyn Gubernya [Wolyn Province]. Then it was part of Russia; now it's part of Poland. My father grew up in Odessa but he was born in another shtetl in Wolyn called Antenufka—I think it was the model for Sholom Aleichem's Anatefka."

"*Ostjuden* or German Jews," Nathan was waving his eyeglasses again. "Hitler won't make any distinction once he gets power."

"Listen to me, Nathan," Papa Herz spoke irritably. "Hitler's nothing but an Austrian housepainter. How far back can he trace *his* German ancestry? My family has been in Germany for generations, and I myself was decorated with the Iron Cross in the Great War. I'm more German than he is."

Frau Herz said worriedly, "Otto, you're getting too excited. Go lie down for awhile."

With Papa Herz out of the room, Nathan pulled a leaflet out of his pocket and passed it around the dining-room table. "Look at this, look how Hitler tries to seduce the farmers suffering in this depression. It's not the *Ostjuden* he blames. It's all Jews."

I read the leaflet and shuddered.

GERMAN FARMERS

Farmers, it is a matter of your house and home!

Factories, forests, railway, taxes and the state's finances have all been robbed by the Jew. Now he's stretching his greedy fingers towards the last German possession—the German countryside.

You, farmer, will be chased from your plot of earth, which you have inherited from your forefathers since time immemorial. Insatiable Jewish race-lust and fanaticism are the driving forces behind this devilish attempt to break Germany's backbone through the annihilation of the German farming community.

Wake up!

I gave the pamphlet back to Nathan. "How do 'greedy fingers' and 'race-lust and fanaticism' rob factories and railways and farms?" I asked in disgust.

"You expect logic from the Nazis? Here, keep this pamphlet. Take it back to America when you go home." He looked toward Papa Herz's bedroom. "Some people think because they've lived in Germany for generations, nothing can happen to them."

Mama Herz stood up. "I don't like to hear things like that. I'm going to bed. I'm in the middle of a good novel."

10

The next Sunday evening, Nathan came with a newspaper under his arm. He opened it at the dinner table to a full-page photo of Brownshirts marching with their arms shot forward.

"One hundred thousand Nazis marching in Harzburg," he said. Papa Herz studied the photo. "*Gefährlich* [terrible]. But it's only one town."

"Now it's one town," Nathan said. "Next month it will be ten towns. Every day the fire gets stronger. Last year there were twelve Nazis in the Reichstag. Now there are a hundred and seven."

"And in the university?" I asked.

"They're still a small minority. But they're getting there. The ones who are there are getting cockier every day."

"What about the professors? What about Ernst Bertram, my Nietzsche professor? My friend Johann insists he's not a Nazi."

"Whether he's a member of the Nazi party or not, I don't know." Nathan stroked his chin as if he were stroking a beard. "But from what I hear, he has three *bêtes noires*. He hates foreigners. He hates women; he never invites them to his Friday night soirées. And he hates Jews. Does that make him a Nazi?"

"Come on, Nathan," I protested. "You see a Nazi under every bed."

"Just keep your eyes open."

If I was curious about the students, they were equally curious about me. Friedrich von Harzvogel, a blond student with a Kaiser Wilhelm mustache and a scar on his right cheek, sat next to me in Art History. "We have some foreign students here," he told me one morning before the class began, "from France and England and Italy and from countries far away like Japan and India. We even have a few *Neger* from Africa." I flinched. "But most of us have never met a student from America. We have monthly meetings where lecturers speak to us. Would you be willing to be the next lecturer?"

"Oh no. I'm not equipped to give a lecture."

"Of course you are. We'd like to know about life in an American university. For instance, the difference between American and German education."

"I don't really know enough about German universities. I'm here to learn, not to give a lecture."

"True, you're here to learn about us, but maybe we can learn something from you." The scar on his cheek seemed to redden. "You owe it to us. Our next meeting is one week from today."

All week I made notes and discarded them. I tried ideas out on Luisa, on Johann, and on Nathan. I read up on German universities, studied the faces of the students in my classes. Could I really give a lecture in Germany—and in German? In high school, I had been in the Debating Society, but there I had team security. This would be solo—one hour, 360 slow-ticking seconds, standing, quaking, maybe drowning in a sea of strange faces.

The October sun shot warm morning rays across the students in the cavernous lecture hall, but I was sitting on a bucket of ice. My hands shook, my teeth chattered; I clutched my knees to calm them. Before me was a blurred landscape of German faces.

I heard von Harzvogel introduce me: *"Fraülein Gruber aus Amerika."*

Shakily, I stood up. What do you do with your hands? I finally squeezed them together until they ached. *"Meine Freunde,"* I began. My voice was high and tight.

A plump young woman in the front row, with a braid of flaxen hair crowning her head, smiled encouragingly. I tried to bring my voice down a notch.

"I once heard somebody say that the best time to write a book about a country is after you've been there eight days. Then you're sure you know everything and you're an expert."

I paused, still quaking. "If you spend more than eight days, maybe you've learned too much and you're totally confused."

I stopped again. "If you spend a year, forget it."

The young woman with the flaxen hair laughed. The rest of the audience was silent.

"I've been here more than eight days, in fact a month, so I guess I no longer qualify as an expert."

I heard a few more students laugh. The faces became less blurred.

"Herr von Harzvogel asked me to describe some of the differences between your university and mine. I will try."

I took a deep breath and began to speak rapidly.

"I have discovered that most of you choose someone—maybe someone like two of my professors, Professor Bertram or Professor Schöffler—and you come to sit at their feet. In America we apply to the university we would like to go to, and very often we're rejected." I had not meant to say anything negative about America. But the words came out. "For instance, I might have liked going to Harvard or Yale. They were barred to me except in the summer. Can you guess why?"

"No," a student in the middle of the room called out. A few shook their heads.

"Because I'm not a man."

I heard a little more laughter. I let my hands fall at my side. The faces were becoming more defined.

"In America we enter college after high school; you enter after the *Gymnasium*; it would be like our entering the junior college year in America. So most of you, when you come, are at least two years older than American freshmen. Your *Gymnasium* is stricter, much more rigorous, than our high school, but your universities—they're like sudden freedom."

Several nodded. I picked out those who looked genuinely interested and talked to them.

"You all seem so eager to learn. The other day a woman who I think must be seventy years old came to sit beside me in Professor Bertram's class. 'I heard you're an American,' she said. 'Ah, maybe I'll learn something new.' "

The young woman with the blond braid clapped her hands silently. I hoped it meant that she too was learning something new.

"In America," I went on with more courage, "we have to take midterm and final exams. You don't have to take exams until you're ready."

Several more heads were nodding.

"You yourselves decide when you're ready, then you write your thesis and take your oral exams. I've even met some—you call them *ewige bemooste Studenten* [eternal moss-covered students]—who tell me they've been working for six or eight years to get a doctorate and haven't gotten it yet. Maybe for some people, both here and in my country, the university is a refuge from the terrible problems of the world."

A mature-looking student near the front pointed to himself.

"I would like now to interrupt," Friedrich von Harzvogel said.

"Please do." I remained standing.

"What you said is interesting," he began, "and I admit we know next to nothing about American universities. But what we do know is your culture. You have the hangovers of a pioneer civilization. You think extensively, in terms of quantity, in terms of size and wealth. We in Germany, with our culture and our long traditions, we think intensively, in terms of quality." He puffed his chest out. "We know your culture well from movies and novels."

"*Jawohl*," a few voices called out.

I shook my head. "Some of our movies and novels are fantasies that may have misled you. I'm amazed at how many Germans are convinced that every American girl who comes to Europe wants a duke or a count for a husband."

The young blond woman laughed. But Friedrich von Harzvogel seemed annoyed.

"We don't want your culture to contaminate us. We are not materialists like you, we're idealists. We are Germans, we want to remain Germans."

I stared at him as if I were seeing him for the first time. He isn't interested in the differences between our universities, I thought. If he were, even if I bored him to death, he wouldn't have stopped me this way. Is he trying to humiliate me? Or is he trying to show me and any other foreign students in the hall the superiority of German culture over American?

"*Verzeihen Sie* [Excuse me]," I said. "I know Germans who think in terms of quantity and Americans who think in terms of quality. I know German materialists and American idealists. These are stereotypes."

In the rear of the room, a student jumped up, aiming his forefinger at me like a pistol. "You have quotas in your universities against Jews, don't you?"

"Yes. And it's nothing we're proud of."

"Then you're stupid. You ought to be glad you have those quotas or you wouldn't have space in your universities for anybody except Jewish pigs."

Someone shouted, "That's no way to talk. You're a Nazi."

"That's right. I am a Nazi. You ought to be one too."

"Hold your mouth," someone called out.

"You hold your mouth," the heckler shook his fist. "Hitler is right. We should have quotas here, then we can keep out people like you and the rest of the swine."

I felt my lips trembling with anger and apprehension. All over the crowded room, students were leaping from their chairs, shouting at each other, "We are the master race."

"We need *Lebensraum*, living space."

"You're a Nazi!"

"You're a Communist!"

"You're a Jew!"

I felt naked, violated. The young blond woman hurried toward me. "You were brave to come and to say what you did." Taking my arm, she steered me out of the hall.

"I don't feel brave," I said dismally as we reached the street. "Just disgusted with myself. I should have fought back against that Nazi."

"You wouldn't have accomplished a thing. Please don't think I'm impolite, but are you Jewish?"

I nodded.

"I don't know whether most of the students in that hall realized it," she said. "I sensed it. I am too."

With her flaxen braid and bosomy figure she looked like the girls on German travel posters. "My name is Miriam Levy. I would love to invite you home for Shabbos. I go home Friday afternoons to Dinslaken; it's just north of here along the Rhine. Would you come sometime?"

"Sure."

I walked back to Agrippina Ufer disconsolately, the words ringing in my head: *You're a Nazi! You're a Communist! You're a Jew!*

11

Miriam Levy talked excitedly as we left the train in Dinslaken and hurried to her house. "I have four little brothers and sisters, and they've never seen a live American. The only Americans they know—when my mother lets them go to the movies—are people like Joan Crawford and Lillian Gish, and you don't look like any of them."

On the quiet street, her little sisters and brothers, all blond and blue-eyed with apple-red cheeks, climbed over her with bear hugs, then stood shyly as she introduced me.

Inside the house, her parents shook my hand. Her mother was plump and flaxen-haired like Miriam, her father tall like Papa with graying hair. The smells of fresh-baked challah and roasted chicken flooded my senses. It's Brooklyn, I thought, Brooklyn in Dinslaken on the Rhine.

Mrs. Levy blessed the candles, Mr. Levy sang the *kiddush* prayer over the wine, we ate gefilte fish and roast chicken and chanted songs and melodies from the Bible. During the singing I shut my eyes, letting the warmth of Friday night envelop me.

The next morning in a little orthodox synagogue, Miriam and I sat with the women in the balcony, the men on benches below us, praying in German accents.

I whispered to Miriam, "Four thousand miles from America, and here I am reading and chanting the same Hebrew prayers, only the translations are in German."

Miriam smiled, the same smile that had helped my knees stop shaking in the lecture hall.

We returned to the house and assembled around the dining table for *chulint*, the Saturday afternoon stew of *gedämpfte Brust*—pot roast and potatoes. Since orthodox Jews may not work on the Sabbath, Mrs. Levy had prepared the *chulint* on Friday and kept it on a low flame all night.

After lunch Mr. Levy herded his blond children into bed for a nap. In Miriam's bedroom, I lay awake thinking of the Herzes and their friends, the less devout ladies whom Mama Herz met in cafés for coffee and cake, who went to synagogue only for Bar Mitzvahs and weddings, never for ordinary Saturdays like this one.

Thinking of the Herzes brought Johann back into my head. I sat up with a start. He had told me that though he was a Lutheran, religion meant nothing to him; he did not go to church. Why had I never invited him to the house? I had invited other students who were not Jews. Why not Johann? Was I worried that they might not approve of him?

A few days later, I chose my words cautiously. "Frau Herz, I'd like to invite one of my friends—not for lunch or Sunday night supper, just for tea or a glass of wine in my room. It's his birthday."

Her eyes sparkled. "You never asked me if you could invite somebody to your room before. He must be something special."

"In a way."

"Then we'll make it a real nice birthday." She brought out a lace tablecloth to cover my desk. I bought a bottle of wine, a tall candle, and a flowered paperback of Rainer Maria Rilke's *Ausgewählte Gedichte*, his *Collected Poems*.

Johann arrived punctually as the clock in the hall struck seven.

I introduced him to the Herzes and Luisa, who were already in their coats, ready to leave for an engagement party. Mama Herz smiled, Luisa winked approvingly, Papa Hertz was polite.

As soon as they left, I led him to my bedroom. We sat, stiff and formal, in the two chairs I had carefully placed, with space between them, in front of my desk. "To you, Johann," I toasted him.

"To you," he raised his glass. We both used the polite German form "*Sie*."

We sipped self-consciously until I handed him my present.

He tore the wrapping, leafed through the pages and turned to Rilke's "*Liebeslied*," his "Love Song."

"Let me read it to you," he said.

I settled back in my chair and closed my eyes as he read:

> Everything that touches us, you and me,
> pulls us together, like a violin bow
> that draws one voice out of two strings.
> Out of what instrument are we bonded?
> And what player has us in his hand?
> Oh sweet song.

Like a violin bow that draws one voice out of two strings. I repeated the line to myself. If this were a movie, I thought, this is where the violin strings would begin to soar. But it's not a movie. And I'm here in a small bedroom with a down-covered bed and a lace-covered desk listening to Rilke's "*Liebeslied*" and wondering if I'm truly in love.

Johann continued reading poems Rilke had written of childhood and the women I was sure he had loved. The candle threw a gold light on Johann's face. His head is like a Roman sculpture, I thought.

He stopped reading and leaned forward. "I like you a lot."

I poured him another glass of wine.

He took a sip. "You are like nobody I ever met in my life—"

"You probably never met an American before."

"Quite so." He set his glass down. "From a little boy, I knew what my life was to be. I would be an elementary schoolteacher, just like my late father. My life was set. I asked no questions. Then you came here like a wind, and you make me want the kind of freedom you have."

"You don't want to be a schoolteacher any more?"

"Oh yes I do. I dream of being a teacher and training young minds. The younger the better. The sooner we train children, the more influence we have."

A shadow fell on the room. That was what Hitler was saying in his speeches: "Give me a child up to six—and I own his mind for the rest of his life."

Johann was still talking. "I would like to have the kind of freedom you have. Freedom to leave your family." He smiled at me and the shadow lifted. "You left America, a girl alone."

"I had to fight hard to do it."

"That's what I mean about you. You know what you want to do, and you do it. That's freedom. And that's what you represent to me. Forgive me for being so forward, but what do I represent to you?"

I thought for a while. "First I'll tell you what I think you're not. You're not like the students who tried to break up the talk I gave in the lecture hall. They were Nazis."

"I'm not a Nazi."

I nodded. "I can't picture you talking about Jewish pigs or spouting those Hitler theories about *Lebensraum*—"

He put his hand on mine. "You said what I'm not. Now please tell me what I am."

"I think you're sensitive and idealistic and—"

"Yes? And what?"

"And romantic."

"I think you are much like me," he said. "And I must tell you, I find you most attractive."

I became aware of the silence in the Herzes' apartment. I sensed his body though our chairs were far apart.

"Do I have permission to kiss you?" he asked. It was the first time he had used the familiar *du*.

I murmured, "Yes."

He went further. "Before I kiss you, would you permit me to turn off the light?"

Again I nodded, unable to speak.

He switched off the light. We stood up from the desk together. He put his arms around my shoulders. My body began to tremble. I felt his trembling too. Yet somehow I knew *we* were projecting our own romantic fantasies on each other. In the dark bedroom, Nietzsche's words began singing in my head. *Night am I, ah that I were light.*

Then slowly, as if he had practiced each movement, he bent his head ready to press his lips to mine.

I raised my head, and at that moment the Herzes returned. We stood holding each other, not kissing, afraid to move. I heard Papa Herz go to the kitchen and return to his bedroom. We waited, still frozen in our embrace, until we thought they were asleep. Then I tiptoed to the front door to let Johann out.

Papa Herz heard us, rushed out in his pajamas, and screamed, "Who is there? Thief! Stop! I will call the police!"

"It's no thief, Herr Herz," I said. "It's only me."

"What were you doing?" he demanded.

"*Wir haben nur das Licht ausgeknipst* [We only switched off the light]."

"*Licht ausknipsen ist verboten in meinem Haus* [Turning off the lights is forbidden in my house]." I felt humiliated.

"Get out," he shouted to Johann. "And Ruth, go to bed."

12

Professor Herbert Schöffler, chairman of the Department of English Language and Literature, invited me to his office.

He motioned me to a chair while he hoisted himself up on the edge of his desk, a short, stout man with his stomach hanging over his belt, and a jovial, round face.

"I would like you to work for your Doctor of Philosophy degree."

I was stunned. "You're very kind, Professor Schöffler. But my fellowship is for only one year."

"Then write and ask to have your fellowship extended."

I shook my head. "They would never grant it, and even if they did, my parents would never agree to my staying two or three more years."

I thought of Papa trying to bribe me not to go: *Don't go, Ruthie. I'll give you anything you want. Only don't go.*

Professor Schöffler moved from his desk toward me. "I have a special motive. I would like to have one of my students do original literary research in the writings of Virginia Woolf. She is my favorite modern English author. But my students are Germans; their English is not good enough. I don't know when I shall have another American or English student. I would even prefer that you write your thesis in English."

"I would love to study her work," I said. "But I know I can't stay beyond this year."

His face seemed to grow rounder as he smiled. "No one has ever gotten a Ph.D. in one year. But let's try."

Dazed, I walked out of his office. I had nothing to lose, I assured myself. It would be another challenge.

I rushed downtown and canvassed the bookstores to find Virginia Woolf's books. I bought all that she had written thus far, published in hard cover by her own and Leonard Woolf's Hogarth Press in London, and paperbacks published by the Tauchnitz Press in Leipzig. Professor Schöffler was the director of the Tauchnitz Press.

In my bedroom, I plunged into her world, feverish with excitement. I filled notebooks, wrote on the margins and the endpapers of her books, met her strong, creative women and her sensitive, poetic, or hypercritical and destructive men.

I reveled in her determination to describe life as a woman with "obstinate integrity." "We think back through our mothers if we are women," she wrote.

On sheets torn from my notebook, I copied lines from *A Room of One's Own* and lay them across my desk so that they were the first words I read when I woke and the last before I went to sleep.

> So long as you write what you wish to write, that is all that matters; and whether it matters for ages or only for hours, nobody can say. But to sacrifice a hair of the head of your vision, a shade of its colour, in deference to some Headmaster with a silver pot in his hand or to some professor with a measuring-rod up his sleeve, is the most abject treachery.

*　　*　　*

In November I wrote home:

> Dear Mom and Pop, I've been asked if I would like to join several other American exchange students in Germany. We've been invited to spend our Christmas vacation on a ski trip in the Bavarian Alps. It costs $75. Would you send me the money? I'd like to go.

In December, a letter came back from my brother Harry, who was interning at Kings County Hospital in Brooklyn.

> Dear Ruth, As usual, you stirred up quite a ruckus on Harmon Street. Mom and Pop think skiing is too dangerous for a girl; they're always worried about you anyway. They'd like you to just finish this year and come home. But I convinced them this is a good way for you to see more of Germany. Who knows when you'll get another chance? So here's a money order. Love from us all, and don't fall off a mountain.

I hurried to the university to share the news with Johann.

"How lucky you are to go to Berchtesgaden," he said. "Soon you'll know more of my country than I do."

"That'll never happen. Let's go downtown. I have to change the money order for Reichsmarks, and I want to go to a bookstore. There may be more books by Virginia Woolf."

We walked along the banks of the Rhine. I talked excitedly, still elated from Harry's letter. "As soon as I get back from Berchtesgaden, I'm going to start writing my dissertation. I've even figured out the theme. It's her will to write as a woman."

Johann said nothing. I went on blithely, "I'm so happy I'm doing this study of Virginia Woolf."

"Why?" He sounded sullen.

"It's helping me understand Germany."

"How can that be? Virginia Woolf helping you understand Germany!"

"It's that Virginia Woolf and Rilke are meshing together in my head: Virginia Woolf paving the way for women to write as women, and Rilke capturing the beauty, the essence of Germany."

"I can't see it at all. What does Rilke have to do with Virginia Woolf?"

"She makes me feel about London the way Rilke makes me feel about Germany. I know her streets and flower markets the way I'm beginning to know the streets of Cologne. It seems so . . . so . . . " I wanted to use the Yiddish word Mama used all the time, so *beshert* [so destined], but I knew Johann wouldn't understand it. Instead I said, "so symbolic that I should be discovering her here. As if she's helping me in Germany chart the course of my life."

Johann said nothing. His dark mood puzzled me.

"Did I say something wrong?"

"No," he said brusquely. "Just forget it."

We had left the Rhine and reached the Old Town, heading toward a bookstore along Hohestrasse, the main shopping street where no cars were allowed. Solid bürghers, carrying leather briefcases, entered little stores to buy tobacco or newspapers. Women in long woolen coats and helmet-shaped hats talked together. Prostitutes stood, openly soliciting. We passed the great glass windows of Tietz, the largest department store in Cologne, owned by the Tietzes, a prominent Jewish family, until we came upon a bookshop. Hitler's two-volume sets of *Mein Kampf* were the only books in the window.

Inside the shop I asked a clerk for books on Virginia Woolf. They had none. Was this, too, *beshert*? *Mein Kampf* and no Virginia Woolf. I bought the two volumes of *Mein Kampf*.

"Why are you buying them?" Johann demanded.

"I'm going to read them on the train."

"It's not exactly what one takes on a holiday."

He was still preoccupied as we left the shop, crossed over to Schildergasse, another street free of cars, and made our way to our favorite square. Above us, the Cathedral stretched its latticed arms into the sky, the symbol of all that was noble and spiritual and idealistic in Germany.

"If you finish your thesis this fast—." Johann suddenly stopped.

"What do you mean?"

"You'll be ready to take your orals this year. I won't be ready for another year, probably two more years. It bothers me that you'll get your degree before I do."

I spun around to look at him.

"Is that why you seem so irritable today?"

"I should be getting my doctorate the same time you get yours. I'd feel better about us."

"What difference who gets it first?" I asked.

"It makes a difference. The man should get it before the woman."

"I can't believe you're saying this."

He stopped. "I shouldn't have said anything. I don't know what got into me. Forgive me."

He took my hand. "I'll never forgive myself if you let these words come between us."

"Let's walk back quickly," I said. "There's so much to do before I leave for Berchtesgaden."

13
Christmas 1931

The train pulled out of Cologne's Hauptbahnhof.

I sat on the wooden bench in the second-class compartment looking out the window. Johann's words had baffled me.

Maybe, I thought, even subconsciously he's swallowed all that Nazi propaganda about women and the three Ks—*Kinder, Kirche, Küche* [Children, Church, Kitchen]. Imagine me in that category! I wonder if we know each other at all.

Facing me on the opposite bench, a worn-looking mother, with a baby wrapped like a mummy in her lap, took a roll out of a wicker basket and munched it loudly. A middle-aged man sat humped over his newspaper, his nose a map of broken capillaries. A young skier hoisted his skis into the ledge above our heads and went to sleep. Do all these passengers, so *echt Deutsch*, such real Germans, do they all believe in the three Ks? I opened *Mein Kampf*.

"On April 1, 1924," Hitler began his preface, "because of the sentence handed down by the People's Court of Munich, I had to begin that day, serving my term in the fortress at Landsberg on the Lech."

His motive, he said, was "to set forth the object of our movement, to draw a picture of its development . . . [and] to destroy the evil legends created about my person by the Jewish press."

I had heard how he had been arrested after the famous Munich *Putsch* in November 1923, when he tried to overthrow the government. He had fled from Munich, but army troops had tracked him down. He was arrested and spent his months in jail dictating this mélange of autobiography and polemics to his devoted follower, Rudolph Hess.

He's no great German writer, I thought, as with mounting anger and disgust, I marked line after anti-Semitic line.

I shut the book and looked at my neighbors. Did the worn-looking mother and the middle-aged man, now snoring over his newspaper, believe all this? Did the skier, lost in a paperback mystery, believe it? What chord did it touch? What made the Germans buy *Mein Kampf* as if it were their new Bible?

In the Hauptbahnhof in Munich I boarded another train and was soon transported into a scenic wonderland of snow-covered mountains. The train pulled into Berchtesgaden, and in minutes I was in a horse-drawn sleigh sloshing through a quaint storybook village.

In an equally quaint ski lodge, I met several of the American exchange students who had arrived from other German universities. Our American chaperone greeted us as we checked in.

"Tomorrow," he announced, "we will all ski."

I had never skied; I had never even ice-skated or ridden a bicycle in Brooklyn. I was prepared to learn.

The next morning, in woolen pants, heavy underwear, boots, and skis, I was barely on the snow when I fell. I tried again, sailed a few feet, and fell again. After an hour of tripping and rolling, I admitted to myself that I was no athlete and never would be, and I made my way back to the lodge. In front of a huge blazing fireplace, I warmed my hands and feet and then joined the skiers for the obligatory shot of brandy and a delicious Bavarian lunch of chunks of wurst floating in pea soup.

I spent the next mornings falling on my skis and the afternoons stomping through the white enchanted village with its lovely chalets and painted wooden balconies. *"Grüss Gott"*—Greet God— shopkeepers welcomed me, offering to sell me dolls in Bavarian costumes, German pastry, or German *schnaps*—whiskey. I needed no *schnaps*. I was happy drinking in the pure mountain air.

One evening our American chaperone announced in the lobby, "We have been invited to a party given by some of the townspeople." It was to be in a local *Bierstube*, a beer parlor. "Wear your best clothes, and be there punctually at seven."

At seven we were greeted by hospitable-looking buxom women in dirndl skirts and snow-white blouses and muscular men in leather weskits, knee-high socks, and *Lederhosen* [leather pants]. A few of the men were bareheaded, but most wore green felt hats with jaunty bird feathers perched in the band.

We sat on benches facing each other across narrow wooden tables, each American student between two villagers. The tables, covered with red-checkered cloths, were laden with knockwurst, potato salad, coleslaw, and richly decorated beer steins with metal lids. At my left was a burly young man in his twenties, with brown hair pasted back, brown eyes, and a round head.

"Ich bin Heinz," he said, shaking my hand so vigorously it stung.

"Ich bin Ruth," I answered.

"Ah, Ruth. How do you like our village?"

"It's like a German fairy tale. I have to pinch myself to be sure I'm really here."

He was pleased. "And how do you like this weather?" Before I could answer, he went on, "Tell me, do you have such good skiing weather in America?"

"I'm afraid I don't know much about skiing weather. I'm trying, but I'm really a ski-failure."

"Stay longer among us," he said. "I will teach you myself. Will you let me be your teacher?"

I was not sure how to take his offer. I was spared from answering when someone began to yodel. Soon most of the men were snapping their hands like whips across their *Lederhosen*. After the yodeling, we began to sing the familiar German song: *"Du, du, liegst mir im Herzen."*

> You, you lie in my heart,
> You, you lie in my mind;
> You, you give me much pain;
> You don't know how good I am for you.
> Yes, yes, yes, yes,
> You don't know how good I am for you.

By now we had stretched our arms around each other's waists and were swaying from side to side. The singing and swaying were like a German ritual, romantic, sentimental, but the words "You give me much pain; you don't know how good I am for you" seemed arrogant. Johann flashed across my mind. Yes, his arguments were arrogant. I felt the rift between us.

Someone began "Die Lorelei," Heinrich Heine's fantasy of the mermaid luring sailors to their graves in the Rhine. *"Ich weiss nicht was soll es bedeuten . . ."*

> I don't know what it means
> that I should be so sad;
> a fairytale of ancient times
> I can't get it out of my head. . . .

My reference points were nearly always in my beloved New York, and as we sang I thought of the Heinrich Heine monument on the Grand Concourse in the Bronx. The Lorelei, the mermaid, sat like a Greek goddess on a marble pillar, forever looking down at Heine. Three more half-naked mermaids rested at her feet. Water spouted from dolphins into a pool where New York children waded, unaware that the monument of a famous German poet, born Chaim Heine, had landed in the Bronx after German anti-Semites had denied it a place in his native city of Düsseldorf.

I was mulling over the tragedy of his life when I realized the singing had stopped and once again people were munching knockwurst and potato salad and clinking their beer steins.

Heinz wiped some foam from his lips and put his arm around my waist. "I want to tell you something. I don't like Americans. They're all loud and vulgar. But you're different."

A ball of anger rose in my throat. Was this to be a replay of the scene in the Art History class? I, who could not wait to escape from Brooklyn, had never felt so patriotic.

I tried to be polite. "I don't agree with you that all Americans are loud and vulgar."

Heinz took another draught of beer and squeezed my waist again. "Americans are bad enough, but American Jews are the worst. They're all bankers or communists. Hitler is right. We have to get rid of them before they take over the world."

My anger seemed to choke me.

I yanked Heinz's arm away and stood up. "I am an American and a Jew, and I will not listen to such talk."

The room grew silent. The students and the Germans all stared at us.

"I didn't know you're a Jew," he said, sobering a little. "But you're different. I told you that."

"I'm not different. And I'm proud of what I am."

I stalked out of the *Bierstube*, followed instantly by the American chaperone. "You had no right to speak to that man the way you did. I want you to go back and apologize."

"Apologize! He insulted me."

"You are here as an ambassador of the United States. The way you act influences how the Germans see us. I insist you apologize. This man is one of our hosts."

"Hosts don't insult their guests."

"Nonetheless you must go back and apologize."

"You expect me to apologize to someone who denigrates America and hates Jews. Let him apologize to me."

"Of course he won't apologize to you. That's the way he thinks."

"Then I don't want to be in the same room with him. I'm leaving."

In the ski lodge, I packed my bag and tried to sleep. There was no heat in the bedrooms. Even the hot bricks that the chambermaid brought to warm my feet were no comfort. I was freezing with rage.

In the morning I took the train across the Alps to Vienna.

Vienna! The fabled city where Beethoven composed and Freud analyzed his own and his patients' dreams. I was sure that in Vienna I could put last night's bitter experience out of my head.

I registered in a small pension and telephoned Norman, one of my sister Betty's friends. A victim of the quota system, he had been turned down by every American medical school to which he applied. Fortunately he had been accepted in Vienna.

He came quickly, tall, thin, hungry for news of America. Satisfied that Betty was fine, he said, "Vienna is all yours today. What do you want to see first? The Imperial Palace. The gardens. The Opera House. Museums. Coffeehouses. The university. You choose."

"Let's go to the university," I said. "I want to see where you're studying."

Norman bit his lip. "I'm not sure you'll like what I have to show you."

"What do you mean?"

"You'll see. I was there this morning."

At the university, we made our way to the chemistry lab. I clutched my stomach. The lab looked as if a bulldozer had plowed through it. Glass beakers and test tubes were shattered. Chemicals were spilled across the tables with the nauseating smell of ammonia and sulphuric acid. The floor was littered with notebooks ripped apart.

"Nazis?" I hardly heard my voice.

He nodded. "Nazi *students*. They must have come in the middle

111

of the night. Just to this lab—they knew most of us were Jews. Months of work, all destroyed."

"Were they punished? Did the university do something to them?"

"Nothing. It was not the first time."

"Do Austrians outside the university know about this vandalism? Are there stories in the newspapers?"

He shook his head.

The ball of anger was rising in my throat again. "What will you do now?"

"Start the experiments all over again. I can't leave. I have no place else to go."

"My God," I blurted out. "There are Nazi students at Cologne, but I never heard of them doing anything like this."

Norman's face was ashen. "The Austrians don't admit it, but they're just as anti-Semitic, maybe more—if that's possible—than the Germans. Don't forget, Hitler was born in Austria."

"They're exceptions," Johann said, trying to explain away the drunken villager in Berchtesgaden and the wanton destruction in the Vienna lab.

We were walking hand in hand along the Rhine. The winter sun threw shafts of light on the water. Traffic on the river was heavy with commercial ships and barges.

Johann had come to the house soon after I returned, to apologize again for his irritable outburst. "It was a bad day for me," he said. "I couldn't tell you that my mother had lost her job. But she has a new job, and I realize what a fool I was. Forgive me."

I nodded. I wanted to forgive him. And I wanted his help in understanding what had happened in Berchtesgaden and Vienna.

"It's only a handful of Nazis," he said, and repeated," Just exceptions."

I looked at him more closely. "Who are these exceptions?"

"Mostly *Lumpen,* ruffians."

"But it was Nazi *students* in Vienna who wrecked those experiments. You can't call students *Lumpen.*"

"They're not the majority," he protested. "I know I'm right. And you must not let those experiences affect our friendship."

He put his hand under my arm and held it tightly. "I've never felt toward anyone the way I feel toward you. You must believe me."

"I want to believe you, Johann," I said, still searching for answers.

The next months became an exhausting tug-of-war as I sought to hold on to my faith in Germany. I felt there was something holy in Germany but something shameful, sinister, evil, too. In the playgrounds, children playing "Cowboys and Indians" now called the game "Aryans and Jews." In the schools and universities, Baldur von Schirach, the Nazi Youth Leader and his eager followers, faculty and students, were preaching two things: ultranationalism and anti-Semitism. Each day more students surfaced in our classes in brown shirts.

"Why is it happening so fast now?" I asked Johann a few days later. We had just left Bertram's lecture hall. "I look among the students and I wonder who are the Nazis not yet in uniform."

"If they're not in uniform, they're not Nazis," he insisted.

"But who *are* the Nazi students? Are they the sons of Junkers? Are they the children of the proletariat, or are they middle-class? Who are they?"

"You ask me that as if you suspect I may be one of them. I'm not a Nazi. I'm not a member of any party. I suppose I'm closest to the German Nationalist party. It's right-wing, but it believes in the Weimar Republic. We believe in the dignity of Germany. In its history. Its culture. Its language. I repeat, Ruth, I am not a Nazi."

"Of course you're not."

We walked a short distance in silence. The questions were still tormenting me. "Remember one of our favorite lines in Rilke, about 'learning to live with questions that have no answers.' I can't help

113

it, Johann. I need to have answers. Is Nietzsche being misread? Is his Superman the excuse to make Germans feel superior to everybody, especially to Jews?"

He put his arm through mine. "Listen to me. Germany is going through a terrible crisis. Workers have no jobs; even the middle class is pretty poor; people have lost most of their savings. My mother and I have very little. What's happening is the result of the Treaty of Versailles."

"That's what Hitler says in *Mein Kampf*. Everybody in Germany blames the Treaty of Versailles."

"But it's true. It's what the Allies did to us after the Kaiser was defeated in 1918. You don't know what it was like here during the inflation. German marks were worthless. You had to haul the paper money in a baby carriage to buy a loaf of bread. I don't know if you—I mean, if an American—can understand what it was like in Germany and what it's like today."

I felt the warmth of his arm against my body. I wanted to assure him that I believed in him. Instead I heard myself say, "Germans aren't the only ones suffering. We're having a depression in America too. But that doesn't make us want to make our country a dictatorship with a madman like Hitler turning thugs loose. You haven't answered my question. Why are so many university students wearing brown shirts?"

Johann shook his head. "I don't know. But *I'm* not like them."

"Of course you're not." I took his hand.

"They won't win," he said. "You'll see."

14
February 1932

It was Carnival time in Cologne.

Ruth Jacobi, a dress designer and a friend of Luisa's, came to the apartment with colorful fabrics and in one short afternoon sewed up costumes for us. Luisa stood in front of a long mirror smiling at herself as a Renaissance princess in a flowing skirt and lacy top; I was a Harlequin clown in a shiny yellow-and-green sateen jumpsuit.

Mama Herz told me, "*Liebchen*, Darling, in Cologne tonight you must let any man kiss you who wants to, and you must not come home until morning."

Luisa and I, our faces hidden by masks down to our chins, sauntered through the narrow medieval streets crowded with Marie Antoinettes, Madame Récamiers, Napoleons, eighteenth-century officers in tricorner hats, Gretchens, Greek Helens, soldiers in periwigs and red and blue breeches, Arabs, Eskimos in fur parkas, sailors, toreadors, and dozens of Mephistopheleses trailed by little devils, all dancing, singing, blowing horns and trumpets, reveling in the last bacchanalia before the penitence of Lent.

"If we get separated," Luisa said, "we'll meet my parents in the Gürzenich." For five hundred years, the Gürzenich had hosted emperors and nobility. Now it hosted fashionable shops and a banquet hall where every year Mama and Papa Herz met their friends at Carnival.

Like two boats lashed to each other, Luisa and I were swept up in a flood tide of rolling, shoving, drinking, raucous, masked human beings. I looked for Johann. I knew I would recognize him even in a mask. But I could not find him.

Suddenly a mock-Indian with a feathered headpiece grabbed my arm.

"Stop," I screamed, "you're hurting me." In the raging crowd, I lost Luisa.

Clutching me tightly, he smashed through the maelstrom toward a side street, shouting demented war cries in German.

I struggled against his clenched hand. "Whoever you are, let me go," I tried to shout across waves of people, most of them drunk.

Suddenly a masked man in a forest-colored cape and a shock of silky white hair eddied toward us.

"*Lass sie gehn* [Let go of her]," he commanded. He wrenched the mock-Indian's hand off my arm and steered me back into the main current.

"How can I thank you," I gasped.

"I didn't like what he was trying to do to you."

He tucked his arm gently in mine. "I knew you were American even before you spoke. There's something about Americans. Maybe it's the way you walk or the way you hold yourself. I didn't want you to think badly of us."

I would have liked to have seen his face. I was sure he was handsome, like Ronald Colman or Walter Pigeon. But instead of removing his mask, he bowed, kissed my hand, and vanished into the crowd.

I found Luisa at the Gurzenich, and once again we were back on the streets, swimming through the reckless tide.

It was six in the morning when we dragged our feet along the Rhine and up to Agrippina Ufer.

Papa Herz was on the balcony in his pajamas, waving us home.

The next weeks were frantic ones—attending classes, working on the dissertation, stealing time to walk with Johann.

The two volumes of *Mein Kampf* stared at me from my bookshelf. Hitler's voice blared hysterically through the radio each time I listened to the news. I tried to block it out while I immersed myself in Virginia Woolf, writing for hours each day and often, in the middle of the night, jumping out of bed, rushing to my desk, and writing some more.

Each Friday afternoon I sent a letter home, trying to describe the warmth of my life with the Herzes. I wrote nothing of politics. I had given Mama and Papa enough pain by coming to Germany. Why give them sleepless nights worrying whether I was safe?

The storm troopers in their ugly brown shirts and laced-up ugly boots marched down the streets more brazenly than ever. Gang wars made walking precarious. Spring elections for the presidency of the Weimar Republic were approaching. Nazi slogans surfaced everywhere, promising the dispossessed and the unemployed an end to their misery: "Work and Bread for All," "The Needs of the People Before the Needs of the Individual," "Down with the Tyranny of Investment Capital." Hitler was running against the eighty-five-year-old president, ex-Field Marshal von Hindenburg, and huge posters carrying their faces were plastered on billboards and on thick columns all over town.

Election day, Sunday, March 13, 1932, was unseasonably warm. It was a good sign; the balmy weather would bring more people to the polls to defeat the Nazis. I walked the streets with Johann to see what elections were like in Cologne.

Gangs in Nazi uniforms were chanting, "Vote for our glorious *Führer*." We knew the Communists would vote for Ernst Thaelmann. The Catholic center would vote for von Hindenburg. The

German National party, the one Johann felt closest to, the right-wing party claiming to be nationalists but not Nazis, would vote for Alfred Hugenberg.

But how would the majority of the middle-class bürghers act when they entered the voting places? Would most of them vote for the aging president and keep the Weimar Republic? Would they wash away the center and embrace the right or the left and destroy the republic?

We returned to the Herzes' apartment and listened to the radio on my desk. We kept the door of my bedroom properly open. No more *Licht ausknipsen.*

"Von Hindenburg," the announcer reported, "has failed to win a complete majority."

"Oh no," I moaned.

"President Von Hindenburg has won only 49.6 percent."

By German law, the ruling party had to win over 50 percent.

The announcer continued: "Hitler and his National Socialist party are second, with 30.1 percent."

"Thirty percent!" I blurted. "Thirty percent of the German people want Hitler! It's sickening. What's wrong with them?"

Johann shook his head. On the air, the announcer was still talking: "The Communists are next with 13.2 percent, and the Nationalists have only 6.9 percent."

There would be a second election in a month.

On the streets, fights between the Nazis and the Communists grew bloodier. Thugs in brown shirts marched insolently, stopping pedestrians, halting traffic, screaming their curses: "Death to the Jew–Weimar Republic. *Jüde Verecke* [Croak the Jews]."

The German Nationalist party withdrew from the elections, telling their followers to vote for Hitler.

"That's disgusting," Johann said. "I'm through with them. They've completely capitulated."

The days became more ominous. What would it mean if Hitler won in this second election for the presidency, scheduled for

April 10? What would happen to the Jews? the Herzes? Would I have to rush home to Brooklyn before I finished the school year?

April 10 was a dark, brooding day with intermittent rain. I did not walk the streets; instead I sat with the Herzes in the living room, listening to the radio, dreading the news. Mama Herz's knitting needles made the only sound in the room. Luisa slumped in her chair, looking pale and vulnerable. Papa Herz pretended to read a newspaper; it lay open on his lap.

At last the announcer's voice came through the air. "Von Hindenburg has won 53 percent of the vote."

"*Gott sei dank.*" Thank God. Tears ran down Mama Herz's face.

"Hooray!" we embraced each other.

Herr Herz filled our glasses with sherry.

"To the Weimar Republic," he raised his glass.

"To the Weimar Republic," we answered.

The republic was standing.

At the university, the anti-Nazis among us congratulated each other. "The majority of Germans," we told each other, "have seen through Hitler's antics. He's on the way out."

I went back to my dissertation on Virginia Woolf.

But a month later, von Hindenburg abruptly fired Chancellor Heinrich Bruening, who had fought to keep the Nazis in check. In his place, Hindenburg appointed Franz von Papen.

"Von Papen is a fool, a clown," Papa Herz said. We were eating the usual potato pancakes at the Sunday night dinner table.

Nathan, sitting next to Luisa, openly smitten by her, agreed for once with Papa Herz. "You're right. Everybody laughs at von Papen. He has no experience and no judgment."

He turned to me. "Did you know that halfway through the Great War, von Papen served in Washington as a military attaché. Your government threw him out. Why? America wasn't even in the war yet and they found him planning to blow up your bridges and railway lines."

The potato pancake turned sour in my mouth. "Why would von Hindenburg pick a clown to run the government?"

Nathan replied, "I'm sure one day we'll discover the Nazis had a major hand in getting von Hindenburg to do it."

The next election was called for July 31, the third national election in four months. The first two had been for the president; this one was for seats in the Reichstag.

"It's the last election I'll see," I told Johann at the university. My year's fellowship was scheduled to end in August.

To fill the Parliament with his followers, Hitler unleashed Nazi speakers on street corners to scream venomous attacks against all the other parties and against Jews. The city was plastered with new Nazi posters exhorting people to vote the list of the NSDP (National Socialist German Workers Party). Newspapers carried front-page photos of Hitler electioneering before tens of thousands of followers in a sea of Nazi flags.

Fear settled over the household. Few guests came. We seemed to be pulling ourselves into a bomb shelter, protecting ourselves against the storm we could see on the horizon.

I was glad my dissertation was almost finished. It was harder each day to concentrate; rumors were spreading around the university that Hitler would win a majority in the Reichstag.

We sat in bleak silence in the living room on the night of July 31, listening to the radio, the focal point of our lives. Hope or despair, tragedy or survival, the fate of Germany, the fate of Jews—we would learn it all with the flick of a knob and the sound of a disembodied voice.

"Hitler's National Socialist party," the voice announced calmly, as if it were giving a daily weather report, "has won 230 seats in the Reichstag."

Papa Herz banged his fist on the table. "Awful. Awful. They were a nothing party in 1928. And now, in three years, look at them. The biggest party in Germany." His blue eyes were bloodshot.

"But Herr Herz," I said, searching for a spot of light in the menacing darkness, "there are 608 seats in the Reichstag. They still don't have a majority. The majority of Germans still don't want him."

Mama Herz looked at me sadly. She seemed to have aged in the last hour. "Yes, Rütchen, we mustn't give up hope."

15

Luisa typed the Virginia Woolf dissertation in her father's office, and the day after the elections, I brought it to Professor Schöffler.

Days passed. I paced the bedroom floor. I fingered the card on my desk and reread Virginia Woolf's credo: "So long as you write what you wish to write, that is all that matters."

I had written what I wanted to write. I had tried to be analytical, critical, and at the same time show how much I admired her. Schöffler's delay made me fear he would reject my thesis the way the *Atlantic Monthly* had rejected my freshman essays at NYU.

Finally, the call came. Schöffler summoned me to his office. "You've given me just what I wanted," he said.

"You really like it? Really, Professor Schöffler? You're not just saying this because . . . because I'm an American and . . . and . . . because . . ."

"You've done a splendid job." He was still talking, but I no longer heard.

The oral exams loomed next. For my three majors, I would have to appear before Professor Bertram on Nietzsche, Professor Schöffler on Virginia Woolf, and a professor from the Art History department on German medieval and Renaissance art, analyzing especially the woodcuts and etchings of Albrecht Dürer.

I spent hours studying my notes on Nietzsche, poring over art books on Dürer, and rereading Virginia Woolf's books.

The day before the exams, Luisa, home from school with a cold, called me to her bedroom.

"Do you know how many times you've been to the bathroom today?"

"What are you talking about?"

"I've been counting. You've run to the toilet sixteen times already. And it's only two o'clock."

"Oh God."

Early evening, she called out again. "Six o'clock, and it's up to twenty-seven."

The orals were scheduled for eight in the morning. I went to bed early, to be fresh for the examination. Instead I tossed, tormenting myself. What questions will they ask? What answers will I give? Professor Schöffler may be friendly, but what will Bertram be like? He doesn't know me. How could he know me in that huge lecture hall? What if he really is a Nazi, despite Johann's denial? He'll surely fail me.

I fell asleep for a little while and woke up with a start. Nathan's words were spinning through my brain. *Bertram has three bêtes noires: he hates foreigners, women, and Jews.* I fit into all three categories.

I finally fell asleep.

In the morning Mama Herz, still in her bathrobe, said, "Come have breakfast. Here's a nice hot roll."

"I can't eat."

"You must put food in your brain."

I nibbled the crust. "I can't eat any more."

She took me to the door. "Do well, *Kindchen*."

Johann was waiting outside the university.

"You didn't have to come," I said gratefully.

"I know how I would be feeling in your place."

We took seats on a hard bench outside Bertram's office. Four scared-looking young men scheduled to take their orals after me joined us on the bench, our fears mirrored in each other's faces.

"Your hands are ice," Johann said.

"But I'm sweating. I've heard how many students fail and keep taking their orals over and over. If I fail, that's it. I can never take them again."

The door opened. It was Bertram himself.

"*Fräulein Gruber, bitte eintreten*, please enter," he said.

In my state of ice-cold hands and sweating brow, I saw his office as a German inquisition chamber. Everything was frighteningly *ordentlich*—orderly desk, orderly bookshelves, orderly hard chairs in an orderly semicircle, even orderly shuttered windows. My head felt as if orderly bricks were pushing it down.

The three inquisitors—Bertram, Schöffler, and the art professor—sat in the orderly semicircle while I stood before them, a prisoner about to be executed.

Bertram was first, interrogating me in German. Nathan's list of his three bêtes noires flashed through my head. I tried to control my chattering teeth.

"What stands out most for you in Nietzsche's philosophy?" he asked.

I took a deep breath. "His search to lead the German people to new heights, to help Germany rise above even the evils we see confronting her today."

I stopped short. Did he think I meant the Nazi evils? If he really was a Nazi, how would he react to that? But he was already asking the next question.

"What do you think of Nietzsche's approach to the Old Testament?"

I inhaled the orderly air. "He admired the strong figures in the

Bible, he admired the beautiful language, the majesty, and the strict, inflexible commandments."

The questions continued, questions about Nietzsche's life, about *Also Sprach Zarathustra*. I kept my answers short until I startled myself by shouting my favorite Nietzsche line: "*Nacht bin ich, ach dass ich Licht wäre* [Night am I, ah that I were light]."

After an eternity, probably ten or twelve minutes, Bertram motioned to Schöffler to take over. Beads of sweat ran into my eyes.

"In your thesis," Professor Schöffler began, "you describe how much more sympathetic Virginia Woolf's women are than most of her men. Please explain it."

"For Virginia Woolf," I said, "woman is the creator, man the destroyer. Many of her women are heroic, her men often weak, with no heart, no mind."

Now why did I say that, I wondered. From the corner of my eye, I saw Bertram and the art professor sitting straight, listening hard.

"You called her novel *The Waves* a 'rhythm of conflicts.' What did you mean?"

I managed to pull out of my brain sentences still fresh from my thesis. "It's the struggle between light and darkness. It is the law of polarity, of conflicts as irreconcilable as night and day, of poets versus critics, that reverberates through all her writing. It is her final solution to her problem of style and the riddle of life. No truth is absolute, no style is supreme. We live our lives in a polarity of conflicts."

Professor Schöffler turned the questioning over to the art professor, who interrogated me about Albrecht Dürer.

Half an hour had passed. The three men looked at each other and nodded. Their faces were stony, expressionless. "That will be all." Bertram rose from his chair.

Schöffler led me to the door. "Please wait outside."

On the bench Johann tried to stop my hands from trembling.

A few minutes later Schöffler came toward me. "I am proud to tell you, Fräulein Gruber, you have won your doctorate *mit sehr gut*. It's the German equivalent of your American *magna cum laude*."

I wanted to throw my arms around him. "Thank you, Professor Schöffler. Oh, I thank you. And I thank Professor Bertram. I . . . I . . . I don't know what to say. I thank you all."

The door opened again. Professor Bertram emerged and thrust his hand out to shake mine. He smiled benignly: "*Schicken Sie uns recht viel Jugend genau wie Sie* [Send us many more young people just like you]."

Professor Schöffler then handed me two sheets of paper. "These are Professor Bertram's and my critiques of your dissertation."

My hands shook as I read Schöffler's first: "It is a critical study of a woman by a woman. A man could never have written this work. It possesses deep critical powers and a profound knowledge of English and world literature."

Still trembling, I read Bertram's page: "This work could be a model for modern criticism. The struggle of the poet with the critic is seen very sharply, very clearly. The work shows amazing maturity and originality."

Johann squeezed my hand. "Congratulations," he said and left for his class. I ran all the way to Agrippina Ufer to share the news with my German family.

"So it's *Fräulein Doktor*." Mama Herz looked delighted. "I'm going out to buy the best cake in Cologne."

I tried to reach Nathan on the telephone. No answer. Finally, toward evening, I found him home.

"Nathan," I talked rapidly into the phone, "you were wrong about Bertram. He doesn't hate foreigners or women or Jews. How can he? He told me to send more people just like me to Germany."

The phone seemed dead. "Nathan, are you there? Do you hear me?"

"I hear you," he said. His voice sounded as if he had been weeping. "I really can't talk," he said.

"Nathan, what happened?"

"Someone broke into my locker at the university and stole my dissertation. I have no copy."

I screamed. "It's like murder. It's like murdering a child. They murdered your years of work. Can I do something for you, Nathan? How can I help you, Nathan?"

"You can't help. Nobody can help. I'm finished, Ruth. It's over. I'm going to get out of this country."

16

I could not leave Germany without visiting Goethe's house.

Johann came with me to Frankfurt, where we headed straight for the *Goethehaus* on Grosserhirschgraben Street No. 23. It was a five-story rococo town house, the home of a wealthy eighteenth-century family, with red damask chairs, gold clocks, oil paintings, and black silhouettes hanging on the walls.

We hurried through the rooms, impatient to climb up to the attic, the small gabled room where Johann Wolfgang von Goethe, Germany's greatest poet, playwright, novelist, had sat at his desk. We stood in awe.

Here, with a quill pen, he had written some of his masterpieces. Here he had read his plays and poetry to his circle of young friends. Here he had defined the two souls that lived in his breast, the two souls that were Germany—good and evil. Here he had written the first version of *Faust*.

"Johann, remember how *Faust* begins," I said. "He's sitting alone in his room—a room, I imagine, like this attic—asking him-

Nazi storm troopers marching
down main streets of Cologne,
exhorting Germans not to
buy from Jews

Gruber in her study at
Cologne, 1932

Otto and Frieda Herz, the family Gruber
lived with in Germany from 1931 to 1932

Gruber with Luisa Herz, their daughter, in Cologne, 1932

Agrippina Ufer, the street where Gruber lived with the Herz family

Cologne street scene; in the background the Kölner-Dom, the Cathedral, and the river Rhine, along whose banks Ruth walked each day

Carnival in Cologne, 1931

The Gürzenich where
Gruber met Luisa Herz
after escaping from her
attacker in the carnival

self, 'In the beginning was—what? The deed? No. In the beginning
was the Word.' "

"In the beginning was the Word," Johann repeated.

"To capture with it what one thinks and sees and feels. To hold
it, to be ennobled by it, to understand oneself and the people one
loves—and it's all through the Word. That's what Goethe taught
us."

He, too, seemed inspired. "And no word that's spoken is ever
lost. Every word has an effect upon someone. Every word stays
somewhere in the universe."

"Only Goethe used the Word to create. Hitler uses it to kill," I
said.

Johann nodded.

Reluctantly we tore ourselves away from the attic into the warm
June sunshine. We were hungry, but lunch in a restaurant would
have taken more money than we had. From a street vendor we
bought cornucopias of cherries, walked to the park-zoo, and sat on
a bench, joyously nibbling the fresh ripe fruit. For a fleeting moment, I remembered sitting on the bench in Washington Square
Park with Joseph Ostro. *You are light in my dark soul.* Washington
Square Park seemed light-years away from Goethe's Frankfurt.

"You know you don't want to go back to America," I heard
Johann say.

"That's not true. I'm ready to go back."

"You love Germany."

"I love *this* Germany, Goethe's Germany, not the Germany that
destroyed my friend Nathan's thesis."

"Ruth, I want to marry you."

"You don't mean that." I suddenly moved away from him.

I tried to picture him in Harmon Street. I saw Mama, in black,
her dress torn above her heart, sitting on a little mourner's bench,
mourning me as if I were dead. I saw Papa shaking his head, his
gray eyes saddened by my treachery. I saw Zayda turning away
from me, as if I had sunk to my knees to worship a forbidden idol.
There was no place for Johann in Brooklyn.

He seemed to sense what I was thinking.

"Of course, we wouldn't live in America. We'll live in Cologne. We can live with my mother."

"With your mother!"

"She likes you."

"We've never met."

"I've told her about you. She knows we'll always take care of her. I'll work hard to get my Ph.D. It won't be bad. I'll get it just a year or two later than you. We'll teach together. We'll write together. We'll change the world, Ruth. We can."

I looked at Johann, trying to return his confidence in our love and at the same time trying not to ask myself if he was seeing me as his escape out of a frightening Germany.

I shook my head. "Johann," I said, "let's not be so serious. Let's picture our future lives. I see you married to a nice plump woman, sitting home evenings, marking schoolbooks, smoking a pipe in a big armchair, disciplining your children, calling your wife to bed at nine o'clock—."

"That's unfair. What a boring, Philistine life you picture for me. You see me stuck in the mud, a plodding schoolteacher, while I see you going from one place to another, wandering over the whole world, bringing restlessness to every man you meet, forcing them all to strive higher." He paused. "Aren't you afraid sometimes?"

"Maybe I'm too dumb to be afraid. Maybe I don't know all the hazards. Or, if I know them, maybe I push them away. The way I'm going to stop this conversation right now. Let's treat ourselves to coffee and cake."

We entered an elegant-looking restaurant, and I headed straight for the ladies' room. I stopped inside the door. An attendant with a breast projecting like a bulwark was screaming at a small, elderly woman. "You pig. You asshole. You dog manure! I clean these stinking toilets and you give me one pfennig."

"But that's all the money I have." The lady hunched her body protectively.

"You're a stinking liar. Get out now, before I tear you apart."

I opened the exit door for the poor woman to flee, while the attendant stamped on a rumpled newspaper, still yelling to anyone who would listen, "I keep these shitty toilets clean, and all I get from these farting pigs is this damned pfennig."

She moved away from the newspaper to collect money from another woman. Something drew me to look down. The face she was tramping on seemed strangely familiar. I picked up the newspaper. It was a photo of me. What was my face doing in this German newspaper? And why had this foul-mouthed ogre been stamping on me?

I read the caption:

20 JAHRE ALT - UND SCHON "FRL. DR." IN EINEM JAHR GESCHAFT

[20 years old and already Fräulein Doctor. Achieved in one year]

Was it symbolic? A German stamping on a Jew.

I used her facilities, handed her a fistful of pfennigs, and hurried out to show the newspaper to Johann. It was the *Frankfurter Zeitung*. Together we read:

> At 20, she is the youngest Ph.D. in the University of Cologne and the youngest Ph.D. in Germany. As exchange student she came for one year of study in Germanistik and Anglistik and Art History. When her great talents were recognized, it was suggested to her that she try to work on her doctorate. After one year, she had the Doctor Diploma in her pocket. Our young doctor, despite all her knowledge, has still remained very young, and is overjoyed to be in Germany.

"I can't believe this. First that woman with a face like a nightmare stamps on my face. And now this crazy article."

We boarded the train back to Cologne. I had scarcely put the key in the door when Mama Herz rushed toward me.

"*Kindchen*, the office of the *Oberbürgermeister* [the Lord Mayor] telephoned. They made an appointment for you to come to the

Rathaus tomorrow morning at nine o'clock. The Lord Mayor wants to see you."

"Why? What's this all about?"

"You'll find out when you meet him," Mama Herz said. "How many people do you know who get called by the mayor to the Rathaus?"

Once again I spent a sleepless night, trying to figure out why the Lord Mayor, Dr. Konrad Adenauer, wanted to see me. I knew that the Herzes and their friends admired him; they had voted for him in every election. Now fifty-six, he had been mayor since 1917. He had reopened the University in 1919; he had rebuilt the medieval Green Belts around the city; he had organized the Cologne Trade Fair in 1924, he had helped Cologne try to recover from the wreckage of the war and inflation. Why would such a man want to see me?

Early the next morning I took a bus downtown to the Rathaus, a massive stone building lined with Romanesque arches, built in 1150 in the Jewish quarter. I stood for a moment studying the street sign: *Judengasse*, the Street of the Jews.

"We should drive the Jews out," the Nazi heckler in the lecture hall had shouted, as if Jews were newcomers in Cologne. But the Rathaus and the *Judengasse* were living proof that they had lived here for more than eight hundred years.

Slowly I mounted the broad carpeted stairs to a huge chamber flooded with sunlight. Heavy drapes were drawn back from windows that reached from the ceiling to the floor.

A fatherly man with high cheekbones, a prominent nose, and skin the color of ivory, towered over me. He shook my hand heartily.

"I congratulate you," Dr. Adenauer said. "You have done what no German student has done." I murmured an inaudible "Thank you." It was unreal. What was I doing in this sun-filled chamber of Cologne's town hall on the Street of the Jews shaking the hand of the Lord Mayor?

"I have a present for you from the people of Cologne." He led me to a highly polished table on which lay two art books, one in orange leather with gold lettering, the other off-white cloth with red lettering. The title of the orange book was *Köln: Werden - Wesen - Wollen einer Deutschen Stadt* [*Cologne: The Making, the Character, and the Will of a German City*]. The off-white book was *Der Goldene Schrein: Ein Buch Über Köln* [*The Golden Shrine: A Book About Cologne*].

The *Goldene Schrein* looked exactly like the *Song of Songs*, the beautiful art book printed in Palestine that Joseph Ostro had given me. Circles within circles Germany and Palestine! Cologne's Rathaus on the Street of the Jews!

"The books are magnificent," I whispered.

He opened the art book to show me full-page photos and color reproductions of paintings that told the story of Cologne, its founding in Roman days, its art treasures, the great Cathedral, and the bridges over the river I had grown to love, the Rhine.

"We hope you will come back to Cologne, Fräulein Doktor," Mayor Adenauer said. "Until you do, I trust these books will help you remember your year among us."

I held the books close to my body.

"They have more meaning for me than I can tell you. I promise you I will never forget this year—nor you."

He placed his hand on my head as in a benediction. "Bless you, my child. May God go with you."

17

It was early August. In the foyer at Agrippina Ufer, I kissed Mama and Papa Herz and Luisa goodbye.

Tearfully, Mama Herz hugged me. "Rütchen, you're like my own daughter." She hurried into her bedroom.

Papa Herz shook my hand. "Will you ever come back?" he asked.

"If I can."

His protruding blue eyes clouded over. "But will you want to?"

I hesitated for a moment. "Somehow I think I'll always want to come back."

"Luisa," I embraced her. "Come see me in America."

"I wish—"

Johann was waiting at the station. We sat on a bench holding hands.

"I want to marry you, Ruth. As soon as I have a job. Tell me you want it too."

I shook my head. "How can you ask that, with the Nazis getting more power every day?"

"The only thing that matters is two people in love. We'll keep the world outside our door. We'll live our own lives. We'll make a sanctuary for each other."

"I need time to think. I need to put distance between us."

The train whistle blew. "*Einsteigen* [Climb in]," the conductor called out.

Standing on the train steps, I looked at Johann, hoping he would take my face in both his hands and kiss me. Instead, he shook my hand with strong up-and-down strokes. We had so often held hands, walked arm in arm, felt each other's closeness. I knew he was angry and disappointed.

At the dock in Hamburg, I climbed aboard the sleek white steamship, the *St. Louis*, the flagship of the Hamburg-Amerika Line. In 1939 it would become famous as the ship that carried one thousand Jewish refugees from Germany, only to have them shamefully refused asylum in Cuba and then in Florida, forced back to Europe where most of them were trapped and later killed.

I stood at the rail watching the ship break foam as it headed into the North Atlantic. The sea and sky were sapphire blue. Last year, on the SS *Milwaukee*, I had wanted to meet everybody; now I wanted to be alone.

I thought of the prophecy of Mama's friend Gittel, "the witch": "If you let her go to Germany, you'll lose her forever."

No, you haven't lost me, Mama, I thought. But I'll try to get a job as soon as possible. Maybe with a newspaper. Maybe at a university. Then I can move to Manhattan and get a room of my own.

On the last day of August the *St. Louis* entered New York Harbor and sailed past the Statue of Liberty. Passengers, officers, crew members, rushed to the rails waving their hands at the mythic woman holding a torch welcoming us home.

An elderly woman standing next to me sobbed. "*Lieber Gott.* Dear God. To leave Germany and to see this statue! Do you know what that means?"

I put my arms around her. "I think maybe I do."

A tug pulled the *St. Louis* into the harbor.

Mama and Papa were on the dock. I waved to them wildly. But who was that handsome young man beside them? Could it be? Yes, it was. It was my little brother Irving. A year ago he was a fourteen-year-old in knickers, trying out the mattress on my upper bunk. Now he was six feet tall, in slacks. The year had stretched him too.

A porter helped me down with my bag. I saw a crowd of reporters and photographers at the bottom of the gangway. I looked back at the ship. Some movie star, I thought, must be coming down from first class.

"Miss Gruber," I heard someone call. I turned to see a photographer aim his camera at me.

Suddenly I was surrounded. Men with press cards sticking up from the ribbons of their battered felt hats, women with press cards protruding from the bosoms of their summer dresses, seemed like hunters crowding in for the kill. After Germany, the crush resonated like an invasion.

A tough-looking reporter yelled, "How does it feel to be the youngest Ph.D. in the world?" I gasped. How do you answer reporters? I had never been interviewed. Protectively, I hid my face in my hands.

"Get yesterday's *New York Times*," a young woman called out. "The Germans said you were the youngest Ph.D. in Germany. The *Times* says you're the youngest in the whole world. How do you feel about that?"

They seemed to be leering, ready to pounce.

"What do you think about Adolf Hitler? When do you think he'll take over Germany?"

I no longer heard their questions. I was back in the Nazi melee in the lecture hall.

I had to escape.

"Let me through! I want to get to my family."

Blindly I elbowed my way through the mob and reached Irving. I grabbed his arm. "Get me out of here. Let's move fast."

In the car, Mama said, "The phone doesn't stop ringing. All day reporters, radio people, photographers. They keep asking, 'When is

your daughter coming back?' The Baerenklauses, the Schiffen-
deckers, all our neighbors are sending you flowers. The house looks
like the Botanical Garden."

Papa said thoughtfully, "I guess we were wrong trying to stop
you from going."

We drove east down Delancey Street, then across the Williamsburg Bridge. My private bridge. Brooklyn looked ugly; Harmon
Street looked ugly; our castlelike gray house looked ugly. Strangers
were lined up outside the black front gate; more strangers were
sitting on the stoop. More press cards in battered hats. More reporters. They too looked ugly. I hated it all.

"Papa. Don't stop. Drive right into the garage. I don't want to see
them."

I fled through the backyard and through the kitchen door, raced
up the stairs, and locked my bedroom door. I threw myself on the
bed and wept.

Books could make me cry and sad movies. But this was different.
I could not understand why I was crying. It was as if I were looking
at myself lying on the bed, shaking with sobs. Whom was I crying
for?

I looked around the familiar bedroom, at the vanity bench Betty
had painted black, the books I loved, the books Joseph Ostro had
given me.

I realized that the girl who had slept in this room a year ago was
no more. I cried for her, and I cried because I was safe while a black
cloud hung over the Herzes, over Nathan, over Miriam in Dinslaken, over the Jews of Germany.

"Come down for dinner," Mama called from the bottom of the
stairs. The reporters had gone.

Around the big dining-room table, Bob, Harry, Betty, and Irving talked excitedly about a game at Ebbets Field when some
batter had slammed a home run with the bases loaded. "You
won't believe it," Irving said to me, "but I fainted, right there in
the bleachers."

I listened in amazement. The Dodgers. Was that what counted?

A baseball game when Germany was marching toward disaster? They're my family; I love them, but I've become a stranger. I don't belong any more. Maybe the witch was right.

Papa changed the subject. "In the barber shop, everybody's asking, 'Who's gonna run for president?' We've gotta make sure Governor Roosevelt wins. Hoover's been telling us if we elect him again, we'll have a chicken in every pot."

"A chicken in every pot," Mama snickered. "Where they gonna put the chicken if they don't have a pot."

The phone rang all the next day, reporters asking for interviews. Mama lied bravely, "She's gone out of town. There's no way to reach her."

For three days I stayed indoors, fearing a reporter might jump from behind a tree.

On Saturday Mama came to my room. "There's a reporter outside. He says he's from the *New York Herald Tribune*. I told him you don't want to see anybody. But he says he'll sit there all night if you don't talk to him. He says it's his job."

"I don't know how to talk to reporters. Tell him to go away."

"Ruthie, you learned so much already, you'll learn this too. Go wash your eyes out and go down and talk to him."

"I just can't, Mom."

"It's not right. You can't let the poor man sit on our stoop all night. Go outside. He won't chop your head off."

I went into the pink-tiled bathroom, washed my face, and descended to the stoop. On one of the lower stairs, I saw a middle-aged man with a face as creased and battered as his felt hat. I sat on the stoop beside him.

"I appreciate your seeing me," he said gently. "I guess you're overwhelmed. I would be too."

"I really don't know what you want from me."

He patted my arm. "This is my job. I don't want to upset you, but if I don't get this interview, I can be fired, and I've got a family to feed."

On Sunday, September 4, his article appeared with the caption:

GIRL PH.D., 20, BEWILDERED BY
FUSS OVER FEAT

RUTH GRUBER FEELS HUNTED,
SHE SAYS: FEELS ACHIEVEMENT
WAS NOT UNUSUAL

HAD FUN WHILE STUDYING

JUST WANTS SOLITUDE A WHILE
TO GET HER BEARINGS

The dam was broken. More reporters demanded interviews. Clippings arrived from across the country with a cartoon sketch in "Strange As It Seems." A man in the Midwest mailed his photo, offering to marry me if I would send him the fare. I was beginning to relax a little and was even able to laugh when Betty and I, lying in our double bed, read an editorial in the *New York Evening Post* titled "Sex and Intellect."

> Forty or fifty years ago, if a girl had obtained the degree of doctor of philosophy at the age of twenty, it would have been her sex, but not her youth, that would have been regarded as the astonishing feature of her achievement. Miss Ruth Gruber's return from the University of Cologne with a Ph.D. *summa cum laude* [I giggled, I've already been promoted], after a single year's residence, has aroused a great deal of admiring public attention; but one discovers no sign of surprise at its being a young woman, and not a young man, who has performed this extraordinary feat.

In the next weeks, Mary Barnicle, who had sent my freshman essays to the *Atlantic Monthly*, invited me to lunch. Professor Meyer, my first German teacher at NYU, invited me to tea. And Mr. Hug-

139

gins, my black history teacher at Bushwick High, came to Harmon Street with a gift—a box of calling cards that had not one but two titles: *Dr.* Ruth Gruber, *Ph.D.* Proudly he told me he too had just received his Ph.D. from Fordham in African history.

The next afternoon, Zayda Gruber telephoned Papa. "Come pick us up. We want to see Raquela." It was my Hebrew name.

In our backyard, the sun sent shafts of light on Zayda's gray beard and on Baba Gruber's tiny humped body and her orthodox wig, too big for her gently lined face. I had often tried to imagine how, less than five feet tall, she had borne nine children and survived the death of four of them. I knew that she faced her own and everyone else's problems with faith: "*Gott wett geben* [God will provide]."

In the yard, Zayda took my hand. "Raquela, for a whole year while you were in Germany, I prayed to the Almighty to watch over you and bring you home safe. You know, because I tell everybody, you are my favorite grandchild. I thank the *Rabboinische L'Olam* [Master of the Universe]. He answered my prayers."

18

In October, Zayda Gruber opened a tiny store to sell grapes. "You don't need to work," Papa had told him. "We can support you."

"Bob is getting married in February," Zayda explained. "He's my first grandson. I want to give him a good wedding present."

I knew it was a ruse. Zayda wanted independence as I wanted independence. We wanted no one to support us.

On Leonard Street, half a block from the four-story walkup where he lived, Zayda found a shop not much bigger than a kiosk. His white beard bobbed with pleasure as he hammered up a wooden ledge and stacked it with baskets overflowing with stalks of ripe purple grapes.

Grapes were important to the Jews in the neighborhood and to the Irish and Poles and Germans who ventured into the ghetto. With grapes they could make their own wine and defy Prohibition. The grapes sold for thirty-five cents a basket. In the Great Depression, thirty-five cents was a fortune.

The Depression hit whole chunks of the Brooklyn I wandered

through. Buildings were abandoned, streets were desolate. The Italian shoemaker who used to sing "O Sole Mio" while he nailed rubber heels on my shoes had vanished. The candy store where I had bought ice cream cones and charlotte russes was bolted. On Bushwick Avenue, black signs "Apartments For Rent" hung outside four-story buildings. "For Sale" shingles swung on the gates of deserted brownstones with tattered shades fluttering like ghosts in empty windows. Families huddled together in tents and shanties.

I had to find a job. I worked up a résumé and filed job applications with NYU, Barnard, Cornell, Wisconsin.

Form answers came back. "We regret there are no openings."

I went to the *New York Times* and applied for any kind of job. "Sorry, no experience."

I tried the *Herald Tribune*, the *World-Telegram*, the *Mirror*, the *Daily News*, the *Brooklyn Eagle*. The answers were the same.

Papa, seeing my restlessness, made an offer: "You're always talking of wanting a room where you can do some writing. Maybe you can fix up the room over the garage."

It was the loft in the former carriage house where Harry and his premedical school friends had dissected pregnant cats, the loft where they scared my girlfriends when they pulled a baboon pickled in alcohol out of a barrel.

You entered the loft by climbing a ladder inside the garage and pushing up a latch-door. Once hay had been hoisted up through the big front hatchway for the horses quartered below. Harry had turned part of the loft into his operating lab, the rest was the *avayra* room, for things that were an *avayra*, a shame to throw out— family portraits, diplomas, clothes to be sent to the relatives in Europe.

I converted the front part of the loft with its hatchway and two small windows into my idea of a studio in Greenwich Village— bookshelves propped up with bricks, a rolltop desk, and an imitation Persian rug tossed over a cot. I pasted Virginia Woolf's picture on the brick wall and set her book *A Room of One's Own* in the place of honor on top of the desk. Here I lived and read and wrote poetry and typed letters to Johann and Nathan and Luisa in Cologne.

Presidential elections were coming in November. The boss of the Knickerbocker Democrats, puffing a four-inch cigar, came to Harmon Street.

"I read all that publicity about you." His black suit reeked of tobacco. "We'd like you to run for woman district leader."

"What would I have to do?"

"Just be at the Sunday night dances and give free milk to babies. We'll do the rest." I didn't run.

In Zayda's little grape shop, I heard people ask each other, "Who you voting for?"

"For Governor Roosevelt," Zayda said. "And you?"

"Roosevelt." "Roosevelt." "Roosevelt."

From open windows, Roosevelt's patrician voice boomed out of radios, pledging to lift us out of the Depression.

On election day I entered the polling booth reverently, as if I were entering a temple, to cast my first vote for Roosevelt.

Two weeks later, Zayda Gruber leaned against his ledge of baskets of grapes, clutching his heart. He managed to walk home, and with Baba Gruber's help, undressed and lay in bed.

I was home when the news reached us. I rushed to Siegel Street, up to the second floor, to sit with him.

"Don't die, Zayda," I cried.

He opened his eyes, looked at me, and closed them again.

"Zayda, I need you. I love you—Zayda, don't die."

A day later he was dead.

I had never told him, nor anyone in the family, about Johann. Yet the morning of the funeral, standing in the stairwell outside his apartment, I knew what he would have said.

I entered his bedroom, where he lay like a bearded monarch on the high white bed. I whispered to him, weeping, "Zayda, I heard you."

That afternoon I wrote to Johann. "It's like a fever that has broken. I know now it can never be."

For seven days we sat in Zayda's apartment, mourning his death. Papa and his brothers sat in stocking feet on little wooden boxes, the rest of us on chairs, as neighbors came to comfort us and tell us what Zayda had meant to them.

On the eighth day, the telephone rang in Harmon Street.

"My name is Abraham Silverstein," the voice said. "I'm calling from Newark. We'd like the youngest doctor of philosophy in the world to speak about the oldest philosopher in the world."

Was this a prankster?

The voice went on. "It's Spinoza. We're going to celebrate the three hundredth anniversary of his birth here in New Jersey."

"Spinoza—the oldest philosopher?" I started to say. "What about Aristotle . . . Plato . . . ?"

"Well, so maybe he's the oldest *Jewish* philosopher. Maybe there were even some Jewish philosophers before him. But the Jewish community is honoring him in a big tercentenary celebration. The Dutch consul general is coming to bring greetings from his country. I'm the chairman of the committee; I'm also a reporter on the *Newark Chronicle*, and I'd like you to be the principal speaker."

"I'm honored but, but I. . . ."

"Come on, no excuses. It's Sunday, December the tenth."

"That's only two weeks away. There's not much time to prepare."

"You don't need much time. You come out to Newark by train. We'll meet you at the railroad station. We expect hundreds of people. Okay?"

Each day, with Spinoza's *Critique of Revealed Religion* and several more of his books under my arm, I walked up Bushwick Avenue to Highland Park where, wrapped in a winter coat and a wool scarf, I sat on a bench under a bare oak tree, working on my speech.

144

What a chance for irony, I thought. A Jewish community in New Jersey honoring a Jewish heretic.

I decided to call my speech "Spinoza—God-intoxicated Jew." I prepared for it as intensely as I had prepared—was it only four months ago?—for my oral exams. I dreamed up new phrases and tried them out, hurling them into the wintry sky.

At Lord and Taylor, I found a long black silk skirt topped by a white silk bodice and a green cummerbund. The long skirt would hide my knees when they knocked together.

Sunday, December 10, I woke to the sound of winter rain rattling the bedroom windows. A fitting day for a philosopher-heretic.

Mama sent me off with a blessing: "*Sei mazliach bei Gott un bei Leit* [May you give pleasure to God and to people]."

In New Jersey, in the dark twilight, a committee greeted me as I stepped off the train. Abe Silverstein's face was red with excitement. "Welcome, doctor, to Newark. And call me Abe."

He then introduced Mr. Montyn, the Dutch consul general, who had arrived on the same train, and the elders of the Jewish community, all of them in black homburgs and long, wet winter coats.

Tucking one arm under mine and holding an umbrella over us with the other, Abe led the way to a limousine. In front of the car a corps of policemen sat on motorcycles, the rain washing down their faces.

A motorcycle escort to honor Spinoza!

With sirens screeching, the cops wove through Sunday traffic to the Ezekiel Home on Clinton Avenue.

Inside the hall, Abe said proudly, "It's Standing Room Only."

We pulled off our wet coats and mounted the dais.

I looked out at the sea of faces. My knees shook under the long skirt, but I seemed to be gaining control. Had I learned from that failed talk to the students in Cologne not to be intimidated? Or was it that this audience seemed familiar—like my family—looking up, smiling, as if they were saying, "Come on kid, we're with you all the way."

After the opening ceremonies, Abe returned to the podium. I

145

heard words like "astonished the world . . . youngest . . ." I sent up a silent prayer, "Dear God. Make the words in my mouth reach their hearts—."

The silk skirt rustled as I walked to the podium and began.

"They have called Spinoza an atheist. If seeing God as he saw Him, through the necessity of his own vision, his own belief, is being an atheist, then Spinoza was an atheist."

I looked out to see the audience's reaction, but they were in darkness. A yellow beam of light circled me as if I were alone in the hall. I was treading dangerous ground. But I lurched ahead, daring and naive.

"If seeing God manifest in everything—in trees, in beasts, in rivers, in man—is to be an atheist, then Spinoza was an atheist. Only he who has known the tragedy of having doubted, who has been tormented by the whys of existence, ought to be given the right to call himself a believer. Only the God-seekers who have spent sleepless nights, tossing on beds with questions they could not solve, and at last found faith, are the true believers."

I sat down. The audience applauded. Abe asked us to rise again and sing "*Hatikvah*," the song of hope.

I went back to New York with the consul general, who said, "Let me recommend you to a lecture bureau." On the train, he wrote a warm letter to his friend who ran the bureau.

The Newark newspapers were kind. "Her intellect, poise and subject matter fairly captivated her audience. . . . Although some persons felt her indictments too severe, they did, however, acknowledge her ability to state the case."

Soon I was speaking to small groups and appearing on a radio program called "The Voice of Brooklyn" on station WLTH. I prepared a weekly series on famous women of the past. Even Papa found the series boring. I never heard from the consul general's friend in the lecture bureau.

I tried my hand at writing articles. I had never taken a course in journalism. I had no idea how to fashion an article for publication.

I drafted a critique of D. H. Lawrence, the high priest of love, and sent it to the *Atlantic Monthly*. It came back with a cold rejection slip.

I tried a political article on poverty in postwar Germany and the elections I had witnessed. It too was rejected.

I worked up an article called "Right- and Left-winged Literature in Germany" and mailed it to the Sunday *New York Times*. Instead of a rejection slip, Lester Markel, then Sunday editor, wrote, "This is an interesting piece of work, but it is, after all, an essay in literary criticism and so, it seems to us, belongs in a literary monthly rather than a newspaper."

But no literary monthly wanted it.

The walls of the studio-loft were being papered with rejection slips.

Then, on January 30, 1933, the blow fell in Germany. Hindenburg, weakened and growing senile, appointed Hitler chancellor.

I sat in my loft mourning the death of the Weimar Republic. There had been no revolution, no bloodshed, not even a new election. Hitler had done it all legally. He had used each election to maneuver himself closer to power until he murdered the republic.

The German bürghers will have their wish, I thought—a dictator they can follow eagerly, *ordentlich*, without questioning.

A letter arrived from Luisa. "My father has been thrown off the commodities exchange. He left Köln and is now in Amsterdam trying to find an apartment and see if he can start a new business. My mother and I are taking care of the apartment house on Agrippina Ufer and will join him as soon as we wind up our affairs."

Her next letter came from Amsterdam. "We're safe now. I couldn't tell you in my last letter from Köln how dangerous it is for Jews to live in Germany."

I was still jobless. I decided to write an article about the place I knew best. Brooklyn. The article painted the landscape of Brooklyn like the countries of Old Europe, with an Italian section, a Jewish ghetto, a Greek quarter, and gypsies crossing all the frontiers.

The Sunday *New York Times* accepted it. I framed the twenty-five-dollar check and pasted it on the wall next to the rejection slips.

Suddenly the articles were selling, especially to the *New York Herald Tribune*. I prowled the city for features. In a restaurant in Greenwich Village I met a former convict who told me how drugs were being smuggled into prisons. Money could buy anything. Prison guards were corrupted. Wives and girlfriends stuffed chocolate candies with cocaine or morphine, reshaped the candies, and brought them in fancy boxes to the jail.

"Stay with the *Herald Tribune*," a reporter at the *Trib* told me. "The *Times* is like Macy's where you find everything; the *Trib* is like Saks Fifth Avenue; it's class."

19
Summer 1934

I first met Vilhjalmur Stefansson, the Arctic explorer, at Romany
Marie's restaurant in Greenwich Village. It was his favorite restaurant and soon would be mine.

"You pronounce my name, 'Vill'-hjoul'-moor Stef'-an-son,' "
he told me, "but you can call me 'Stef.' "

Nearly every evening Stef would be greeted at the door by Romany Marie, a short, ebullient Romanian Jew dressed like a gypsy,
with cascades of glass beads and a nicotine voice. Marie led him to
the long front table that was exclusively his.

There he sat like a Viking king with a rugged and furrowed face,
thick white hair and disheveled eyebrows framing oddly gentle blue
eyes. Surrounding him were explorers, inventors, writers, folksing-
ers, admirers, and occasionally strangers whom he invited to join
the group.

Not yet a regular at the table, I sat in silent awe. He had commanded three scientific polar expeditions, charted over a hundred
thousand square miles of hitherto unknown polar territory, and
written a score of books. He seemed to know every modern explorer

149

dead or alive. He talked knowledgeably about Hitler, Mussolini, Stalin. He corresponded with presidents and prime ministers and kings. He set the table laughing with his one-liners, like "False modesty is better than none" and "Women knit in order to have something to occupy their minds while they are thinking."

Sometimes he turned the entire evening over to one of the guests; often it was Sir Hubert Wilkins, the Arctic explorer, or Buckminster Fuller, who had invented the geodesic dome. It was on my fourth or fifth evening that Stef turned the table talk to me.

"Ruth, what do you make of this new bloodbath in Germany?" he asked.

Hitler had just ordered the murder of Ernst Röhm, the homosexual leader of the SA (*Sturmabteilung*). Once Hitler's closest ally, Röhm was said to have plotted to overthrow Hitler and the government. Each day the figures of Röhm's followers executed as traitors by Hitler escalated: two hundred, then three hundred, then a thousand. "Everyone must know," Hitler warned the Reichstag, "that, if he raises his hand to smite the State, his fate is certain death."

Day after day I had sat in my studio-loft glued to the radio. Thank God, the Herzes were safe in Amsterdam, but Nathan was still in Cologne, trying to get a visa to come to America. Miriam was still in Dinslaken. Were they in danger? What was happening to Johann?

"I should have foreseen the bloodbath," I said, as Stef and those around the table listened. "The signs were there."

"What signs did you see?"

The table was silent as I tried to describe the violence, the thugs marching on the streets shouting *Jude Verecke*, the roller-coaster elections hurtling Hitler to power.

Stef's blue eyes squinted, then darkened, as he listened.

Just before midnight, I stood up to say goodbye, ready to go back to Brooklyn. Stef stopped me.

"I'm looking for a part-time researcher who knows German. Are you free?"

"When do you want me?"

"Tomorrow."

At nine the next morning I was in his office, the front room of his one-bedroom apartment on Morton Street in Greenwich Village. The smell of coffee perking came from the kitchen. He introduced Olive Wilcox, an attractive young woman who sat typing rapidly, and who, I learned, managed the office. Another young woman stood before a row of green filing cabinets that filled an entire wall. Bookshelves reached to the ceiling. Stef had the largest Arctic library in the world.

He cleared a small table and set a stack of German documents before me. He was preparing a massive study for the United States War Department on the whole Arctic world.

"I'd like you to excerpt these documents," he said. "I pay a dollar an hour." It was the same salary I had earned ghostwriting for the baron. But now I was a researcher, not a ghost.

I began to leaf through the papers. My picture of the Arctic—a vast frozen wasteland of ice and snow—had come from school-books and the movies. Nobody, I was sure, lived up there except Eskimos who ventured out on dogsleds in blinding blizzards to hunt walruses and then spent the rest of their time in igloos trying to keep warm.

Stef punctured most of my misconceptions. He gave me copies of all his books, "introducing" me, he wrote on the flyleaf of his *Northward Course of Empire*, "to ideas about the Far North which are among the hobbies of Vilhjalmur Stefansson."

From *The Friendly Arctic*, I learned that you could live in the Arctic. There was ample food—caribou, walrus meat, fresh fish. No need to take lemons to the North to prevent scurvy. Eskimos never saw lemons and never got scurvy. If you lived as they lived, hunting and fishing, you could stay alive—and healthy.

From *The Northward Course of Empire* I realized that the top of the world would soon become the shortest air route between America and Asia. Stef was the prophet of transpolar aviation. And from *My Life with the Eskimos* I learned about Eskimo culture and even

151

believed the rumor, which Stef never confirmed or denied, that on one of his polar expeditions he had fallen in love with an Eskimo woman. Stef was now a bachelor, and in 1939, at sixty, would marry Evelyn Schwartz, a young dynamic folksinger who had been married to Bill Baird, the puppeteer. Stef taught her to be a librarian and a skillful writer.

He was a teacher who loved teaching anyone who would listen. He taught those of us who worked for him discipline in work, thoroughness in research, skepticism before accepting standards and values merely because they were time-honored. He taught us when to work and when to stop. "You do the best job you can," he said. "But there comes a time when you shut your eyes and say, 'This is it. It's finished.' Whether it's an article or a book, you hand it in. Otherwise you can go on revising for years."

And mostly he taught us to respect and then love the Arctic. He was fascinated by what the Russians were doing in their vast polar empire. He was not a communist, nor, so far as I knew, were any who worked with him. Hitler was the villain, not Stalin, who even then was murdering millions. We knew of the forced collectivization of farmers, but we had no idea what it meant in terms of destroyed lives and destroyed farmland. Still, in the mid-thirties, idealists like Stefansson had high hopes that some of the experiments being tried in the Soviet Union would work. For Stef and for those of us who worked with him, the opening of the Soviet Arctic held the promise of a bright new world where people could live with adventure and excitement.

One night, Romany Marie's French husband, Marchand, the fortune-teller, read my palm. "I see a big trip for you. I see you in a cold place wrapped in a lot of furs with people with brown skin."

Stef, who hated superstitions and enjoyed shattering myths, had no patience with fortune-tellers. He waved Marchand away.

"Don't write him off so fast, Stef," I told him. "Some day I'm going to go to the Arctic and try to live, as you did, off the land."

20

On a summer night, Harry Roskolenko joined Stef's table and entered my life.

Harry was a poet and a political left-winger who raised and lowered the Harlem River drawbridge to let tall ships sail out to sea. From nine to five, he sat in a little cage on the side of the bridge over the river, and in the intervals between opening and closing the bridge he wrote poetry. Often I sat with him. We began to spend my free weekends together and Sundays took the ferry to Staten Island, quoting T. S. Eliot and Edna St. Vincent Millay to each other as Johann and I had quoted Rainer Maria Rilke, walking along the Rhine.

Where Johann was tall and handsome, Harry was short and ruddy-faced. Where Johann was philosophical and romantic, Harry was volatile and political. Where Johann was a conservative and a nationalist, Harry was a radical and an internationalist, closer to Trotzky than to Stalin, whom he loathed. Both men loved words, but while Johann weighed each word before he pronounced it, as if he believed it would be immortal, Harry used language the way Trotzky used a soapbox.

"What do you believe in?" Harry demanded one day. We had been wandering through the woods in Staten Island, delighting in our discovery of a forest just across the water from Wall Street and the Battery.

"I believe in creativity," I said.

"Not fame or fortune?"

"Fame? Sure, I'd like to get my work published. Fortune? Who needs fortune? I don't want a mink or a Buick, and I hate property. It drags you down when you want to fly off. I'd like to earn just enough to live on, so I can write."

"You can't earn enough unless you change the political state."

"I'm not interested in the political state. I'm interested in the individual. I'm interested in the Woman of the Future." I said it slowly. I wanted him to hear the capitals in my voice.

"She's a figment of your individuality," he shouted, "of your destructive nihilism." Other walkers in the woods stopped to hear him. "Why don't you forget your Woman of the Future and begin to build the Society of the Future?"

"What if I deny Society and tell you I worship life? Will Society start an inquisition and put me on the rack as a heretic?"

"You are so damn naïve. This is just more of your decadent recidivism." He spat out the word. "To live you must be social-minded. That's what living is."

I laughed. "So I've never lived. So I'm dead. Even now, while I feel hot blood racing to my head, I'm dead. I'm dead while my body is aching with life."

He pulled me toward him and kissed me, obviously prepared to end the argument. I was not.

I opened my bag and pulled out a sonnet I had sent him. He had sent it back, with red ink scrawled across the top of the page: "Your literary passion is sadly misplaced because it has the energy of youth and not of art."

"I carry this with me like a talisman," I said. "I like 'the energy of youth,' even if it's not art."

A week later I sent him another poem. It came back, scrawled over this time in black ink: "It has force, but without the ring of social historic truth."

"A fine phrase but rotten criticism," I wrote him. "You would like to rhyme love with factory sweat and life with party propaganda."

The next day he sent an angry poem ending with the lines: "I should sink your feet/ In my blood,/ For your admiration."

I shot back a poem, equally gory and ridiculous: "I am glowing and laughing and quivering/ With your blood deluging my feet."

He telephoned. "How about the ferry to Staten Island next Sunday?"

We spent the afternoon arm in arm, forgiving each other for our bad verses, stopping to kiss, strolling through the picturesque little towns, watching the Staten Islanders rake the red and golden leaves that carpeted their lawns, gather them into neat piles, and set them aflame.

Back in Harmon Street that night, I lay in bed thinking.

Are you in love with Harry? I queried myself.

I'm not sure. He excites me. His tirades challenge me.

And Johann? Were you really in love with him?

I don't know. Maybe I was in love with the idea of love.

What attracts you to two such different men?

I think it's Goethe's two souls again. The good and evil in each of us attracted to the good or the evil in someone else.

Good and evil, eh? I wonder if Johann has become a Nazi.

He had continued to write, though after Zayda's death I had stopped answering.

Why are you still curious about him? Why don't you drive him out of your head once and for all?

Our neighbors were burning leaves in their backyards, and the night wind ferried the fragrance up to my bedroom window. I opened a notebook and wrote my final farewell to Johann:

Leaves burning in the autumn, burning
In the twilight of the autumn, smoke
The air with the evanescent yearning
Of your lips beneath my beating throat.
Though you are dead, buried deep at least
In the mind's cold yard of lovers,
Leaves burning in the night release
The choking sorrow, fling the futile covers
Of remorse to autumn's flame. Night
Will lose its terror now, and dreams
Their prophecy of loss, despite
The burial I gave you. For it seems
You will not lie there, buried in the past
While leaves are burning in the dying grass.

Poetry magazine printed it.

I sent a copy to Johann who answered in the next mail: "I will not lie there, buried in the past. Reconsider. Come back to Köln. We belong together."

21
June 1935

"I'm going to wake up tomorrow morning and find I dreamed this whole thing."

I was in the city room of the *Herald Tribune* showing a letter to George Cornish, tall, courtly, with horn-rimmed glasses and a low Alabama-accented voice, whose mild manner hid the power he held as the *Tribune*'s assistant executive and later executive editor.

He read the letter in one swift glance. It had come from the Guggenheim Foundation.

> At our recommendation, you have been awarded the Yardley Foundation Fellowship of the New Jersey Federation of Women's Clubs to travel abroad.

"I'm a millionaire, Mr. Cornish." I showed him the check for two thousand dollars.

He smiled. "What do you plan to write about?"

"It's a freewheeling fellowship for 'creative research.' I'm free to write about almost anything 'creative.' I'd really like to do a study of women under fascism, communism, and democracy—what's happening to them while the map of the world is being redrawn."

"I guess you've decided what countries you'd visit."

"England, France, Holland—to study women under democracy. Then Russia for women under communism and Germany, of course, for women under fascism."

He nodded thoughtfully and scanned the letter again.

"While you're abroad, I'd like you to be our Special Foreign Correspondent. Come see me when you're ready to leave. I'll give you press credentials. Cable us whenever you find an important story."

I thanked him, said goodbye, and hurried through the city room. Men in shirtsleeves were pecking letters on big desk typewriters. Cigarettes seemed to be burning on every desk. I wove my way hastily past reporters talking on telephones, taking notes, beating deadlines. I wanted to absorb this incredible luck lest it suddenly be snatched away.

Except for the part-time research job with Stefansson, I had been unable to find any work. Now suddenly to get a new fellowship *and* an overseas assignment from the *Herald Tribune*! It was the dream of every journalist.

I took the subway to the Williamsburg Bridge, climbed up to the walkway, reached the center of the bridge, and stood clutching the rail. I looked down at the dark river. The map of Europe seemed to spread across the water.

Did I have enough knowledge, enough skill? I would work hard. I would try to keep my eyes and mind open. I would write about people.

In London, maybe I could even meet Virginia Woolf. If she agreed to see me, I would tell her how she had helped shape my thinking and writing, how I saw her as the liberator of women writers.

Then I would go to Amsterdam and visit the Herzes, and from there go to Köln to try to find Nathan and Miriam. What had happened to them since Hitler had come to power? Were they safe? And Johann? Should I see him? Would seeing him reawaken feelings I had long suppressed?

At home, Mama and Papa were distraught.

"Why do you have to go back to Germany?" they asked with anguish.

"I have to. Germany is the centerpiece for my study. I have to find out what's happening to women in that fascist country."

"You're crazy," Mama wept. "They can kill you."

"I have an American passport."

"Big deal. They can't shoot a bullet through an American passport?"

"I'll be careful."

"My *meshigena* [crazy] daughter has to go running all over the world. It's time you got married already. When I was your age, I had four children. You want to be an old maid? Look at your friends. Most of them are married with two or three children already."

"There are things I want to do first, Mama."

"Always things you have to do first. What comes first now?"

"This study of women."

"So study women in Brooklyn."

"They don't give you a fellowship to study in Brooklyn."

"God better watch over you." She lifted a corner of her apron and brushed more tears from her eyes.

Nearly everyone I knew wanted to help. Charles and Mary Ritter Beard, the historians, invited me to their home in Connecticut and gave me letters of introduction to women writers and feminist leaders in Europe. Stef wrote a letter to the scientists who were opening the Soviet Arctic.

Printed copies of my dissertation *Virginia Woolf: A Study* had just arrived, published three years after I had written it. I sent one to Mrs. Woolf in London. Would it be possible, I wrote diffidently, to interview her for my study of women?

I waited impatiently. Would she hate the dissertation? Would she even answer? Finally a note arrived inviting me to call her when I came to London.

22

Armed with letters and credentials from the *Herald Tribune*, I sailed to London and telephoned Virginia Woolf. A voice answered: "Mrs. Woolf is in the country, and will return on October the fifth. She will be pleased to see you the fifteenth of October."

Coming back to London would cut into my travel budget. Never mind. I would eliminate one of the democratic countries on my itinerary.

In the British Museum, I sent a two-sentence note to Johann. "I shall be arriving in Cologne on Tuesday. If you want to see me, come to the Kölner Dom Hotel at 5:30 in the afternoon."

As the train crossed into Germany, I pulled my American passport out of my purse and held it tightly. Soon the coach was filled with uniforms. A border policeman studied my passport. The customs man searched my suitcase as if I were a jailbird. Storm troopers came aboard and stared at me suspiciously. I sat in silence, trembling.

The border policeman stamped my passport. The customs man closed my suitcase. The storm troopers clomped out. The uniforms moved to the next compartment. The train rushed on. I relaxed. At every railroad station from then on, I watched armed soldiers surround the train as if this were wartime and the soldiers searching for the enemy.

In Cologne I hurried from the Hauptbahnhof to the Kölner Dom Hotel. The lobby was filled with more soldiers. More storm troopers.

In my room, I was too restless to unpack.

I telephoned Nathan. No answer. Had he managed to get out of Germany?

I tried Miriam in Dinslaken. Her mother answered the phone.

"We are here," she spoke cautiously. "But Miriam is away."

"Where?"

"I really don't know," she whispered.

Her fear made me afraid.

"When you hear from her, please tell her I called."

I sat on the edge of the bed, shaking. What had happened to Miriam? At least the Herzes were safe in Amsterdam. Outside the heavy German drapes the sun was shining.

I unpacked quickly, descended to the lobby, and walked to the pedestrian Hohestrasse, where I had walked countless times with Johann. It was still crowded with people hurrying with briefcases, but there were signs on shop windows: NO JEWS ALLOWED. Flags waved in the warm wind, blood-red flags with black swastikas in a field of white.

I entered the bookshop where I had tried to buy Virginia Woolf's books and instead bought Hitler's. *Mein Kampf* was still in the center, surrounded by piles of other books with swastikas on their jackets. People were browsing through the shop, buying, chatting with salespeople, as they had done three years before.

Then suddenly Hitler's voice rasped through a loudspeaker and the shop went silent. Everyone stood transfixed as Hitler ranted about the damn Jews and the damn Treaty of Versailles that had tried to grind Germany into the ground after the Great War. His voice crawled like a snake down my back.

I hurried out and walked toward the Cathedral.

A whistle blew. I saw Gestapo officers in black uniforms and shiny black boots herding some twenty men and women and children in the gutter. Some walked with their heads up. Most were marching in obvious terror. The Gestapos kept them together in orderly fashion. *Ordentlich.*

I was trapped on the sidewalk by a wall of people. Onlookers pushed me forward so that I could almost touch the people being herded down the gutter.

A Gestapo officer turned to look at me. Mama's words rang in my head: *They can't shoot a bullet through an American passport?*

I remembered ripping the beer-besotted Nazi's arm off my waist in the *Bierstube* in Berchtesgaden.

One of the women in the gutter walked bent over, as if her whole life was focused on one thing—protecting the elderly hunchbacked man clutching her hand. As she passed me, she looked up. Her eyes burned into me.

A middle-aged man standing next to me blurted out. *"Gott in Himmel*—dear God. It's Mrs. Mueller and her father."

"What's happening?" I whispered.

"They're my neighbors," he answered in a low voice. "There must be a new *Aktion* [roundup]."

Under my breath I said, "They're Jews, aren't they?"

He nodded. "First they took the communists. Then the socialists. Now the Jews."

"Where are they taking them?"

"To some kind of camp . . ."

I went back to the hotel, my body tight with anger.

At 5:30 there was a knock. I walked swiftly to the door. When I saw Johann wore civilian clothes, I breathed a sigh of relief.

"Guten Abend, good evening." He shook my hand and kept holding it. I pulled it away.

I motioned him to a big overstuffed chair and sat on a straight chair facing him. The three years had aged him; his face was still lean and handsome, but the poetry had gone from it.

He spoke, his voice almost breathless. "Your brief note from

163

London—tell me, it means you've changed your mind, doesn't it?"

"I haven't changed my mind at all," I said. "I wrote because I wanted to know what was happening to you since Hitler—"

"Ah, what is happening to me." He straightened his body to make himself taller. I had seen that gesture hundreds of times, his back shooting up, like a soldier ordered to stand erect. "I worked very hard at the university. I received my Ph.D. in two years, and now I have a job teaching in an elementary school."

"So you got what you wanted after all."

"Yes indeed. I'm a happy man."

I could not tell if this was sarcasm.

"And your mother?" I asked. "How is she?"

"She's proud of me. Now I earn enough, so she doesn't have to work. And you? Tell me about you."

"I've come back to do a study of women under fascism, communism and dem—"

I stopped abruptly.

"Johann," I blurted out, "what's happening here is terrible—frightening—a nightmare."

He tried to make himself even taller.

"You mustn't believe everything you read. Hitler has rejuvenated us. He prevented us from having a civil war. He's created an optimism even greater than the optimism you had when your President Roosevelt was elected."

"You speak of Roosevelt and Hitler in the same breath?"

"Yes, because he has taken young men who were without jobs and without hope off the streets. He has put them into military labor, into agriculture, into—"

"Johann, did you become a Nazi?"

"Well, not . . . not really."

"What does that mean?"

He pulled a handkerchief from his pocket and wiped his forehead. "I had to join the party. It was the only way I could get a job teaching."

My voice was choking, "You—joined—the—Nazi—party?"

"Ruth, I would have been unemployed. How could I support my mother?"

I put my hands over my face.

He came toward me. "I've never loved anyone the way I love you."

He opened his arms, ready to put them around me.

I jumped up, shoving him away.

He paid no attention. "You and I, we'll be different from all the others. We'll hold on to our beliefs, our values. We'll teach them to the children we both want."

He came toward me, trying once again to put his arms around me. I freed myself and ran to the door.

He followed me. "Ruth, don't," he cried. "We belong together."

"Get out. Leave me alone. You're a Nazi! How could you?"

I flung the door open, pushed my hands against him, shoved him out. And I locked myself in. My poet had become a monster.

23

I sat in the hot second-class coach headed for Berlin, pretending to read. I would not show fear to the men in their felt hats and double chins and the buxom women in their shapeless dresses and sensible shoes. I fingered the papers in my bag—my ticket to Poland and the USSR, my passport with its pages stamped with visas for half of Europe. Everything was in order, yet my heart was racing.

An SS man with polished boots flung the compartment door open. His narrowed eyes slowly surveyed me. I felt like a spy.

The Berlin Hauptbahnhof was crowded with soldiers, SS men, police, and travelers. Was I being followed? I tried to walk nonchalantly out to the street. Did those SS men eyeing me see that the hands carrying my suitcase and typewriter were trembling? I hailed a taxi and gave the driver the address: Oranienburger Strasse 28. Did he know it was the *Jüdische Gemeinde*, the office of the Jewish community?

Berlin looked clean and orderly. A mild wind rustled the leaves along the broad Unter den Linden and sent swastika flags waving.

Posters with Hitler's face were plastered on nearly every street column. Army trucks packed with soldiers honked as they rolled by.

The cab pulled up in front of the "Neue Oranienburger Strasse Synagoge," still called the New Synagogue, though it had been built in 1866. Three six-pointed Stars of David rose delicately above its three domes. It looked like a Moorish Alhambra.

It was not the synagogue I wanted but the simple office building next to it, the community building that was the center for many of Berlin's 160,000 registered Jews.

I climbed a flight of stairs to a small unpretentious office, bare save for a desk and two straight chairs. A middle-aged woman with sharp brown eyes sat behind the desk.

I introduced myself.

"How can I help you?" A small sign gave her name—Anna Sommers.

"Why don't the Jews all get out of Germany?" I asked abruptly.

"Before I answer," she said, and turned on the radio sitting in front of her. Loud music filled the room as she went on in a low voice, "Now you'd better tell me something about yourself."

"I'm an American."

"Obvious."

"And a Jew."

"Sit down. What's an American Jew doing in Berlin?"

I slipped into a chair and handed her my credentials from the *Herald Tribune*. She scrutinized my face slowly and waited.

"I'm trying to find out what's happening to Jews and to women in the Third Reich. I came to get some answers."

"You came five thousand miles to get answers? Are you brave or stupid?"

"I want to know why Jews aren't rushing to get out."

"You can't be that naive."

The collar of my dress was wet. "*Some* get out. The family I lived with in Köln is already in Amsterdam."

"Lucky people. What country wants us? Go to the American

consulate. You'll see people lining up every day to get a number. It's a long and slow process. If you get a number like five thousand, you may have to wait five or six years before you can leave—if ever.''

"And if they have relatives in America?"

"Have you seen the documents your State Department makes American citizens fill out to prove they can take care of their German relatives? They want bank accounts, income tax records, employers' recommendations, proof that our people won't become a burden on your government.''

"But Americans *do* fill out the documents, don't they?"

"Many do. But some send letters with excuses. I have copies on my desk. 'We would love to help you, but we don't have a job.' 'We don't have a big enough apartment.' 'We're sending three children to college.' ''

"You make me ashamed of my countrymen."

"Some of our people have given up trying to get into America. Instead, they're trying to get certificates from the British consul for Palestine.''

"Then why don't they all go to Palestine?"

Her eyes grew dark. *"Wir sind unbeweglich."* [We are immobile.]

"What do you mean?"

"When your family has lived in a country for hundreds of years, it's hard to move. You have a house. You have a business. It's hard to leave it all. And there are many who say, 'We've been through crises before. Germany is a civilized nation. What can they do to us?' I don't know what your father does. But can you picture him just leaving everything and running?''

I tried to picture Papa piling the trunk of the Buick with suitcases, Mama on a ladder taking down her homemade curtains, the rest of us filling cartons with pots and pans. I shook my head. "You're right. We are immobile."

She began to speak more passionately. "We all know America has its own diseases. Our Nazi papers run ugly pictures about those young Negroes, the Scottsboro boys, saying how Negroes rape white prostitutes. And our German-Jewish papers write about fascists like that priest in Detroit, Father Coughlin. But you live in America without fear. That's how we lived in Germany until two years ago."

"I—I said all the wrong things. I had no right to press you so hard."

She turned the radio up even louder. I leaned forward to hear her words.

"You're a journalist, yes? You have more questions?"

"How do Jews who've lost their jobs stay alive?"

"They come here to us. We support them. The state gives us the money."

"The Nazi government gives you money?"

"Oh, it's all Jewish money. We're taxed for it. It was this way even before the Nazis. Every Jew, every Christian, every citizen must pay a 'religious tax' to the government. The state then gives each religious community the money to run its own institutions."

"So then the government knows exactly who is a Jew or a Catholic or a Protestant?"

"Of course. Any time you move, you have to go to the police, give them your new address, and of course, fill in the line about your religion."

I thought of the people being herded down the Hohestrasse in Cologne. "That means the Gestapo and the police have every name; they don't even have to search to find someone." Somehow just saying it frightened me.

She looked at the radio playing loud music on her desk. "You say you're interested not only in Jews but in women?"

"Yes."

"We're not yet as endangered as Jews, but we're getting close to losing everything we won under the Weimar Republic. Pushed back a hundred years. Told to go home and bear children. Told to forget politics, ambition, careers."

"Are women fighting back?"

"With what? Votes? Guns? Power? Jewish women who've spent

years working for their degrees are being thrown out of the universities. Women studying to be doctors are dismissed from their labs and hospitals. Anyone known to be, or suspected of being, a communist or a socialist has already been arrested. Some of my friends have been shot"—she drew quotation marks in the air— " 'trying to escape.' "

"And Aryan women?"

"Aryan communists or socialists have the same fate. Only those who join the Nazi party are on pedestals. You've heard of the BDM girls, the *Bund Deutscher Mädchen* [the League of German Maidens] who march in their brown uniforms. Their faces all shine— you should see—with love for the Führer. A real passion, as if they wanted to sleep with him."

Somewhere I had read a joke about the BDM girls: "Those girls are so in love with their leaders that they have a picture of Goebbels tattooed on one breast and a picture of Goering on the other. After a few years think what long faces Goebbels and Goering will have."

Through the closed window came the sound of drums and brass, of soldiers marching.

"May I give you some advice?" she asked suddenly.

"Of course, Frau Sommers."

"Get out of Berlin. Get out of Germany. You don't have to wait in line like the rest of us for a visa to leave. I know what you're going through. You want to see with your own eyes what Jews and women are experiencing. You feel the terror and the danger in your heart. And you want to write about it. You're a young woman starting her career. I don't want to see you end it here."

"I'm not afraid," I said, but even as I said it, I felt my stomach tighten. "What can they do to me—an American?"

"Nobody is safe anymore. They don't need an excuse. They can pick you up and say you were trying to change dollars on the black market. Do you think your United States consul can save you? How do you know some secret agent didn't follow you here from the railroad station?"

"I was careful."

Her eyes glanced at the radio and then around the room to the shuttered windows.

"I'm talking to you as if you were my daughter. I have a daughter your age and I wish I could help her get out. Maybe things will change here. Maybe they'll get better in a year or two. Come back then. I promise I'll answer any questions you have. Only please take my advice. Go. Go now. Go today. You can help us."

"I would love to help. But how?"

"Go home to America and *scream*. Scream about what's happening here. Maybe if people learn . . ."

She came from behind her desk, put her arms around me, and kissed me.

She said again, "Get out."

Part Three
THE SOVIET ARCTIC

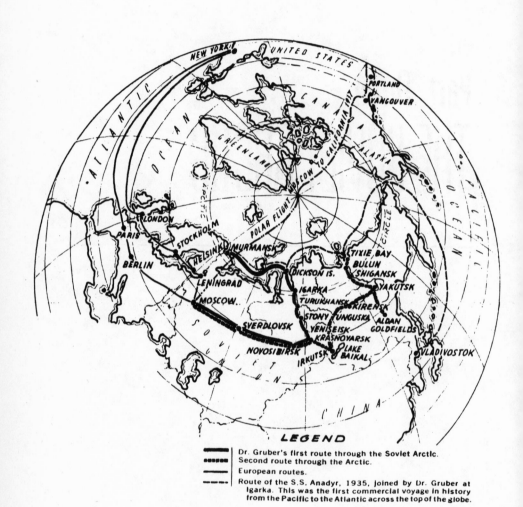

LEGEND

▬▬▬▬ Dr. Gruber's first route through the Soviet Arctic.
▬▬▬▬ Second route through the Arctic.
──── European routes.
─ ─ ─ Route of the S.S. Anadyr, 1935, joined by Dr. Gruber at
       Igarka. This was the first commercial voyage in history
       from the Pacific to the Atlantic across the top of the globe.

24

At the Berlin railroad station, I sent a telegram to Mama's Aunt Mirel in Beremlya in the Wolyn Province of Poland. I had promised I would try to see her relatives in the shtetl where she was born.

I boarded the train for Warsaw and stared sightlessly out the window.

It was early evening when the train reached the border of Poland. German uniformed officials in shiny black boots gave way to Polish uniformed officials in shiny black boots. Polish officers opened the door of the compartment, stamped my passport, and stared suspiciously. Polish soldiers with guns guarded the railroad tracks, entered the train, and marched up and down. Still, I was out of Germany, and I could not believe the sense of freedom that suddenly enveloped me.

Midnight. The train pulled into Warsaw. A burly man in Polish peasant pants, a threadbare shirt, and torn boots came toward me. His face was pockmarked.

"You are Ruth," he said in Yiddish.

"How did you know?"

"You look so American. I am Yankel, your mother's cousin, Mirel's son. Come quickly."

He picked up my bag and typewriter, slung my Leica camera over his shoulder, and led me to a horse and cart.

"Jump in. And hide under the hay."

"Can't I sit up front with you?"

"Not safe." He covered me up to my chin with a coarse blanket that smelled of grass and horse manure.

"Why are you hiding me?"

"They can kill you."

"Who? We're not in Germany."

"Bandits, maybe, if they saw you get off the train." He spoke impatiently, as if I were a brainless child. "They think Americans are all millionaires. You're probably carrying more money in your pocket than they have seen in their whole lives. Or it could be soldiers. Or police. They kill easy here. Don't ask any more questions. I have no time to talk."

Yankel flogged his horse and cursed at it in Yiddish to go faster.

I lay wide awake in the black night, up to my neck in hay. It was two in the morning when we entered a small, dark, dirt courtyard in Beremlya. Yankel called out, "Wake up, everybody. *Gnendel's tochter is gekimmen.*" [Gussie's daughter has come.]

Candles appeared in the windows. Doors flung open as the dark courtyard came alive with aunts, cousins, uncles—some twenty or more—laughing, crying, until Mama's Aunt Mirel drew me into her little cottage. The others squeezed in behind us.

They made me sit in a low chair at a wooden table, while they crowded around me, touching my face and hands, kissing me, forcing black bread and kasha soup on me, interrupting each other's questions.

"How is my sister Dora?" Mirel asked about my elegant grandmother, Baba Rockower. "Who is alive in the family? Who is dead? Who got married?"

"Tsk, tsk, tsk," they marveled to each other. "An American. And she speaks Yiddish. Even though it's more like German. But she understands us, and we understand her. Who does she look like? Who has green eyes like that in the family? Maybe Gnendel. But who remembers what Gnendel looked like? She was five years old when they left for America. So you're not married? Tsk, tsk, tsk. You couldn't find a good man yet? What brings you to Beremlya?"

Smiling, happy, excited, I tried to answer all their questions while they kept stroking and embracing me as if they would have liked to swallow me whole.

I looked at the women with orthodox kerchiefs on their heads, the men in loose pants held up with rope, the barefoot children staring at me as if I had dropped in from the moon. Here, I thought, in this little shtetl, my ancestors came together, slept together, and passed on to me the shape of my face, the size of my bones, the color of my skin, and forged my Jewishness, my existence. These warm, kindly people—they are my link to the past, and I am their link to the present and the future. I, Gnendel's daughter, link them to the dream world of golden streets that they had lacked the courage or the money or the precious *Schiffskarte*, the steamship ticket, to escape to.

"Do you go to school?" I asked Hannah, a fifteen-year-old with a shining mane of black hair, fair skin, and hazel eyes flecked with gold. She wore a one-piece housedress; her feet were bare.

Hannah shook her head shyly. "I went only enough to read and write."

"What do you want to be?"

She looked down at the floor. "They'll pick somebody for me to marry, and I'll have children."

She had blood like mine. In America she might have gone to NYU and Wisconsin. Here she was shackled.

My Great-aunt Mirel, who seemed to be the matriarch of the family, adjusted the cotton kerchief over her forehead and pushed back a few stray strands of gray hair.

"We have to find a dowry for Hannah. If not for the money your father sends us every month—God should only bless him and keep him alive till a hundred and twenty—we would starve. We plant a little so we have with what to eat. But we don't have doctors, we don't have medicine. Our children get sick and every year we bury a few more."

She stopped for a moment.

"Over us is a big fear. Pogroms. When will they come with knives and guns to kill us? When will they come to Beremlya and do those terrible things to women? Before, our shtetl was Russia. After the war it became Poland. For us it's all the same! Russian Cossacks! Polish peasants! Everybody wants to kill us."

I tried to break the pall that the word *pogrom* had thrown on the crowded room. "How is Dvora doing in Palestine?" I asked Mirel.

Mama's cousin Dvora had written to Papa a year before, telling him she had joined a Zionist youth group and was training to go to *Eretz Israel*, the land of Israel. "But I need a *Schiffskarte*."

Papa had sent her the money the next day.

Mirel rubbed her hands roughly over her eyes and cheeks. "Dvora! A burning Zionist we needed yet in the family. As if we don't have enough *tsurus* [trouble]. We all tried to stop her. 'You can't go live with those Arabs,' I told her. 'I hear they ride on horses and chop off Jewish heads. How will you live? In a tent like Abraham in the desert?' But who could talk to her? Every day I expect to get a letter that she's dead."

Mirel rocked back and forth in her chair. "When she left, we sat *shivah* for her."

Hannah changed the mood. "Eat something." She offered me more black bread. "Yes. Yes. Eat." The voices came from around the room. Food is love, I thought, as Aunt Mirel dished more hot soup out of a pot and placed a steaming bowl in front of me. I worried that I was eating what might be their next two meals. But I knew I could not refuse them.

I had gone back to Germany to reconnect with my student year and had failed. Instead, I had found this instant, almost unbelievable connection with my family in Poland.

"Hannah," I beckoned to my young cousin. "Come sit beside me." I took her hand in mine. I needed to feel her closeness as much for myself as for her.

"Tomorrow," Hannah said, "we'll take you to the wonderful bathhouse your grandparents built for us."

We were still talking when early morning light filtered through the window.

"Let her go to sleep already," Yankel said. "She had a long trip."

"That's right," Aunt Mirel said. "We should let her go to sleep."

"I'm not sleepy. Really. I'm so happy to be here."

We heard a heavy knock on the door. Yankel went to open it.

Two policemen in full uniform with waxed mustaches and leather boots, one tall and straight-backed as if he were corseted, the other short and stout, burst into the tightly packed room. Hannah put her hands over her mouth in terror.

"Who is she?" The tall one pointed his nightstick at me. "Someone has reported a stranger—"

"She's my sister's grandchild." Mirel tried to sound unafraid. "She came from America to see us."

The two policemen swept their eyes over me, then turned to my portable typewriter and camera case. I realized the typewriter and camera were making me suspect.

"Your passport." The corseted policeman stretched out his hand.

I opened my purse and carefully extracted my passport. He studied it so slowly I wondered if he were illiterate. "So you just came from Germany last night. And where do you go from here?"

"Russia," I said. Oh God. The two neighbors Poland feared the most. Both enemy lands, possible invaders.

"Open your suitcase," he snapped.

The policemen took turns lifting each garment, even my underwear, up to the gray light at the window. They left the clothes in a heap on the table.

The short policeman paced in a small circle around me as if his eyes were X rays that would ferret out anything I might be hiding.

"What are you doing here?" he hissed the words.

"I'm a student and a tourist." I tried to sound casual, praying they would not make me open my purse. The *Herald Tribune* credentials would make them even more suspicious.

"We want you out of here in one hour," the tall policeman ordered. "If you're not gone by then, we'll come back and arrest you."

They stomped out of the house. I clutched the table. To be jailed here! In a shtetl in Poland!

"You better go immediately," Yankel said. "God only knows what they can do to you."

"Yes," one of the uncles insisted. "You better go. We will never see you again."

Hannah pressed my arm. "Don't go yet!" she whispered.

Her eyes kept searching my face as if she wanted to imprint me in her brain.

I can go home to America, I thought. But she's trapped. They're all trapped. *When will they come with knives and guns to kill us?*

My clothes still lay disheveled on the table. I selected my favorite dress, a turquoise blue silk with a stand-up lace collar and lace cuffs and two sets of underwear and handed them to Hannah. Her mouth fell open.

"For my wedding," she cried. She pressed the dress against her body and then helped me repack.

I stood up and one by one kissed Hannah, Mirel, Yankel, my aunts and uncles and cousins, who, six years later, with everyone else in the shtetl, would be herded to the river's edge, forced to strip naked in a Polish killing field and shot by Germans. Only Dvora, the burning Zionist, would be alive in Palestine.

In the courtyard my Polish family stood weeping while Yankel hoisted me into his wagon and covered me again, this time hiding even my face.

He drove his horse like a madman back to Warsaw.

25

On the train to the Soviet Union, I thought of the stories on Germany and Poland that I might write. But the next days were too full even to send a query to the *Herald Tribune*.

Stefansson had given me a letter of introduction to Professor Rudolph Samoilovich, the director of the Arctic Institute in Leningrad.

"Find out what you can about the Soviet Arctic," Stef had suggested before I left New York. "The Russians are carrying out a multiplicity of scientific and exploratory activities in their Arctic empire, but no foreigner, man or woman, has been allowed to see exactly what they're doing."

The Arctic Institute was housed in an old Czarist palace with red moiré silk walls. Professor Samoilovich came around his desk to the center of the former ballroom, shook my hand, and said in German, "I am so happy to see you. Our good friend Vilhjalmur Stefansson has already written me about you."

His entire head was shaved, his eyes peered merrily through thick glasses, and his mouth was covered by two unexpectedly large tusks of a mustache. "So you've just been in Germany. What do you think of the changes since you studied there?"

We talked in German. Though my Russian was adequate for conversation, I was far more fluent in German. Like many Russian scientists born before the Revolution, Samoilovich had studied in Jena, and his favorite expression of amazement was a long German "Zo-o-o? Zo-o-o?" each time with a little greater delight. I wondered why he seemed so animated, but he soon explained it by a question: "I understand you're making a study of women? Do you know about the work our women are doing in the Arctic?"

"Women in the Arctic? You mean there really are some Russian women up there besides native tribes?"

"Thousands of them."

"But I thought explorers never took women north. Stefansson never did."

"Zo-o-o. What a pity you didn't come a month ago when our last expedition left. You could have gone along and met some of our women yourself."

A month too late.

"But look," his face brightened. "When you get to Moscow you must see Otto Yulyevich Schmidt. He is in charge of all our Arctic work. He can give you much more information."

He moved the papers on his desk and wrote a note of introduction to Professor Schmidt.

I decided to take the night train to Moscow. I tried to sleep in the wagon-lit, with its red carpets, green window blinds, and yellow lampshades. But sleep was impossible. A month too late!

Early the next morning I found a room in the Novo Moscovskaya hotel and hurried over to see Professor Schmidt. Stef had told me that in 1932 Stalin had placed Schmidt at the head of the newly formed Northern Sea Route Administration and commanded him to open all the territory north of the 62nd parallel. It was the Soviet's Arctic Empire and Schmidt was its Czar.

Close to the Kremlin, I walked through a rambling courtyard into a white three-story building. Telephone bells were ringing, typewriters tapping, wireless machines chattering, while groups of men in naval uniforms held excited conferences in the corridors.

I knocked lightly on Schmidt's door. When no answer came after several minutes, I looked into a small, crowded room. Without rising, a young man in uniform asked me what I wanted. I handed him Samoilovich's letter. He read it, disappeared, and returned within moments. "Professor Schmidt will see you directly." Other visitors, who looked as if they had been waiting for hours, seemed not to mind.

He led the way into a large inner office. Models of Arctic ships, trophies, animals and art objects carved from walrus ivory stood on top of filing cabinets and special stands. Huge colorful maps of the Arctic hung on the walls. A conference table, covered in red, dominated the center of the room.

Schmidt, seated at a desk at the end of the table, had the same dramatic effect on me as his room did. He was tall and broad, with dark hair and a graying beard that made him look like a twentieth-century prophet. From his canvas shoes to the commander's cap that lay close to his telephone and the starched naval jacket buttoned to his throat, he was dressed in crisp Arctic white. He had melancholy gray-blue eyes and a mystic, dreamy face.

He stood up, hand outstretched, while I wove my way precariously through the Arctic trappings. *"Es freut mich sehr* [It pleases me very much]," he said, as though he were picking up the thread, even in German, where Samoilovich had left off. I imagined Samoilovich had telephoned him from Leningrad.

"I understand," he said, "that you are making a very interesting study of women. What can I do for you?"

I launched into the question of women in the Arctic: Did they belong? Why were they going? What was their status? What of the old sex prejudices—the dangers, the hardships, the cold?

He threw his head back and laughed. He was no prophet now, but a jovial human being to whom the prejudices against women looked deliciously absurd. "Do women belong in the Arctic? Why not?"

He grew serious: "You ask me why women are going north. For the same reasons that men are going north. We want to open new land. We want to build cities. We want to find gold. We want to explore. We want to build polar stations for weather reports. These people are human; they want especially to earn more money.

"Let me show you," he said, getting up from his desk and going to the large Arctic map that hung nearest him, a colored map crowded with symbols.

"Here's Igarka." He pointed to a town in Siberia, north of the Arctic Circle. "Five years ago there was nothing here but tundra. Today it's a thriving lumber town. And the leader of Igarka," he said pointedly, "is a woman."

I must have looked startled, because he went on, "There is nothing in the Arctic that women can't do, and do just as well as men. Sometimes I think even better. You want to know what they're doing, how they're living. What can I tell you? . . . you'd have to see it."

Hesitantly I said, "It would be rich material."

"Yes, yes, very rich material . . ."

I saw him looking at me the way a father studies a young daughter. "You know we've never sent a foreign correspondent to the Arctic." He paused. "But we can send you; we can give you your transportation and wireless facilities. You'll find out about women in the Arctic, I promise you."

I left his office unbelievingly, hailed a droshky, and sat forward as the horses rushed me back to the hotel. I telephoned Ralph Barnes, the Moscow correspondent of the *New York Herald Tribune.*

"I've just spoken to Professor Otto Yulyevich Schmidt and—"

"What? You've seen Schmidt? Hold on, I'll be right over."

Barnes came driving up, tall, hatless, excited. "How in the world did you get to see Schmidt?"

"Through Stefansson. Why?"

"Don't you know every correspondent in Moscow, not just me, but Walter Duranty, Maurice Hindus, men who've written books about Russia, we've all been begging to see Schmidt. It's the hottest story today. We're expecting one of their pilots, Levanevski, to fly across the Pole from Moscow to California. And Schmidt's making the plans."

"He mentioned it."

"Did he tell you when the plane takes off?"

"No. But he's offering me a trip through the Arctic."

"What!" Barnes leaned toward me, amazed. "How did you manage it?"

"I don't know. Maybe he liked the woman angle."

Barnes settled back in his chair and sighed. "That's probably why he decided to send a girl after he turned down all the men. He may feel that if a young woman can travel easily around the Arctic, people will realize the Soviets are really solving the problem of transportation in the north. Whatever his reasons were, you've got a real scoop."

We cabled our arrangements to the home office. I was to go as special foreign correspondent for the *Herald Tribune* and wireless my articles to Moscow from radio stations in the Arctic. Barnes would transmit them to Paris and to New York.

In the next crowded days, newspaper correspondents and others came to the hotel to give me advice on the Arctic. Several insisted that I would have to undergo a complete physical examination; every Arctic explorer did. Professor Samoilovich traveled down to Moscow, and at a little midnight dinner he gave to celebrate my going, I asked him about the examination.

"It would be wise," he said, "to be examined. I require it of all the people on my expeditions. We can't take any unnecessary chances."

The next morning when I saw Professor Schmidt to make final arrangements I mentioned that people were suggesting an examination. He looked me over from head to toe.

"An examination?" His beard shook with laughter. "Of course you can go to the doctor of our clinic if you want one. But I certainly don't think you need it. You look as healthy as a good apple. Just make sure you take warm underwear."

Coming from Schmidt, it seemed like excellent advice. I took the warm underwear and skipped the examination. Gifts began to pour in from enthusiasts who had never been to the Arctic. Some brought fur-lined mittens, others caviar, bologna, canned liver, canned eggplant, Soviet Swiss cheese. Americans who had carted boxes of chocolates six thousand miles brought them as an offering to the Far North. I was beginning to feel like an explorer until a woman brought two hot-water bottles.

After hours of sorting and cramming and stuffing, I went to Moscow's huge department store, the *Mostorg*, and bought a canvas duffel bag with two compartments. Then, heartlessly, I went through the supplies. Food? Stefansson had taught me you could live off the land. I decided to give all the food to Muscovites. Clothing? I would be flying into both extremely hot and cold weather. Flying in open cockpit planes would be cold. But the Arctic, in the summer at least, would be quite warm. Accordingly I packed into one pocket of the duffel bag the Compleat Explorer's Equipment:

> one woolen dress
> one silk dress
> two pairs woolen underwear
> two pairs silk underwear
> a bathing suit
> one pair mittens
> one pair galoshes
> two hot-water bottles
> mosquito netting
> one Boy Scout compass

The other pocket was filled with notebooks, typing paper, pencils, and a little library of books and newspapers that I would be leaving with the people who were, I was sure, starving for culture. I drove to the Moscow airport, where I slept that night.

26

At five in the morning seven Russian men and I climbed into a small twin-motored plane.

We studied each other surreptitiously, but none of us spoke. I held myself tight as the plane rolled down the tarmac, then rose smoothly, swiftly, easily, over Moscow.

Ralph Barnes had cabled the *Herald Tribune*: "Please telephone Ruth's family telling them they may not hear from her for months. She is flying to Siberia, then north to the Soviet Arctic."

I could see Papa's face, tense with worry. I could see Mama at the dining-room table. "Dave, we should never have let her go."

"And who could have stopped her?"

Below us, the Kremlin with its prisonlike red brick walls, the huge nothingness of the Red Square, even the multicolored onion domes of St. Basil's Cathedral grew shapeless in the yellow of the rising sun.

With two maps on my lap, one in English and one in German, I followed our route over the Central Russian Plateau. We were cruising at just over a hundred miles an hour, skimming and bouncing over an uninterrupted expanse of earth and trees and waving wheat fields without fences.

We landed in towns with names like Arzamas, Kazan, and Yanaul, and each time we entered a new time zone I set my watch back. The USSR spanned eleven time zones, but the clocks in the airports were all on Moscow time. Thus, Muscovites were probably eating dinner, when, at midafternoon, our ANT-9 plane dropped its wheels and landed in Sverdlovsk, the new name for Ekaterinburg, where the last Czar and his family were murdered.

"In less than ten hours," I jotted in my notebook, "we've reached the great Ural Mountains, nature's wall between Europe and Asia."

The airdrome had a small wooden hotel to which a porter carried my duffel bag and typewriter. I followed him down a hall of doorless bedrooms with men sprawling fully dressed on iron cots. I seemed to be the only woman.

"*Vot.*" The porter dropped my bag in a small room with a double bed that extended wall to wall. I felt a surge of relief. The bed was occupied not by a man but by a buxom young woman. Lying on her back in a long, old-fashioned serge skirt and jacket, she smiled warmly and moved to make room for me. I stretched out and for a few minutes felt the world turning dizzily.

"My name," I heard her say in Russian, "is Olga Ivanovna, and I'm flying to Vladivostok. I'm going to live for a month with the Red Army in a camp in Okhotsk."

I sat up in the bed. The dizziness had evaporated. I saw the beginnings of a story about a woman in Siberia. "Are you a soldier?" I asked.

"No. I'm an electrician. I won the trip as an award because I organized lectures, plays, music classes for my union. And you? Where are you going?"

"To the Arctic."

She looked unbelieving. "You going to work there?"

"No."

"How can you go then? I didn't think anyone could go without a contract to work."

"I'm going as a correspondent."

"For a communist paper?"

"Why no."

She looked even more incredulous. "What paper?"

"The *New York Herald Tribune.*"

"Of course, the *New York Gerald Triboon.*" (*H* becomes *G* in Russian.) "But you won't be able to write what you see, will you?"

"Who is to stop me?"

"Your paper, of course," she said indignantly, as though I were questioning an axiomatic truth.

I decided to show her my letter from Professor Schmidt. It was addressed to all the officials of the Northern Sea Route Administration, telling them that "the American correspondent, doctor of philosophy, Rut [there is no *th* in Russian] Gruber was traveling through the Soviet Arctic for the *New York Gerald Tribune,*" and requesting them to give her any aid she might require.

"So you know Otto Yulyevich Schmidt," she breathed his name. "Do you know how lucky you are? Is he as handsome as his pictures?"

"Even more so," I said.

She was already my friend. "Let's go have some tea."

"I'd like to wash up first," I said, "and go to the bathroom."

"The outhouse is back of the hotel," she said.

I made my way to a two-holer with seats so high I was sure they had been built for Cossacks.

The next day the clock in the airport read 3:00 A.M. Moscow time, but the sun was high in the sky when we flew off and began following the tracks of the Trans-Siberian railway. We landed in Omsk to refuel.

A cold drizzle made me pull my coat close around me. I hurried through the airdrome for the omnipresent Russian tea and sipped the brew gratefully, beginning, in that damp air, to appreciate its popularity. One of the passengers told me to arm myself with Narzan, Russia's mineral water. "You can't be airsick if you drink it," he assured me. He was wrong.

After an hour, we climbed back into the plane, which soon began to plummet through a storm. In a little while those of us who couldn't sleep were reaching for the telltale paper bags. After endless hours over the endless steppes, we came to rest at last in Novosibirsk.

A young director named Ilya introduced me to the housekeeper, a woman of nineteen with vivid black eyes, inky hair, and marble-white skin. She gave me a room to myself, with a door but no plumbing.

Each day was bringing me closer to the Arctic, yet no sooner did we reach a town than I wanted to detour and look around. I set out by bus for the city, and near the center I started to walk with a sharpening feeling that I was walking through two eras. I saw both nineteenth-century low wooden blockhouses and steel-and-concrete apartment houses modern even for New York City. Ancient droshkies lumbered over the cobbled streets, with a shiny Model-T Soviet Ford honking past them. Young people were hurrying in and out of mills, factories, modern hotels, while older people waited in a long, patient queue to enter the community steam bath which took the place in Siberia of the warm shower I was beginning to yearn for.

In my bedroom the young housekeeper heated a large stove in the room, then, putting her arm around my waist and calling me "Little Sister," led me outdoors, filled a pitcher with water, and, back in the room, began hovering over me as though I were helpless. She poured the water on my hands and neck, dried me with a warm towel, helped me change my dress, and picked up my shoes to polish them.

I took the shoes from her. "But really," I protested, "I'm perfectly capable of doing all this myself."

"*Milenkaya moya* [my little beloved]," she cried, "don't deprive me of this pleasure. You are the first American I have ever seen, and already I love you."

It took me time to grow accustomed to these sudden outbursts of Slavic warmth. The Russians are no believers in understatement or emotional restraint.

Later in the evening, the young director, Ilya Pyotrovich, approached me. His nose was snubbed, his face freckled, his hair yellow. He had the shy charm of someone who had just come off a farm.

"How about a game of chess?" he asked.

"But I play badly," I said.

He persisted. "Let's try anyway."

A Red Army captain named Leonid in a stiff uniform, with a monocle and a closely shaved head, followed us, smiling broadly, as we walked to a small chess table. Ilya made gallant attempts to lay his chessmen open to attack. It was useless; I was playing true to form.

He struggled into conversation.

"You . . . I mean your paper. What kind of paper is it that you write for? A capitalist paper or a worker's paper?"

There it was again. *"Kapitalisticheski,"* I answered, wishing his face wouldn't fall so.

"Oh, then you are a capitalist?" Ilya persisted.

"No."

"You are a communist?"

"No."

"Mustn't you write like a capitalist?"

I shook my head. Yesterday in Sverdlovsk and now in Novosibirsk. The same questions. Obviously Ilya had never heard of freedom of the press.

There was a long pause. Ilya finally broke it. "You . . . are you married?" he asked. Leonid, standing behind him, dropped his monocle on his chest and chuckled.

"No," I said.

"But why not?" Ilya asked.

I had to hunt quickly for an answer. "Well, if I had a husband I couldn't be here."

"But that isn't true in the Soviet Union. If you were married to someone here, you could travel all you liked. He would never stop you. You would have your work, and he would have his. Do you ever plan to marry?"

"Of course. Maybe when I'm twenty-five. But first I want to see the world."

Before five the next morning, the housekeeper woke me. "You have to hurry. Director Ilya told me to give you these woolen stockings. You have to dress warm today. There are no passenger planes east from here."

I dug into my duffel bag for my warm clothing. The housekeeper helped me pull on my clothes and then led the way to the buffet room. Ilya, dressed in full military uniform, was already there and ordered breakfast for me—hot kasha, hot buns, and delicious hot chocolate.

At the airfield I was surprised to find the pilots, wireless operators, doctors, meteorologists, and ground workers assembled at this early hour.

"You see," Leonid pointed. "They all come to say goodbye to their *Amerikanskaya zhurnalistka*."

"You mustn't catch cold," Ilya said solicitously, while he wrapped me in a huge fur-lined leather coat. "You have to take a little plane to Krasnoyarsk. It's an open-cockpit plane that carries the mail."

Leonid wiped his goggles and tied them around my head. Someone put an aviator's cap on me, someone else was pulling on heavy boots, and when I began to wonder if the plane could take off with that much ballast, they decided to lift me in. I sat on top of the mail, waving goodbye. The pilot had opened his throttle and was about to taxi off when Ilya, standing near the wing, noticed an inch of my chin uncovered. He pulled a flowered kerchief off the head of one of the women, hopped on the plane, and tied it securely around my chin and neck.

In mock disgust, the pilot turned to me, "An American correspondent is a privileged person even in the Soviet Union." He was right. But would a male correspondent have been wrapped so solicitously? There are definite advantages, I thought, in being a woman.

Fifteen thousand feet over the steppes, the pilot turned to see how I was. I tried to give him a reassuring smile through the kerchief, but he had already turned back to his controls, satisfied, I suppose, that I hadn't fallen out.

Three hours later he circled, dipped his wings, and landed at the airfield at Krasnoyarsk, the largest town on the Yenisei River. Someone led me to a room in the small airdrome hotel so that I could change my clothes and return the Arctic gear.

Within minutes, ten young women encircled me.

"What's it like in America?" a wireless operator wanted to know.

"We hear you have millions of people without jobs," said the nurse. "Is it so?"

"We have a depression," I said, and added defensively, "like most of the world."

"Do your women have to give up their jobs for men?" the meteorologist interrupted.

"Sometimes." I thought of my own problems searching for a job.

"We read how you hang black slaves on trees, and how, if your workers strike, you beat them."

"This is what your newspapers tell you about America," I said. "Unfortunately some of it is true. But do your papers also tell you the good things? That we have freedom to say what we want, to think what we want, to elect people to Congress and elect our president." I sounded like a soapbox orator, but I felt more patriotic in Krasnoyarsk than I had sometimes felt at home.

They seemed embarrassed and began fingering my clothes. They watched with wonder as I changed to the summer dress I had brought for a hot day in Siberia.

"A one-piece dress," one of the girls cried. "How practical. May I try it on?"

193

"Of course."

"But it would never fit me. I'm so fat."

"Not terribly."

"But I am fat, and it makes me so unhappy and lonely. Tell me," she implored, "tell me, how can I get an American figure?"

"In Germany, they say you're starving," I said, as I told the starving Russian women not to eat so much.

A jovial freckled boy picked up my bag and drove me to the town, a few miles from the airport. He asked no questions, but kept bursting into laughter at unexpected moments. I finally persuaded him to tell me what the joke was. It was on me. He couldn't believe that an American would look like other people.

Krasnoyarsk housed the regional offices of Schmidt's Northern Sea Route Administration. In a low, brown wooden building, I found the director, a stocky figure in army uniform, his manner crisp, like that of an officer in the thick of war. He stood up and shook my hand with military precision; with precision he asked me to be seated; and with unconscious precision, I handed him Schmidt's letter.

I thought I saw his manner soften as he read the letter. He told me he would make arrangements to have me taken across the Yenisei River to Molokov Island, the seaplane base twenty minutes from Krasnoyarsk. Without precision, I shook his hand excitedly when he assured me I could leave the next morning for the Arctic.

The freckled boy put my bag and typewriter in a motorboat, helped me climb in, and headed for the seaplane base. Near us, flying boats were bobbing in the Yenisei. Slow riverboats filled with people and sacks of flour were sailing northward. Men were loading a seaplane with newspapers, mail, and cartons of medical supplies, all bound for the Arctic.

Molokov Island looked as green as Eden and almost as untouched. Tall pine trees shaded it; the Yenisei cooled it; the Stoloviyie Mountains gave it a dark, breathtaking beauty; and the white flying boats, sitting in pontoons on the water, linking it to the Arctic, made it look restless and alive.

From the foot of the pier I looked up at the hotel where I was to stay, a shining new building of yellow logs that could have been a summerhouse in Maine. Above the entrance, some five times life-size, were pictures of Schmidt and men I did not recognize, framed by a huge red banner proclaiming "Our Fiery Proletarian Greetings to the Heroes of the Arctic."

In my room I slipped into my bathing suit, for the day was as hot as August in New York, and swam in the river. It was my first bath since I had left Moscow, and I surrendered to the water, clear as glass and crystal-blue.

At last, clean and cool, I returned to my room, changed into my summer dress, took my maps and notebook and camera, and settled myself on the steps beneath Schmidt's picture.

Soon a group of pilots and mechanics sat beside me and began the obligatory questions about my newspaper. Capitalist or worker's? I told them I had come to see and learn with an open mind and asked them to help me chart the Yenisei River artery along which I was to fly to the Arctic. The pilots outlined my route and the places to watch for. Each had his favorite stopping place, all of them jawbreakers: Podkamenaya Tunguska, Imbatskoye, Dudinka. A hand and pencil came over our bent heads to draw a large circle around Igarka. It was not yet printed on the map; Professor Samoilovich had inserted it in black ink.

"Ee-gahr-ka," the owner of the hand said in broken English. "You will be much in-terr-ested."

After dinner in the sunny dining room, an economist who had come from Schmidt's office in Moscow suggested a walk through the island. The subarctic white nights were coming to a close; about ten in the evening the sun set slowly. We watched the red and orange flame flush the trees and mountains. The sky lit up, mirroring its last fierce brilliance in the Yenisei. And the midnight twilight began.

We returned to the log house, where the director and some pilots were playing chess and reading the local newspaper, the *Krasno-*

yarsk Worker. I left them reluctantly to go to bed, for tomorrow's early start.

Sleep was impossible. About midnight, I decided to dress again and slipped out of the darkened house. The afterglow of the sunset was still in the sky, and a full moon had risen, casting a yellow light on the Yenisei. I walked slowly, guided by the stream of moonlight.

From the distance I heard the voice of a woman singing. It might have been a song of love or of longing for home. I couldn't make out the words. But she sang with a low, sad tone that moved me, as though I could see the tears welling in her eyes. I walked in the direction of her voice and found a little circle of men and women sitting on the grass. Someone motioned to me to come into the circle and sit down. There sat the pilots and mechanics who had bathed in the river with me, swaying dreamily and singing melancholy, sweet songs.

Tomorrow one of them would be flying me north—north of the Arctic Circle, north to Igarka.

27

Jan Stepanovich Lieb, tall and broad in his brown leather pilot's coat, with a visored brown leather cap and high rubber boots, walked toward me and laughed. "Aren't you afraid you'll freeze to death?" he asked in Russian.

In a summer dress, with my coat on my arm, I was sitting on the river's edge watching workers in black padded jackets refuel a white flying boat. Filled with anticipation, I had been up before five in the morning. Now it was nearly seven.

Jan Stepanovich waved his cigarette in the air. "We'll lend you one of our coats as soon as we get up in the air."

He was an Estonian who had flown in the Great War and in 1918 had smuggled himself across the border to fly for the new Soviet government. His face, pockmarked and windburned, was calm and peaceful. His wife, the doctor at the airport, was as tall as he, but nervous and even more solicitous. She had taken me to her office in the log building and given me a first-aid kit of cotton, iodine, eyewash, and half a dozen other things. "You never can tell what may happen," she kept repeating.

197

On the river bank, she kissed Jan goodbye.

"Aren't you going to wait to see the *Amerikanskaya zhurnalistka* take off?" he teased her good-naturedly.

Tightening her lips, she said, "No." Then she shook my hand warmly and whispered, "I can't bear seeing him off."

Jan Stepanovich and his first mechanic clambered into their open cockpit. I trailed them into a small cabin, followed by two passengers. All we could see as the plane raced through the river was yellow water slapping against the two little windows in our cabin. Molokov Island slanted and dipped like a rotogravure page caught in a wind.

Flying in the seaplane was like riding in a baby carriage, smooth and comfortable and safe. There were no rooftops, no jagged mountains, no badlands where forced landings would be dangerous. The Yenisei River was our route and our landing field, inviting us to come down at almost any point.

Soon the nauseating smell of gasoline and oil filled the cabin and the baby carriage sensation was gone. I needed air. I pushed open a door to the rear open cockpit, found a seat, and, with my head sticking out, looked down at the world contentedly. After two and a half hours, the plane swooped to settle in Yeniseisk, the first fueling base on the route.

When the plane was ready, Jan Stepanovich invited me to sit with him in the cockpit. I was delighted. Now I could have air all the time. The mechanic, young and muscular and good-looking, wrapped me in his leather flying coat.

From Yeniseisk, our route continued northward to Podkamennaya Tunguska and then to Turukhansk, where Jan Stepanovich exchanged mail with a man who rowed out to our flying boat. We refueled in the river and took off.

"Turukhansk," Jan told me as we flew over it, "used to be one of the most hated places for exiles in Czarist times. Even today the government sends anarchists, mensheviks, and counterrevolutionaries here."

"This beautiful river . . ." I shuddered.

"I've upset you, have I?" Jan Stepanovich put his hand on my arm. "But the Yenisei is known for political prisoners. Famous ones, too. Stalin passed several years in Kureyka on the river, and Lenin served a three-year sentence in a place called Shushenskoye. It's south of Krasnoyarsk."

"I wonder how this river must look to a prisoner," I said. He took his arm away.

Eleven hours after our morning takeoff, we saw a sudden break in the watery landscape. A whole clearing was framed below us: houses, streets, smoke, radio masts, ships. Jan Stepanovich was pointing to it; the mechanic was shouting in my ear, "Igarka."

I leaned out excitedly as we circled over a crowded hill of houses. Here was the newest Arctic city in the world, halfway round the globe from Brooklyn.

I felt a wave of nostalgia. From the air, Igarka looked like an American pioneer town, almost a woodcut of old Chicago. Its square wooden houses were mostly one-storied, stained brown with weather and smoke. Ships were in the harbor, smoke was curling up from buildings, logs were floating downstream.

Our flying boat settled in the Yenisei near a pier. "This is *Port* Igarka. The town of Igarka is about half a mile from here," Jan Stepanovich explained as we stood up in the cockpit. I could see a new two-story house of yellow pine perched on a sharp rise. Over the doorway was a huge sign in English: PORT ADMINISTRATION OF IGARKA.

We climbed into a launch, where a stout, bluff-looking seaman with captain's insignia introduced himself in English with a Russian twang. "I Captain Uskov. Captain of port. I been England many times. Live there. Hoboken too." He bowed graciously.

We tied up at the pier and climbed an endless hill of stairs—I stopped counting at ninety—to the bright new Port Administration building, where I met Captain Mikhailov, the director.

"The whole town's excited ever since we got Schmidt's wire," Captain Mikhailov said gaily in Russian. "Especially our women. My wife—you'll meet her soon, she was a ballet dancer in Moscow—

she's been going around telling everyone an American journalist is coming. By the way, the ladies want to know if you brought any dress patterns from New York."

I shook my head. I would have thought women isolated in the Arctic might have wanted toothbrushes, lipsticks, nail polish, books, women's magazines. But dress patterns? Never.

We were in the dining room, its walls draped with red banners greeting Stalin and Schmidt, when a reporter burst in. He was about thirty, thin, bristling, and dark.

"Pavel Nardoyenov," Captain Uskov introduced him.

"A pleasure," he said in Russian, then pulled a stack of folded papers from his hip pocket and showed me a copy of the newspaper.

THE ARCTIK'S BOLSHEVIK was printed across the top, and beneath it "**The newspaper of the Igarka City Committee of the Communist Party, Political Section of the North Sea Route Administration, and Igarka City Council.**"

"Why do you print an English section?" I wanted to know.

"For the foreign seamen on the foreign ships. They want to know how we live, how we care for our workers, what we do for our women and children. We answer all their questions. And now I will interview you."

After the preliminaries—when had I entered the Soviet Union, how had I come, and did I know Igarka's leader was a woman—he asked the inevitable question, "What do you think of Igarka?"

I said I hadn't seen it yet, but I wanted to immediately—and by myself.

He nodded. "Don't get lost."

"Lost!" Captain Uskov roared, slapping the banquet table with his fat hand. "He think you find way from America and get lost Igarka. No, my friend, her good sailor."

I thanked him for the uncertain compliment, took advantage of the laughter around the table, and slipped out.

With only the arctic white night to light my way, I walked over a dark, swampy hill for about half a mile, stumbling over short stumps, tripping on logs, falling almost knee-deep into mud. I met no one. After a while an occasional rumble and shout began to break the silence. Lights began to appear, stretching out like Main Street in a village. I hurried down the hill and came out of the wilderness to a bright, gay, busy wharf. Hundreds of men and women in Russian peasant clothes, others in foreign naval uniforms, were moving briskly, loading lumber. I could see half a dozen freighters leaning against the dock, the English *New Lambton*, the Norwegian *Granheim*, the Belgian *Navex*, the Danish *Fram*, their booms outstretched, their winches turning as they swallowed yellow wood. I understood better why all the signs and a segment of *The Arctik's Bolshevik* were in English.

I breathed in the pungent smell of newly sawed wood. Planks were stacked along the wharf, planks were being tallied, planks were being swung in midair and hoisted into the freighters. Igarka exported wood.

I stepped onto a wide boardwalk, which vibrated with roaring motion. Horses trotted across, dragging lumber down to the ships. Stocky little boys, the flaps of their fur caps flying in the wind and wide leather belts pulled tight around their fur-lined coats, shouted to me to get out of their path, as they rode their horses bareback with pomp and haughty tyranny and screamed bloodcurdling curses into the brilliant white night.

I left the dock and wandered through the winding dirt streets, feeling this city of some fifteen thousand taking hold. Everything around me confirmed Stefansson's views of the "friendly Arctic." Still, I was unprepared for a lumber town bustling with Liverpool seamen and Norwegians who looked like movie stars.

The midnight sun seemed to be riding the sky downward into a brilliant dawn when I returned to Port Igarka. I sat on a bench and dozed off, dreaming of meeting the lady mayor of Igarka.

28

"I should like to see Comrade Ostro-umova."

I was in the *Gorsoviet*, the House of the Soviets. Skirting scaffolds and cans of paint, I followed a secretary to a sunlit office, dominated by a conference table. Standing at the far end was a thin woman of medium height, with black hair cropped short like a man's, in a white mannish shirt and tie and a blue naval jacket.

"How do you do," Ostro-umova said in clipped English, motioning me to a chair at her right. I put my hand out, ready to shake hers. She kept hers on the table and sat silent, with an air of Well, what do you want? Can't you see how busy I am?

I handed her Schmidt's letter. Her eyes raced down the page, confirming my suspicion that she knew every word on it. She had high cheekbones, buck teeth, and, though in her early forties, the slim figure of a sixteen-year-old boy with slightly tubercular-looking shoulders. Someone had told me she had a son and husband in Moscow. Someone else had said she had been Lenin's secretary and Stalin's.

When she looked up, I reached out to retrieve Schmidt's letter, my passport to the Arctic. Ostro-umova hesitated for a moment, then pushed it back to me.

"Are you comfortable in your room? Yes or no?" she demanded.

"Yes, very comfortable," I said.

"We still have no time to build a hotel," she said curtly. "If you want anything, call or write me a letter and I'll see that it's arranged."

Apparently she considered the interview ended. But I needed a story for the *Herald Tribune*.

"I've come here," I said, bringing my face close to hers, "to study how women are opening your Arctic. I want to know just what kind of work women are doing."

"Everything." She spat the word out.

"What are *your* special problems?"

She raised and lowered her shoulders in her naval uniform as if she were addressing a meeting of the Communist party.

"Our most important task is to make life comfortable and healthful for the workers. Better houses, fresh food, water, electricity." How many times had she used these same words? She glared at me. "Finished?"

I stayed in my chair. I still had no story.

"Aren't you building also for war?"

She leaped out of her chair. "Ours is a policy of peace."

She went to the door, motioning me to follow her.

Dejected, I returned to my room at the port. I had not reached her at all.

I would try another woman leader, the chief agriculturalist of the Polar State Farm, Maria Mitrofanovna Khrenikova. I had heard that she was in charge of raising vegetables and livestock so the workers could have fresh food.

The midmorning sun warmed me as I slushed through mud and tundra to reach Maria Mitrofanovna.

She was standing in the door of her house, a soft, round figure, dressed in an old sweater and skirt, with a cigarette in one hand and a pencil in the other.

We moved indoors and sat near each other at her kitchen table. "You?" she acted as if she wondered whether she could ask the question. "You are searching. What are you looking for?"

I hesitated. "I'm supposed to be making a search for women—women in the three different political systems."

"Searching for women, or searching for yourself?"

She's like Tolstoy, I thought. She's searching for my soul.

"I'm groping," I said.

"What motivates you?" She lit a cigarette.

"I want to see—I want to understand the world, especially this new world in the Arctic."

"And after you see the world, then what?"

"Maybe, if I can describe some of it, like the things I just saw in Germany—if I can only find the right words, maybe I can help awaken people to what's happening. Most people in America have no idea what's going on. They can't picture Naziism, fascism—"

"My child, you really have faith that words can awaken them?"

"Karl Marx believed in words. I'm not a Marxist, but I believe in words if they're urgent, passionate, honest, filled with humanity."

"You're not talking about words. You're talking about you, what you'd like to be."

I stopped. "Maybe it is the kind of person I'd like to be. But whether I'm capable or not, I don't know. I wonder, does one ever know—?"

"When it happens, you'll know it. You don't have to think about it. Suddenly you're a whole person, you're doing what you have to do, and you're doing it well. You'll know. I know it in myself when it happens. Like when I see the rhubarb I've planted take root in this so-called frozen north. Then I'm inspired. But most of the time I'm like you, I'm not sure." She inhaled her cigarette and blew a ring in the air.

I sat silently, mulling over her words. She was forcing me to confront myself. I did not resent it.

"Maria Mitrofanovna, we're soul-searching. I came to interview you."

"Ah yes, but my life is not interesting. I'm an old woman."

"Old?"

"Yes, I am old. I'm forty-three. One must be young in the Arctic."

"In America, they're saying that life begins at forty."

"It's not true. Life begins at your age." She puffed restlessly.

"Tell me about your Polar Farm," I said. I still had nothing I could cable to the *Herald Tribune*. "I heard about your farm back in Moscow."

"Come and see it." She went into her bedroom to get her hat, a big-brimmed cotton hat with openwork, and we left for the fields and hothouses to see the vegetables she was growing.

"We're constantly experimenting," she said. "We try about five hundred experiments each year, and so far about thirty or forty have been successful." She ticked a list off on her fingers—potatoes, turnips (the best prevention against scurvy), kohlrabi, which she called Arctic apples, white radish, dill, carrots, cauliflower, lettuce.

"But what in the world are you staring at?" she asked me.

"I was trying to see if things actually grow in the Arctic while you watch."

She laughed good-naturedly. "I've heard that story too. Of course, with the sun shining more than twenty hours a day, crops can grow nearly twice as fast as in the south. But you can stay out here as long as you like and see what will grow before your eyes. Nothing."

I left Maria Mitrofanovna, returned to my hall bedroom in the Port Administration building, and dashed off a note to Stefansson, knowing it might take months to reach him.

"Dear Stef," I typed, "everything you prophesied about the 'Friendly Arctic' is reality here. Even the rhubarb."

Knowing Mama and Papa were probably frantic at not hearing from me, I sent a cable: MAGNIFICENT EXPERIENCE FEELING GRAND WIRE ME HOW YOU ARE ADDRESS IGARKA ON YENISEI USSR. LOVE RUTH

A knock on my door told me that lunch was ready. Would I join some of the captains in the mess hall?

A friendly old seadog sat next to me. "What did you do this morning?"

"I saw two women leaders, Ostro-umova and Maria Mitrofanov-na. But I didn't get very far."

He chuckled. "Maria Mitrofanovna's okay when you get to know her. But don't let Ostro-umova upset you. It's enough she upsets me. I've been a captain for twenty-five years; now I'm her pupil. She can't tell a bow from a mast, and she's supposed to tell me how and when to load lumber ships. She doesn't know a thing about lumber or farming or organizing a new town. I tell you they need a man up here who's experienced."

A young captain opposite us looked up from his soup. "I watched her today. She was out there on the dock at three o'clock this morning. And back again at five. She may be ugly, and she's got a bad temper, but when you think of the responsibilities she's got, you begin to understand her. I admire her. She's as good as any man."

I left the kasha varnichkas on my plate, apologized, and hurried back to my typewriter to record their divergent images of her. I had my story.

My room was two doors down the hall from the wireless room—my link with the outside world. After a week, I brought Georgi, the chief wireless operator, my first two-thousand-word Sunday article. "The ice-trapped Soviet north is being tamed and harnessed," the story began. It was to be a general introduction to Igarka's two women leaders and some of the workers I was now interviewing every day.

Georgi read the copy carefully and said, "Your article will be in Moscow in a few hours."

"Can I stay and watch you transmit it?"

"Of course, but we don't have connections with Moscow until midnight today."

But when I returned at midnight, he said, "There's trouble with Novosibirsk. We won't be able to send your article tonight."

The next day there was trouble with Sverdlovsk. And so it continued. Only when I returned to New York did I learn that my articles took weeks to arrive in Moscow. George Cornish ran them on successive Sundays and syndicated them around the world.

I soon grew accustomed to the wireless delays, to using an outhouse, to scrubbing my body with water brought from the Yenisei in a barrel. Still, I was delighted when Captain Mikhailov offered me a bath in the port's bathhouse.

"A bathhouse!" I shouted.

"We'll call you as soon as the steam is up. I'll ask Eugenia, who works as a secretary, to go with you."

An hour later, the bathkeeper, a tall man with a flowing white beard and long, wavy white hair, announced that the bath was ready. Eugenia and I followed him to the bathhouse, where he introduced his wife, Babushka, and left. Eugenia and I undressed quickly and wrapped ourselves in towels. The steam and hot water and the smell of soap flooded over me.

I shut my eyes. I was a little girl again in Brooklyn in the Turkish bath with Mama, giggling as hot and cold showers beat down on me, then trying to escape a woman attendant hosing me down with a giant rubber pipe that looked like a cannon shooting water. Mama had helped me climb up to a ledge in the sauna where half-naked Polish and Ukrainian women attendants, their big breasts shaking, beat her with heavy leaves.

"Doesn't it hurt you, Mama?" I had cried.

"No," she laughed. "It makes the blood come up to your skin."

I saw myself again waiting on the rim of a small pool, watching her descend the steps and submerge her whole body, even her long curly hair, in the water. When I grew up, I learned that the pool was the *mikvah*, the ritual bath Mama took to cleanse herself so she could sleep with Papa. It was Friday, and it was a *mitzvah* to sleep with Papa on Friday night.

Brooklyn vanished as Babushka led Eugenia and me to a heated room where water and suds sloshed on the floor like water on a ship's deck in a storm. We washed our hair, soaped and rubbed our skin, cleaned our ears and our toes, and poured buckets of hot and cold water over each other. After about seven thorough scrubbings, Eugenia announced, "Now we are clean."

Next we entered the sauna, opaque with hot vapor, its shelves staired up to the ceiling.

"You," Babushka commanded while she climbed after me, "you climb to the top shelf. Lie on your stomach."

With a sheaf of leaves thicker than any I had seen in Brooklyn, she flogged me violently. My back took the stinging and enjoyed it.

"*Ya kulak* [I am a kulak]," she shouted. Kulaks were peasants exiled as "capitalist farmers." "Look at me." She stopped her punishment to pull at her dress. "Here I have no clothes, and at home I had a cow."

"Where was your home?" I managed to turn my head toward her.

"In Krasnoyarsk. I had a cow there and I milked her every day. And I had a horse. And here, here I have to wash your back." She gave my back another sound smack.

"But Igarka is better than Krasnoyarsk, isn't it?" I asked, thinking of my own reactions.

"*Bozhe moi* [My God]," Babushka twitched angrily. "Here I have nothing. There I had everything—*a cow* . . ."

Eugenia interrupted. "What she means, Rut, is that before the Revolution she and her husband had a farm in Siberia. But she doesn't tell you they were bad to their workers. They exploited. Now they must work in the *banya*."

Was it symbolic, I wondered, that in this age-old cleansing ritual, I had come upon Igarka's dark underside—its prisoners. Their term of exile was usually five years, and though they were free to go where they pleased in Igarka, they hated the city. The prisoners made up nearly half of Igarka's five-thousand people. The other half were the pioneers, like Eugenia.

"Me," Eugenia shouted to me, naked on her shelf, "I'm young. I love it here. I'm building for the whole world."

29

On a rainswept autumn morning, the SS *Anadyr* sailed into Igarka, and it seemed that most of Igarka's five thousand people defied the downpour to greet her.

"EAST GREETS WEST," the *Anadyr* signaled with nine gay flags. She was a three-thousand-ton white cargo ship with a hundred people shrieking and waving from her rails.

"WEST GREETS EAST—WELCOME," the foreign ships strung up their answer.

She had left Vladivostok two months earlier, sailed past Japan and Alaska, and now was blazing a route across the Arctic Ocean to reach Murmansk. If she succeeded, she would be the first vessel other than an icebreaker to open the Northeast Passage in one summer linking Asia, America, and Europe across the top of the globe.

After the welcoming ceremonies, a husky young seaman, American-looking from his dark hair, brushed slick, to his gridiron shoulders and his slangy English, invited me to lunch in the mess hall with the officers. He was Vladimir Rudnick, the first mate.

"We haven't had a girl eat in here since we left Vladivostok," Rudnick said. "The men will be spilling wine all over themselves trying to put on their best manners."

Captain Milovsorov entered, smiling. He shook my hand, greeted his men, seated me at his right, and took his place at the head of the table. The steward brought bowls of hot cabbage soup, delicious-smelling pumpernickel bread, and several bottles of red wine.

"Many years ago," the captain said in English, "I visited Nome, Alaska. You been there?"

"No, this is my first Arctic experience."

"I am a great admirer of your American explorer Stefansson."

"He is my friend."

He stopped eating. "You are a friend of Stefansson!" He turned full face to look at me. "What a lucky person. He is one of the greatest explorers living."

"I'll tell him you said that when I get back to New York."

"And I hope you will also tell Mr. Stefansson," the captain said, "we're changing maps the way he did in Alaska and the Canadian Arctic. Tell him we found small islands and rocks in the Arctic Ocean never before charted." He paused, looked around the mess hall at his men, and said, "Please tell him how this crew of men on my ship, a commercial ship, are trying to open the Northern Sea Route before the ice comes."

It was while working for Stef that I had learned how, for three hundred years, explorers had been seeking to open a trade route between Europe and the Orient. That had been Christopher Columbus's goal when he accidentally discovered America. Some voyagers had sought for a northeast passage across Siberia and the Soviet Arctic, others for a northwest passage across Canada and Alaska. If the *Anadyr* reached Murmansk in the next weeks, she would be the first cargo ship in history to open the Northeast Passage in one season.

My desire to join the captain and his crew, to see and know the Arctic Ocean as I had seen Igarka, to experience it, to live it, grew stronger as he spoke.

"Do you think I could join you?" I asked. "Could I make the rest of the journey with you?"

Captain Milovsorov raised his wine glass. "Silence, everybody."

The men stopped sipping soup and lifted their wine glasses expectantly.

"Let us drink to a friend of the great American explorer Stefansson. And to the newest member on our ship."

The men looked at me and, obviously delighted with any excuse, once again drained their glasses.

"More wine," the captain ordered the steward back. The men drank; the captain drank; I pretended to sip the wine, drunk, not with alcohol, but with excitement. I was to sail on a historic ship and start my journey homeward.

The whole pioneer town of engineers, captains, lumbermen, and kulaks seemed to rush down to the dock with Ostro-umova to see us off. The ship carried lumber it had picked up in Igarka, a dozen passengers, a team of thickly furred polar dogs, and two polar bears, Misha and Masha, that had come aboard at Cape Chelyuskin, the northernmost mainland in the world. The polar dogs were destined for Moscow and the bears for children in the Kharkov Zoo.

We sailed past the last outposts along the Yenisei River as it flowed down to the Arctic Ocean, past Dudinka, Golchika, Ust-Port—names that sounded like the chanting of a witch doctor beating his drum. There was something still about this land and river and sky, something arrested in time. But of desolation there was none. Gulls and Arctic terns swooped in our path, crude fishing boats and native rowboats passed us until we stopped at Dickson Island on the ocean itself, its landmark a radio tower tapered like a derrick in an oil well.

Here, just south of the North Pole, two hundred men, women, and children were building a polar radio station—the most powerful in the Arctic, shooting its waves into the world. It chatted with

Moscow; it talked with Paris; it listened to London, Berlin, and Tokyo. It broke the vast silence of the North.

We entered laboratories and wireless rooms, peered into dormitories where men relaxed on triple-deck bunk beds, and talked with hydrologists testing the depth of the water, aerologists sending pilot balloons into the air, and meteorologists studying and predicting the weather. "The Arctic is the weather kitchen of the world," one of them told me. "Weather flows from here to your Alaska."

Back aboard the *Anadyr*, I pulled my coat tightly around me and paced the deck. We were racing to reach Murmansk, lest we be trapped all winter in the ice.

I had imagined that the Arctic Ocean in summer and autumn would be a sinister sea with huge breakers and a screaming wind brushing back the foam. But the ocean was brown and bluish-green, the waves no more choppy and the air not much colder than the Atlantic on a winter crossing.

The peace and silence of the Arctic enveloped me. Water whished against the sides of the *Anadyr*, water that would soon freeze into ice floes. We sailed past icebreakers patrolling the ocean for possible danger. Scout planes flew over us and dipped their wings; polar radio stations guided our path to make sure we would not be trapped in sudden ice.

"I've been wondering what you write about us in your articles," Borisov, the political commissar of the ship, asked me one night after a dinner of potato pancakes and tea.

Borisov was the Communist party's representative and mouthpiece, who could give orders to everyone, even to our sixty-five-year-old captain who knew the Arctic as he did not.

He was twenty-six, good-looking with bright red hair and an athletic body. He talked with a slight lisp. When he grew excited, words tumbled out of his mouth. When he was calm, he spoke like a political handbook quoting party dogma. Excited or calm, he irritated me. Political commissars, I had decided, were either born or trained to arrogance.

212

"I suspect," Borisov said belligerently, wiping his lips after a last sip of tea, "that your articles are like the usual Gearst [Hearst] atrocity stories about our starving people."

"You stereotype me," I answered, equally belligerent, "the way you think American journalists stereotype you."

"Well, if you didn't write that way, why would you be writing for the bourgeois press?"

"Wait a minute," Rudnick, the first mate, interrupted. "I have an idea. Why don't you read us one of your dispatches? I'll translate it for the rest of the boys."

I agreed and hurried past the open boiler room to my cabin. The hum of the ship's engines seemed to beat a warning drum in my ears.

From my desktop I picked up a folder of copies of my articles. Each night, after eleven, I was allowed to cable exactly 150 words to Moscow. It was like writing poetry.

The men lit their cigarettes and leaned forward intently as I read the opening lines of my first dispatch:

> As the first foreign correspondent to fly into the Soviet North, I am experiencing that feeling of zest which goes with exploration. I am in the thick of an historic movement. I am in an era in the making . . .

"*Ochen khorosho* [Very good]," Borisov applauded, and added instantly, "*Vash redaktor nikogda eto ne propustit* [Your editor will never let it go through]."

The *New York Herald Tribune* did not change my articles. But a few months later I had to admit that some of Borisov's suspicions were justified. I was asked to write a series of four articles for NANA, the North American Newspaper Alliance, which serviced some 150 newspapers in America and Canada.

My series began:

Airplanes, icebreakers and radio are opening the Soviet Arctic, breaking traditions of the frozen wasteland of the North. Pioneers are pushing northward, new cities are converting the once uninhabited Arctic into an industrial, livable country.

The *Toronto Evening Telegram* wrote its own lead:

Up over the hub of the hub [was this a typographical error or journalistic emphasis?] of the polar icecap from Canada lies Russia—the Orient separated from the Occident by a few score miles of ice and snow—by a few mere hours of flying. Airplanes, icebreakers, and radio are opening the Soviet Arctic. Pioneers under the banner of the hammer and sickle *are pushing that red rag into the very throne room of the North Wind.* New cities are springing up were [sic] once was only silence and the white bear licking her cubs.

The rest of the story was similarly changed. "In a modern plane," my uninvited ghost wrote, "behind a Russian pilot, I flew into the Soviet northland which is today what the Canadian northland will be tomorrow." And the series, much of which I could have recognized only by my own pictures, ended by having me ask the Canadian public that final stirring question: "When will the Canadian Arctic waken so?"

Vassya, who had been political commissar at Cape Chelyuskin, was the most articulate of the skeptics and woman-haters on the ship. Dark, curly-haired, and muscular, Vassya and I would pace the deck arguing fiercely, indifferent to the weather, even when it began to turn icy cold.

Unlike most of the scientists who spoke English and German fluently, Vassya knew only Russian, and his vocabulary, filled with newly coined and esoteric terms, was beyond my conversational Russian. So we argued through our translator, Leon, a sensitive young man, rather slight, with a pale face, pale eyes, and a gentle voice.

"Expeditions are jobs, not banquets or parties," Vassya would say, stroking the elegantly trimmed black Vandyke beard he had grown in the north. "You can concentrate on your work when you know there isn't a woman along. But one single woman is enough to make a man remember everything he's left willingly behind— comforts and ease and love."

Is he telling me the story of his life, I wondered, as he went on, "I vowed I'd never fall in love again in my life. So far I've been able to keep that vow in the Arctic."

"It seems to me," I said, as we strode the deck, bucking the wind, "that you antiwoman explorers are hanging on for dear life to the Victorian picture of women."

"What's wrong with Victorian women?"

"The trouble with you, Vassya, is that you refuse to recognize there are women just as serious about work and adventure and pioneering as you are."

"You'd have to comb through the country to find such women. I hate women anyway. They lie. They're petty. They're just out to gain their own ends. I hate them, do you hear?"

"I hear, but I don't believe—"

This argument went on day after day. Not yet thirty, Vassya had been chosen political commissar on Cape Chelyiuskin because of the maturity of his political views. In everything but his attitude toward women, he was a child of the Revolution.

To him, the Soviet Union was the glorification of man's hope for paradise on earth. So I became an ardent democrat, extolling America for the political freedom and the standard of living that made it the one and only true paradise. I looked for the flaws in his arguments, he for the flaws in mine. But remembering warnings about the jealousy of men in the Arctic, I was careful not to spend too much time with him.

Late one evening I finished working and went on deck for my regular nightly walk. I carried my notebook with me, jotting down observations about the unexpected beauty I was finding in the Arctic and the mystery of this ocean that reached to the North Pole. I had taught myself the art of writing in darkness by moving my left thumb down the page while I scribbled notes with my right hand.

215

"The ship's engines," I wrote, listening to the rhythmic sounds, "are like a heartbeat propelling us—"

I stopped. Vassya and Leon had appeared at my side.

"Still working?" Vassya asked indulgently.

"I'm finished now."

"Join us for tea."

"Let's walk first," I said. We filled our lungs with the Arctic air and then entered the passenger's mess hall on the upper deck. It was dimly lit and deserted. At the table, Leon sat between Vassya and me. A steward brought us tea and vanished.

Vassya, eyeing my notebook open on the table, wasted no time. He launched into a serious discussion of the scientific work being done to facilitate the opening of the Northern Sea Route. I began taking notes.

"Tell her," he said, with Leon interpreting, "how we make our magnetic observations and send them to the two biggest radio centers, Dickson Island and Tixie Bay, where the Lena River flows into the Arctic. They in turn communicate with the ships and icebreakers opening our path and warning us if we're in danger—"

Suddenly Leon cut into his translation and said in English, "How ironic this is. I am the medium between two people who love each other. Yet I'm in love too."

I stared at him. "What are you saying?"

"Only that I'm not good enough or handsome enough for you."

Vassya went on talking scientific data, while Leon continued. "This is what happens in the Arctic. Two men fall in love with a woman. One is plain but goodhearted. The other is handsome but cruel. The plain one would sell his life for her; she would still hesitate. The dashing one has only to touch her hand, and she would run at his bidding."

Unwittingly I had stirred up the jealousy I had been warned against.

"You wouldn't understand," Leon said softly. "Women don't understand these things. Love isn't something you can put under a microscope. I knew the moment you boarded this ship that I was in love with you."

"*Slushete* [Now listen]," Vassya said, "Tell her that in Vilkitski Strait we made very important hydrological investigations. We studied the currents, the temperature of the water, the salinity, and the physical qualities of the ice—"

"You see," Leon said, "he's in love with you. But his work comes first. You come after the magnetic observations. He is young yet. Maybe he didn't feel his body quiver the moment you stepped on board. But he's human. I think he did."

Vassya reached across Leon to emphasize his words. I could almost feel his breath, but I kept writing to control my confusion.

"You can't help it, of course," Leon said sadly. "You're not to blame for being a woman. I know I'll never even touch your hand, but the memory of the way you walked on this ship, of your laugh, I'll never forget them. They're more important to me than all the work I have done in the North."

"And tell her, too," Vassya lit a cigarette, while I wrote swiftly, "something that should be very important to her as a newspaper-woman. Before, it was necessary to pierce ice for two or three hours before you could measure depth. But this winter one of our mechanics invented a special machine for boring through the ice. It takes only forty-five seconds to pierce ice over six feet deep. She may want to tell her country about it, to use it in Alaska—"

"Maybe you can understand machines," Leon said, "but no one would expect you to understand what an incredible thing it was for me—for most of us starved men—to have you come along. Don't be angry with me for having told you these things. I know you never suspected them. You never suspected I knew you and Vassya were in love."

"It's not true," I said. I was not in love with Vassya. I was not in love right then with any man. Boyfriends, some serious enough to propose marriage, had walked in and out of my life in Brooklyn. Months had passed since I had said farewell to Johann and to the Germany Hitler had despoiled. There were nights when I dreamed of love, yearned to have a man's arms around me. But not Vassya's.

"It's not true," I repeated. "Not true."

"You can never hide those things. I guess you two belong together. You'll still let me talk to you though, won't you?"

"Of course. I'll see you tomorrow, and you'll have forgotten all these things you said tonight."

"Don't jest. You won't be angry, though? I'd never forgive myself if you were. Your coming was a beautiful thing. I should thank you for it. Instead, I can see that I'm making you unhappy, burdening you with it, making you hate me, when I want to be your friend. You do know I'm your friend, don't you?"

"Yes."

"That's all I want. I'll leave you two alone now." He stood up. "Good night," he said to Vassya. "I must go to bed now."

He bowed over my hand.

I stood up immediately. "We'd better all go to bed."

The days sped, growing shorter and colder. We paced the deck. We talked. Nights, after dinner, someone played the accordion or guitar, and we sang Russian and American songs. Once we stopped close to an icebreaker, lowered a rope ladder, and picked up two passengers bound for Murmansk, eager, as all of us were, to finish the voyage and go home.

Sailing around *Novaya Zemlya* [New Land], we were caught in a thirty-three-mile-an-hour wind. The *Anadyr* rocked so violently I could hardly keep from sliding clear across the deck. I managed somehow to get up to the bridge where Rudnick was giving orders to the pilot. He smiled when he saw me.

"I thought you'd be sick like the rest of them. There hasn't been a passenger in the mess hall all day, and now some of the crew are down, too."

"We're running into a pretty bad fog, aren't we?"

He straightened his shoulders as if he were defying the gale. "If we were afraid of the fog," he said grimly, "we should have turned back as soon as we left Vladivostok. Eighty-five percent of our trip is in the fog. Yes, fog, fog and ice are still the major obstacles to opening the Northeast Passage."

Murmansk!

We rushed to the deck to see crowds waving and cheering. Printed banners blew in the wind. Freighters and fishing trawlers honked their welcome. An out-of-tune brass band played the *Internationale*. Reporters raced aboard and tried to interview everyone from the captain and the stoker to me. How did it feel to have conquered the Northeast Passage? What was it like to be on a freighter writing history?

We had no patience for interviews. We waited for entrance cards, dashed down the gangplank, and walked through a still primitive Arctic city of 120,000, whose streets were dirt or planks of wood, and whose houses were weatherbeaten cottages and huts. Our destination was the dining room of the Grand Hotel, a modern stuccoed building, that seemed like a skyscraper in that city of wooden houses. It rose four stories into the air.

First we devoured every orange and grape in the dining room. Then we attacked the caviar, and finally huge portions of beef and fresh cabbage, laughing and joking while we washed the food down with Georgian wine.

For the next two days, we prowled through Murmansk, stuffing ourselves with fresh oranges, and early one evening all the polar heroes climbed aboard the Polar Arrow headed for Leningrad.

"I'll come back," I murmured to the dark Karelian forests as the train rushed south. "I'll come back," I promised Vassya and Leon and Rudnick when none of us could sleep and we sat in a compartment reminiscing through the night.

"I'll come back," we whispered to each other. "I'll come back. I want to die in the Arctic."

30
October 1935

A London fog embraced me. I had traveled directly from Moscow
to keep the date with Virginia Woolf that her secretary had set up
months before.

The Georgian four-story house with its balcony overhanging the
street floor, the serenity of the quiet, narrow street in Bloomsbury,
the clean-washed smell of rain that had fallen all day—the magical
evening turned everything I saw into rapture.

At 6:00 P.M., I rang the bell at 52 Tavistock Square.

A housekeeper opened the door and led me up the stairs. It was
Leonard, Virginia's husband, who met me at the parlor door and
showed me to a winged chair.

She lay curled up on a rug in front of a blazing fire, like an
elegant greyhound, in a long, gray gown, gray stockings, gray shoes,
gray hair cropped short like a boy's, puffing a cigarette in a long,
gray cigarette holder.

Against the back wall, distant from us, sat Leonard, dark and
brooding and protective.

I was too awed to speak. I, the young would-be writer, was in the home of my literary icon, whose photo hung on my bedroom wall.

Her voice was mysterious and sad. Between long pauses, a wave of melancholy moved across her face.

"I looked into the study you wrote about me," she said and blew more smoke. "Quite scholarly."

I could hardly breathe, let alone respond.

"And in your letter," she said, "you wrote that you are a journalist and are planning to write a book about women under fascism, communism, and democracy. I don't know how I can help you. I don't understand a thing about politics. I never worked a day in my life."

I was startled that she did not think publishing ten books, countless essays, and brilliant book reviews was work.

"What have you found so far?" she asked.

Awe gave way to confusion. I had returned to England on my way home just to interview her—to sit at her feet. But it was she who was lying at my feet in front of the fireplace, questioning me. In the cold English parlor, heated only by the blazing fire, my body roasted in front and froze behind.

"I'm still doing research," I said. "I've just come back from meeting a woman mayor and women leaders in a new town called Igarka in the Soviet Arctic."

"The Soviet Arctic?" Leonard repeated. I turned my head to look at him. His face was long and egg-shaped, with soft cheeks that seemed to have no bones. His eyes sank beneath thick black brows, and his hands moved restlessly with a nervous tremor. "I didn't know," he said, "that the Russians allowed any journalists to go up there!"

"They said I was the first."

"Amazing! How old are you?"

"Twenty-four." I had just celebrated my birthday.

"And whom were you representing?"

"The *New York Herald Tribune*."

There was a long silence. I waited for Virginia to talk. Curled up before the fire, she looked helpless and vulnerable. She smoked dreamily, looking into the flames.

Returning from wherever her revery had taken her, she broke the silence. "We were just in your Germany," she said.

Why does she call it *my* Germany, I wondered. I had written her from America. But I did not interrupt.

"We were driving through on holiday," she said. "Our car was stopped to let Hitler and his entourage pass. Madness, that country."

"I was in Germany a few months ago," I ventured. Leonard moved his chair closer. "I was in a bookstore in Cologne when Hitler's voice came over a loudspeaker. A terrifying voice, as if it came not from his lungs but his bowels."

"He has a terrifying voice," she agreed.

I took the courage to go on. "And on the street I watched SS men herding a whole group of people to the railroad station. They were taking them, someone told me, to a prison or some kind of internment camp. There was a woman protecting an elderly hunchbacked man, and he was clutching her hand. She seemed to be asking for help. I wanted to do something. But I was paralyzed."

I stopped, embarrassed that I had talked so long. Virginia lit another cigarette.

"There is such horror in the world," she said, turning her face back to the fire.

I spoke, too quickly. "That's what strikes me so forcefully in your books, the hope that women will help end the horror and create peace. Men make wars, not women."

The housekeeper entered with a tray and offered each of us tea. My hand trembled as I lifted the delicate china cup to my lips. Without tasting the tea, I returned the cup to its saucer. I did not touch it again.

Virginia sipped the tea and then, with a dancer's choreographed movements, eased a fresh cigarette into the holder, struck a match, and blew smoke. A gray shadow fell across her narrow, elegant face. I knew she was fifty-three, but her face and her body, even curled up, seemed to belong to a much older woman. The questions I had planned to ask her lay inert in my head. I must not burden her, I thought. I must leave very soon.

She set her cup in her saucer and ran her hand through her short gray hair. "Once," she said, "we had such hope for the world—" Her voice drifted off with her smoke.

I glanced at my watch. It was 6:30. I stood up carefully, so as not to disturb her. I leaned down to shake her hand, then shook Leonard's and thanked them.

I knew the interview had failed. There was little she had said that I could cable to the *Herald Tribune* or use in my study of women.

But I had met Virginia Woolf!

Half a century later I discovered what she thought of the interview when I consulted her handwritten diaries and published books in the Berg Collection at the New York Public Library on Fifth Avenue.

Her writing in the journals was small, the letters packed so close that some were illegible. Her abbreviations and scant punctuation attested to the speed with which she must have written these pages chronicling her crowded days and nights, her teas, her trysts with lovers, her illnesses, her journeys with Leonard (L in the diaries), the brilliant Jewish husband who nurtured her through her terrifying manic-depressive spells and suicide attempts.

I found my name in the index of *The Diary of Virginia Woolf: Volume Four 1931–1935*: Grüber, Fraülein Ruth.

Virginia Woolf had written about me! But why Fraülein? Why the umlaut? The dissertation, published three years after I wrote it, was in English, my letter was in English, and I had sent it from Brooklyn, USA.

I turned to a passage in the entry dated *Friday 31 May:*

> The usual tremor & restlessness after coming back, & nothing
> to settle to, & some good German woman sends me a pamphlet
> on me, into which I couldn't resist looking, though nothing so
> upsets & demoralises as this looking at ones face in the glass.

And a German glass produces an extreme diffuseness & complexity so that I cant get either praise or blame but must begin twisting among long words.

I reread the complaint: "*cant get either praise or blame.*" True, she admitted she merely "looked" into the dissertation. If she had read just a small part of it, she would have seen how much I admired her.

Next I opened *The Letters of Virginia Woolf: Volume Five 1932–1935*. This time I was in the index without the umlaut.

The letter was to her nephew Julian Bell, who had gone to China to teach and who was later to die in the Spanish Civil War.

> *14th Oct 1935*
> Dearest Julian,
> . . . Now I suppose you are teaching the Chinks about Mrs. Gaskell.
>
> ["Chinks?"]
>
> I must now go and see an importunate and unfortunate Gerwoman who thinks I can help her with facts about Women under Democracy—little she knows—what you do about your poor old Virginia.

Was this what she thought before meeting me? *Importunate? Unfortunate? Gerwoman?* A thin flame of anger was burning my throat. There is not an ounce of German blood in my body.

In the *Diary* I found my name again.

> *Tuesday 15 October*
> . . . couldn't write this morning; & must go up & receive Miss Grueber (to discuss a book on women & fascism—a pure have yer as Lottie would say) in 10 minutes.

Lottie was her housekeeper, perhaps the very one who had brought me tea.

But what was "a pure have yer"?

I asked Ruth Webb, a school inspector in London, who was examining early drafts of *Mrs. Dalloway*.

"A pure have yer," she repeated in a whisper, though we were the only readers in the room. "It's cockney. And I should know. I come from cockney stock. But really I haven't a clue. All I can tell you is, it's derogatory."

I left my papers and books and went to see Catherine Halls, an English librarian, at the information desk.

"Never heard of it," she told me. "It's probably slang. We have a lot of slang dictionaries."

She directed me to the shelves of dictionaries.

I opened Eric Partridge's *A Dictionary of Slang and Unconventional English*. I found the word: *pure* (n.) *a mistress, esp. a kept mistress, a wanton, dog's dung.*

My head exploded. *Dog's dung?*

Wait. Perhaps she used *pure* as an adjective and *have* as a noun. In Partridge's *Slang: Today and Yesterday*, I found: *Have* (*n*), *a deception, a swindle.*

Did she think I had come to swindle her?

I tried to put the pieces of the ugly puzzle together. Maybe, like many self-conscious writers, she thought I had come to get something out of her. But why then did she invite me for tea?

She had written these notes and letters before she met me. What did she think *after* that half hour in Bloomsbury?

I found an entry in the *Letters, Volume Five 1932–1935* and ordered the original letter from the stack. It was written to her seventy-year-old lover, Ethel Smyth, a composer, explaining why she had been unable to work. A week had passed since my visit.

> Monday, [21 October 1935.]
> I've had a poetess reading her works aloud. [Easdale]; I've had a French socialist declaiming against Fascism [Walter]; I've had a German Jewess [Gruber]—no, I cant go into all the vociferations and gesticulations that are our lot in Tavistock Sqre.

A German Jewess?

German? I, who was born in Brooklyn, my language English, my accent obviously, unmistakably New Yorkese? Perhaps she decided I was a poor refugee fleeing Hitler, washed up on Britain's shores, importuning her for help.

I read more of the diaries and letters. In a 1932 letter to Ethel Smyth, she had described a birthday party with Leonard's mother and his nine siblings: "When the 10 Jews sat around me silently at my mother in laws, tears gathered behind my eyes, at the futility of life: imagine eating birthday cake with silent Jews at 11 P.M."

I was appalled. Diaries can rip the mask from their creators.

I reread the letter to Ethel Smyth deploring the poetess, the socialist, and the misspelled Gerwoman who had swindled her of time. Was that why she resented me? Was time-swindling the key? What, after all, to a writer is more precious than time? Was that what "a pure have yer" really meant?

I asked Aïda Lovell, a friend in London, to question Nigel Nicolson. He was one of the editors of Virginia's letters and the son of Victoria Sackville-West, the lover Virginia had pursued. He had known Virginia since childhood.

"Dr. Gruber won't be too pleased by this," he wrote Aïda, "but I was glad to read in VW's diary that she was quite flattered by what Dr. G wrote about her . . . which was rare for Virginia."

Questioning Nicolson's interpretation, I wrote him myself.

"I fear," he answered, "that you may have been hurt by her references to you, but she was like that in her diary and letters, though perfectly courteous in conversation."

As for "a pure have yer," it was slang, he wrote "have yer— Gotcha. It suggests a throw-away attitude, Cockney bravado, suggesting a task forced upon one which needs to be done . . . It's one of the things I deplore about Virginia, her cattiness, contempt for almost everyone who were not her friends, an occasional touch of anti-Semitism, her snobbishness and jealousy. But it's almost heresy to suggest these things to the Virginia Woolf Society of the USA to whom she is Joan of Arc and Mother Teresa combined."

Seeing myself through her English upper-class eyes, I felt rage, then embarrassment, then pain.

All these years I had seen her through the eyes of a naive admirer. Now I learned that even before we met she had confided to her diary and her erstwhile lover that I was from a world that was not hers, a world she could not understand.

After the initial pain, I realized I did not know in 1935 what I learned later. I did not know her sexual preferences; I knew only that the bisexual *Orlando* was my favorite of her books.

For many years I had heard of her anti-Semitism. Now, reading her diaries and letters, I saw her in the context of a British society rife with racism and anti-Semitism.

Nor did I know how many suicides she had attempted before her final walk into the water. Despite my anger and disillusionment, I was moved to see her in a less critical way. Leonard's brilliant autobiography revealed the agony of her madness—her screams, her crazed rejection for days of all food, her abuse of her caretakers, her tearful longing for death to end her pain.

Though no longer infuriated, I understood she had lived her entire life with a will to create as a woman. That was the lesson she had taught me. I had gone with her "To the Lighthouse." Now I was back.

Part Four
THE GULAG

31
1936

The next months at home sped by. George Cornish asked me to write a series of four articles for the Sunday *Herald Tribune* with an accompanying page of photos. NANA (the North American Newspaper Alliance) asked for another series for the newspapers they serviced across the country. Editors created their own headlines with captions like the *Milwaukee Journal*'s "American Girl First Correspondent to Study Soviet's Arctic: Dr. Ruth Gruber Flies to 'Waste' Places of North, Finds Thriving Towns" or the *Boston Globe*'s romantic "ROLLING BACK THE ICE AGE: American Woman Flies to Land of Long Nights and Long Days where Time Has Stood Frozen at Dawn."

William B. Feakins, a lecture agent, booked me on a tour across the United States and Canada to speak on "A New World in the Arctic" and "Women Under Fascism, Communism, and Democracy." I was fulfilling my promise to Anna Sommers in Berlin, who had exhorted me to "scream" about Hitler and Germany.

I was trying to hone two crafts—speaking and writing—and discovered they were two sides of the same coin. Writing helped me

231

organize my thoughts; speaking helped make them sharper and clearer. A novice in both, and still insecure, I found some encouragement in the responses.

"Dr. G gave a perfect talk," the program chairman of the Conference of Club Presidents in Chicago, wrote to the Feakins Lecture Bureau, which then booked me for six more weeks in the Midwest. The first vice-president of the Austin, Illinois, Woman's Club reported, "Her unassuming manner and vivacious, humorous way of telling about her Arctic experiences, made it one of the finest travel talks we have had in many a day."

The comments should have made me feel a little more confident and somewhat more mature. They didn't. I was still searching to find out who I was and what I hoped to do with the rest of my life.

In the spring, I sent the *Herald Tribune* series to Professor Otto Schmidt in Moscow with the news that I had signed a contract with Simon and Schuster to write a book on the Soviet Arctic.

He thanked me for the articles and invited me to come back, live in Yakutsk, the way I had lived in Igarka, and learn what they were doing with their native populations.

Another invitation to visit the Arctic!

I hurried into the kitchen-dining room to tell Mama and Papa the news.

"I've been invited back to the Soviet Arctic."

"No use trying to stop you," Papa said, his voice a mixture of sadness and pride. Mama shook her head in despair.

Once again the *New York Herald Tribune* gave me credentials as their special foreign correspondent.

I packed my bag with a few clothes, a green suede coat and matching profile hat from Macy's, an assortment of big and small notebooks, my typewriter, and my camera.

On a warm spring day, I kissed everybody goodbye and sailed off on the SS *Normandie*.

The clerk at the Europa Hotel in Leningrad regretted that my room was occupied. Foreign fur traders had come for the annual fur auction and taken all the bedrooms.

I telephoned my friend from my first Arctic trip, Professor Rudolph Samoilovich, the head of the Arctic Institute.

"Wait for me in the lobby," Samoilovich said in German, the language we had used before. "I'll be there in a few minutes."

He arrived dressed in white canvas shoes, white trousers, and a white shirt with the sleeves rolled up. He handed me a bouquet of flowers.

"Zo-o-o, zo-o-o," he laughed. "Back in Leningrad at last. I found a room for you in the Institute for Scholars. It's the former palace of the Grand Duke Vladimir, the brother of Czar Nicholas."

The room was palatial, cluttered with gilt chairs, a gold-framed mirror hanging at a strange angle from the ceiling, a three-paneled screen decorated with upholstered fabric, a round wood-burning stove, two single shiny brass beds covered with fat white pillows, and a marble bathroom with a tub big enough to bathe an elephant.

"You must be starving," Samoilovich said from the door. "Let's go down to the restaurant and get you some food."

I left my bag and hat on one of the beds and followed him down a majestic stairway to the crowded restaurant. Everyone in the Institute for Scholars stood up to greet him as we took places at a small table.

"Zo-o-o," he said, "do you know that you will be the first American to visit the Yakutia Republic since 1879? That's when your explorer George Washington De Long and most of his party died trying to reach the North Pole."

He leaned across the table and clamped his hand over mine. "Such a coincidence. De Long went for the *New York Herald*, and you are going for the *New York Herald Tribune*."

I was confused. Was he showing typical Russian warmth and friendship?

"What would you like to do next?" Samoilovich asked after we had downed a cold vegetable soup and a breaded cutlet with rice and potatoes.

"What I'd like is a bath and some sleep."

"I'll order a bath for you," he said. "Then you rest awhile." He checked his watch. "It's eight o'clock. I'll come back about ten and take you for a ride through Leningrad. It'll still be daylight."

My internal alarm system rang a bell, but I refused to let it stop me. "I'll be ready," I said.

I found my way back to my room and started undressing. An old woman entered, looked into the bathroom, came out muttering in Russian "No hot water," and vanished. Soon a younger woman entered, lit a fire in the wood-burning stove and sat patiently waiting for the water to heat. Then she scrubbed and filled the massive tub and smilingly departed.

I hoisted myself up and lay back in the warm water with my eyes closed. Should I have refused to go driving with Samoilovich?

No longer sleepy, I changed into a white linen jacket with an ankle-length black-and-white-checked skirt and a matching ascot, and sat at the French windows looking down at the broad, blue Neva River. On the opposite shore, the tall spire of the Fortress of Peter and Paul rose against the sky. Under the czars, it had been the prison for men and women condemned to exile in the very areas of Siberia where I would be heading.

What a moment to be in Russia, I thought. The Moscow trials were scheduled to begin in August. Waiting in the docks were sixteen founders of the Revolution, chief among them two of Lenin's closest companions, Grigorii Zinoviev, born Apfelbaum, and Lev Kamenev, born Rosenfeld, accused of plotting to assassinate Stalin. Of the sixteen revolutionaries, eleven were Jews.

At ten o'clock, Samoilovich drove up in his open 1931-model Ford. The sun had still not set; the white night seemed to soften the ominous walls of the Fortress of Peter and Paul.

"Are there any prisoners in there now?" I asked Samoilovich as we crossed the Neva and drove past the prison.

"Not any more. But before the Revolution most of our top leaders were in it. I was in prison eighteen times. Things were so bad then you *had* to be a revolutionary."

"How did you survive between prison terms?"

"I lived underground. Every time the police were about to catch up with me, I changed my internal passport. We all lived that way. You took a passport with a dead man's name, or you took passports from your friends who went into hiding for a few weeks until you could escape to another city. I can't count how many different passports I had."

"And now?"

"I'm no Bolshevik. There's nothing more to fight for. We have everything."

"But the arrests of Zinoviev and Kamenev—?"

He turned from the wheel and looked at me warily. It was the way Jews had looked at me in Germany.

"Better not to talk about the arrests," he said. He put his hand on mine again. I chided myself for questioning the reason for his warmth.

I heard the tension in his voice. Like Kamenev and Zinoviev, he was a Jew.

A few days later I left for Moscow and headed straight to the Northern Sea Route Administration to see Professor Schmidt.

"Accept my congratulations on your talented articles." He came forward and shook my hand. His dark hair and prematurely graying beard seemed ruffled, as if he had been running his hands through them, preoccupied with work. "You came just in time. I leave tomorrow evening for Archangel."

"You're leaving tomorrow?" I blurted out. His was the magic name that opened the doors in the Arctic. "Without you, I may never get to Yakutsk."

"No, no. My assistant is prepared to assist you."

I was still apprehensive. "So you're off on another expedition?"

He nodded. "I'll be on the icebreaker *Lütke*. I'll be surveying most of our work, stopping at all our polar radio stations, like Dickson Island, where you were last year."

He turned the conversation to the route I was to travel. I would take the Trans-Siberian Railway across European Russia and Siberia, in order not to duplicate my first trip by air. From Irkutsk I would fly to Yakutsk.

Again Schmidt wrote a note addressed to the officials of the Northern Sea Route Administration advising them that "Rut Gruber of the *New York Gerald Tribune*" was to be given full cooperation. I folded the note carefully in my handbag.

"You'll need another visa," he said.

"But my visa is good for six months."

"That's your Soviet visa. You'll need a special one for the Yakutia Republic. It's an autonomous republic, and they want the right to decide who should enter. But don't worry, my assistant will help you, I promise."

32

"Nye sevodnya [Not today]." An official in a crowded government office shook his head.

"If not today, then when?" It was the eighth day I had appeared requesting the visa to the Yakutia Republic.

A shrug of the shoulders. "Who knows?"

"But when should I come back?"

"Tomorrow. The day after. Suit yourself."

To fill the days of interminable waiting, I spent hours in libraries and museums reading everything I could find in English and German on the Yakuts and other northern Siberian tribes who, according to the historian Gibbon, "alone, among the Sons of Man, are ignorant of war and unconscious of human blood." I was fascinated by the accounts of the shamans, who could heal people with witchcraft and special herbs.

More days passed. Time was my enemy.

"Patience. Just be patient." Maurice Hindus, the distinguished author who was in Moscow writing his fifth book on the Soviet

Union, tried to console me. We were eating borsch and cheese bliniki in the restaurant of the Novo Moscovskaya Hotel.

"You can't speed up bureaucrats," he said. "Remember, they haven't allowed any of us into Yakutsk, though God knows I've tried."

"I'm getting so restless," I said.

"Ruth," he waved his finger at me like a college teacher, "you're not wasting time. Just keep doing what you're doing now—reading, studying. The Russians aren't dumb. They invited you back to the Arctic because you were willing to see with an open mind. You were willing to learn. Some of the correspondents who've been here as long as I have, or longer, are weary or cynical or biased. You haven't gotten to that stage yet."

"You trying to tell me I'm still naive?"

His face, usually dark and melancholy, seemed to light up. "That's your cover, isn't it? Not a bad cover for a foreign correspondent. It helps when the people you're interviewing trust you."

I stared in silence at my borsch. I am naive, I told myself. Naive and female in a tough man's world. I was in a hurry to catch up. I wanted to be a working stiff, like the men correspondents who were traveling across the world with typewriters and cameras.

"Maurice," I asked suddenly, "how would you sum up this summer of 1936?"

He pushed his plate away from him. "Darkness. Blackness. Spain ripped apart by civil war. Ethiopia crushed by Mussolini. Hitler arming troops, terrorizing Jews." Under hooded lids, his eyes swept around the restaurant. "Russia arresting old Bolsheviks, some of them my old friends."

He looked as if he were seeing me for the first time.

"Maybe the Arctic—where you're going—maybe there's some hope for the world up there. Maybe they're doing things we don't know about."

Once again he was the master builder teaching the young apprentice. "Listen to me, Ruth. Talk to the people on all sides of the spectrum. Take lots of notes and for the love of God, aim for the truth."

I had a feeling he himself was not sure where the truth was.

Three weeks later, with the visa finally stamped in my passport, I boarded the Trans-Siberian Railroad and entered my compartment. I found myself in a European drawing room, with a couch that could be made up as a bed, wood-paneled walls, three electric lamps, a red flowered rug, and a writing table at the window.

Soon life on the Trans-Siberian became like life on a cruise ship. There was always time. Time to eat, time to read, to visit, to take long afternoon naps, to sit at the window and watch the landscape change from the Central Russian Plateau with its parched look of drought and death to the life-burgeoning forests of Siberia's pines and spruce.

Early one morning in the dining car, I met a woman in her thirties wearing schoolteacher-like glasses.

"Let me introduce myself," she flung out her hand. "My name is Sophia Nikolayevna. I'm on my way to Khabarovsk."

"Why are you going there?" I asked.

"I'm a geologist and an expert on Arctic flowers. I'm on *komandirovka*—I'm commanded to go, to teach the native peoples."

"You're commanded. You have to go. But the others on the train, why are so many going north?"

"Money. Anyone who volunteers to work above the 62nd parallel gets a double salary, a ten percent monthly bonus, and free transportation. But tell me why you're on this train."

"To write articles and a book."

"You're pretty young to be traveling alone through Russia."

"Twenty-four, going on twenty-five. That's not so young."

"You have a husband, children?"

"I'm not married."

"A boyfriend?"

"Well, a few."

Sophia leaned her bosom on the table with an intimate smile, like a mother whose daughter tells her she's in love. "You know some of them a long time?"

"Some long, some a few months." I felt a sudden rush of loneliness.

"It's good to have a companion," she said. "Nobody should be alone. Today's my birthday." She sucked air through her teeth. "I'm thirty-four."

"And you wish you were spending it with your family."

"How do you know?" she asked.

"Anyone would know."

"*Nichevo* [Never mind]."

"No. Not *nichevo*. We'll give you a birthday party right on the train."

With the help of Nadya, a pretty waitress, and the chef, we took over the dining car. Soon we had the tables with their usual white clothes and glittering glasses stacked with bottles of Tokay wine, shashlik smothered in onions and potatoes, and Swiss cheese and green apples for dessert.

Sophia kept wiping her schoolteacher glasses with incredulity as nearly everybody gave her a gift—a linen handkerchief, a scarf, a bottle of perfume, a book. Nadya, our waitress, gave her two bars of Soviet chocolate. An accordionist was accompanying me singing "Happy Birthday, Sophia" in English when a man jumped up from his table and headed toward us. He had bulging glassy-blue eyes, straw-yellow hair, and a mouth with four astonishingly large gold teeth.

Teeth in Russia were status symbols. Dentists, notoriously incompetent, did little but yank their patients' teeth with pliers. Peasants and workers with little money wound up with gaps in their mouths; the not-so-poor had teeth of stainless steel; and the wealthy and elite proudly displayed teeth of gold.

"Who is that?" I asked Sophia in an undertone.

"His name is Boris. That's all I know."

Boris reached our table and leaned over me. "Look at the river," he shouted. "It's the Volga."

In a basso profundo, he sang *"Ay-da ookh nyem,"* the song of the Volga boatman. A year ago, I thought, I flew over this river, and now it's so close I can almost touch it. It was wide and brown and flowing with boats and barges and fishermen on its shores.

The next evening I climbed down the steps of the train in Omsk, Dostoyevsky's prison town, to post some letters home.

Boris followed me. "Good evening. How do you like the trip?"

"Fine," I said, trying to avoid him. His bulging eyes looked threatening. People waiting to board trains were lying every-where—on the ice-cold concrete walks along the tracks, on benches, on the floor inside the waiting room. Men, wrapped in torn shubas, snored heavily; children, their bare feet protruding from their patched sheepskins, looked wan and hungry; women in rags peered at me with bitterness.

A radio line from Will Rogers ran through my head. "We are the first nation in the history of the world to go to the poorhouse in an automobile." The Russians, I thought, are going to the poorhouse by train—if they can ever get on.

"I see you're disturbed." Boris tried to take my arm. I maneu-vered to draw it away. "You're bothered by these people sleeping in the station. There's nothing wrong. They're just waiting to get onto a train."

"For how long?"

"Days. Sometimes weeks."

I posted my letters and hurried back onto the train.

The next morning I stood in the corridor staring across the tracks. There, on a track parallel with ours, was a train with the heavily barred windows of a jail. Through the bars I could see men stretched out on bare ledges, looking tired, filthy, exhausted.

I was jotting a note—"passing a train that looks like a prison car"—when I felt Boris's breath. I shut my notebook.

"You're fascinated by that prison train," he said in English. His eyes seemed to be reaching out of their sockets.

241

"I am," I said.

"You've probably figured out they're either criminals or counterrevolutionaries, or both."

"Are they bound for Yakutsk?"

"I don't know. Bound for some prison. Does it bother you?"

"Very much."

I opened the sliding door to my compartment to avoid him, but before I could close it, he followed me in. "I want to talk to you," he said.

His blond hair hung long on both sides of his forehead like a girl's. The morning sun lit up the four gold teeth.

"What about?" I tried to be polite.

He leaned against the wall while I took my place on the couch.

"I am a communist, a Marxist, and a professor of philosophy, and I want to marry you."

"You must be joking."

"You will either marry me and live with me here in Soviet Russia, or I will ask the party to send me to America to live with you."

A professor of philosophy! More likely a madman!

He pulled my notebook out of my hand and, leaning against the wall, spoke as he wrote in English, "My reasons for marrying you are these:

> I love you:
> (1) Figure—esthetics
> (2) Intellect
> (3) Ideology (this I will have to change)

"How do I know these things?" He snapped the notebook closed. "I will tell you because I think like a professor of philosophy. Your figure I can see. Your mind also I can read. And your ideology— well, I can imagine that—bourgeois capitalist. I will have to work hard to educate you. Not easy. Still, I love you, because I think your work will be interesting to me, and I think mine will interest you."

Deliberately, he opened my notebook again and wrote:

242

I love you and I think you love me because I have
  (1) The intellect
  (2) The ideology
  (3) The figure

I stood up, retrieved my notebook, and opened the sliding door.
He bowed low, took my hand, kissed it, and walked out.
I lay back on my couch giggling. I had just had my first ideo-
logical marriage proposal from a man with four gold teeth.

33

The platform in Irkutsk emptied of passengers. Long minutes passed, and no one came looking for me. I stared at the tracks as they plunged into the horizon like surrealistic lines in a nightmare.

In the middle of Siberia, I was isolated and alone. I had no addresses. No one to call. Hot and tired, I pulled off my Macy's green suede coat and sat on my suitcase to plan my next move.

Irkutsk was important as a crossroads; from here I was to fly to Yakutsk. But how? In Moscow, I had been assured that someone would meet me at the station.

Finally a young man approached and asked in accented English, "You American girl, yes? Maybe you looking for somebody, yes?"

I explained my predicament.

"Is okay," he said. "I make telephone call. Yes?"

"Yes," I said, warily eyeing my bags, my typewriter, and my camera.

He returned, smiling broadly. "A car come in half hour from Northern Sea Route Administration, take you to Grand Hotel."

"Thank you. I thought for a while I was lost in Irkutsk."

"Lost!" He shook his head. "Nobody lost in Russia. Government know where is everybody."

He waited until a shiny Soviet Ford drove up, and helped me into the car. I shook his hand. "Thank you for rescuing me," I said.

"For me, big pleasure."

The sun was riding high. Even with the windows open, the car was sweltering.

Irkutsk was a paradox. Old dilapidated wooden cottages stood next to modern factories with steam spewing black smoke into the air. Sleepy horses dragged ancient carts on highways broad enough for army tanks.

The chauffeur slowed the car down on Karl Marx Street and finally stopped at a modern building on Litvinoff Street. It was the Grand Hotel. With its boxlike windows and unadorned concrete walls, it could have been a commercial hotel in New York.

A porter ushered me up to my room and returned with a huge bouquet of orange marigolds, yellow daisies, and white petunias.

"From Tovarishch Adamovich," the porter said.

"Who is Tovarishch Adamovich?"

"*Bolshoi chelovyek* [important man] from Yakutsk," he said mysteriously and disappeared.

A few minutes later a stout man knocked at the door and entered. He seemed in his forties, with white hair, almost childlike pink skin, and a stomach that strained the gold buttons of his blue naval uniform. I knew instantly he was Tovarishch Adamovich. Only a *bolshoi chelovyek* would have a full upper plate of sparkling white false teeth with incisors of gold.

"Ilya Andreevich Adamovich," he said, pumping my hand and speaking in German. "Imagine meeting you in Irkutsk."

"I thought I was expected."

"You don't know?"

"Know what?"

His laughing belly made him look like Falstaff in a Russian uniform. "We knew in Yakutsk you were coming. Moscow cabled us. But in Irkutsk they didn't know till they got a telephone call from somebody in the station."

I heard the words again, "Government know where is everybody."

"I'm only in Irkutsk for a few days," he said, "and then I'm flying back to Yakutsk. You can fly with me as my guest."

I spent the next week prowling through Irkutsk, waiting again. War was in the air. I watched children and their parents practice putting on and taking off gas masks. On park benches I chatted with women who told me that evenings, after work, they were learning how to shoot.

"What do you do in America after work?" one of them asked me.

"We don't learn how to shoot or wear masks," I said defensively.

"Maybe you ought to learn."

One afternoon, still waiting, I decided to have my hair cut in the Grand Hotel.

The barber, in a slightly soiled white jacket, waved me onto his movable chair and studied me like a biologist inspecting a new insect. I asked him in Russian if he could trim my hair just a little.

He answered in heavily accented English, "You like fox-trot or circle?"

"I know how to fox-trot," I answered, "but I never heard of a circle."

"Okay."

With a professional flourish, he wrapped a white cloth around me, and with sharp scissors cut my hair short in front and straight across the back like a man's. With a razor he shaved my neck.

"Good?" He pulled the white cloth off. "Now you have Siberian fox-trot."

The would-be sophisticated foreign correspondent saw the startled face of a boy of fifteen or sixteen. I put my hands to my throat to stop from gasping.

It was a week before Adamovich invited me to dinner in the hotel restaurant, saying, "Bring your map along. We'll be leaving any day now for Yakutsk."

At the table, with a red pencil in his hand, he drew a circle marking Irkutsk, then a dotted line along the Angara River and another line down the Lena River. (He pronounced it *Lyenna*, Russian-style; I liked the sound.) Finally he printed a large star on Yakutsk.

"We'll be flying for three days," he said.

"Three days!" I moaned.

I had promised the *Trib* a two-thousand-word article from Yakutsk, and I had already spent a month in Moscow and Irkutsk just trying to get there.

At six the next morning, under heavy rain, we were escorted to the seaplane base by a delegation of men and women who had come to say goodbye to Adamovich.

Perched in the Angara River sat a Junkers monoplane like a slender bird, its body and wings white, its tail red, its pontoons blue. My colors, I thought, with a sudden rush of patriotism—until I read its markings: CCCP–H5 [USSR–North 5].

"This is Victor Galishev, the best pilot in the Arctic." Adamovich introduced a middle-aged flier dressed in a brown leather coat, high rubber boots, a wool scarf wrapped around his neck, and a cigarette dangling from his lips. He leaped across a plank and entered his cockpit, followed by a shy young assistant named Yatzuro.

Taking shelter from the rain, Adamovich and I lowered our heads, hurried over the plank, and entered a pitch-dark cabin under the wings. I groped for the bench, feeling like Jonah in the belly of the whale.

The plane skimmed along the river. I could not see, but I could feel in my body the moment we rose and sailed through the air. Cautiously I walked through the dark cabin to the tiny window and looked down. On both banks and on little islands in the river, yellow trees and green trees rose in exotic, spiral patterns. Mountains circled us. In the distance lay Lake Baikal, the deep wall of water that separated Russia from Outer Mongolia.

Adamovich joined me at the window. "Let me point out some of the sights for you. We're flying over the Alexandrovsky Central, a terrible prison," his finger directed me to a large stone structure. "Many of our leaders were imprisoned inside it or exiled close to it. Stalin, Molotov, others—they were all in this area."

We flew for an hour and a half, following the curves and bends of the Angara River, before the plane taxied to the shore. Men in black padded jackets rushed into the water with heavy ropes, rapidly tied them around our pontoons, raced back to the shore, and secured the ropes to tree stumps. We were in Balagansk.

In a little while, we took off, circled over the Angara River, and then flew over dense forest. We had left our safety net, the river, and for another ninety minutes flew precipitously low over treetops in the rain until, looking down, I caught sight of water. "The Lena River," I sang its name. No river had ever seemed so welcome and so beautiful.

At 4:30 in the afternoon we landed at Ust-Kut, a river port. All I could see, climbing out of the plane, was a log house, a telegraph pole, and a radio-and-weather-bureau station, set down in the middle of the primeval forest. The first day of our flight in the belly of the whale was over.

No one noticed when I slipped out of the log house. At the river's edge, huge mosquitoes and gnats bombarded my face, entrenched themselves in my legs, marched across my neck, massacred my palms, and sucked blood out of my fingers. All I had as defense were some leaves. I fanned wildly, savagely. Somewhere I had read that prisoners in Siberia were often abandoned in the forest and in a few hours died of mosquito bites. I had never believed that story until now as I heard myself screaming, "Get away. Get off me, you bastards."

Across the river, I saw a sign in English, "Harbor Boundary." I realized with a start that this was a frontier. I watched a small band of men with shotguns marching up and down the shore. Ust-Kut was prison country, deep in the gulag.

On the evening of the third day, we reached Yakutsk.

34

My watch said 6:05 P.M., and it was still broad daylight. I sprinted
out of the plane down a wooden plank to the shore, where a
mountainous woman in a brown leather coat jumped out of
a car.

Adamovich kissed her on both cheeks and introduced her, "This
is Tonya Kliukvina."

"*Willkommen*," she said and wrestled my hand like a professional ready to throw me to the ground. "For you," she thrust two
bouquets of scarlet and purple carnations into my arms.

"I told you we'd have a big welcome for you in Yakutsk." Adamovich flashed his pearly-white-and-gold smile. "Flowers, banquets, wonderful friends. You're going to think you're in a regular
city, the City of the Future."

More people came hurrying down the embankment to embrace
Adamovich and Galishev, our pilot. I shed the leather flying coat
Galishev had given me the day before. "It's going to be freezing,"
he had warned me, "even in the plane." He was right. The last two
days of flying had been ice-cold. But now, near the river harbor, an

outdoor thermometer read 80 degrees Fahrenheit. (In winter that thermometer could go to 80 below zero.)

I was watching a boat unload food and equipment when Adamovich took my arm, still wrapped around the flowers, and opened the car door.

"Hop in. This is *my* Ford. I bought it in Moscow last winter." He patted his chest. "I drove it myself across Siberia and down the Lena. I tell you this frozen river was packed down tighter and a lot smoother than the Moscow highway."

He seated himself beside the chauffeur while Tonya towered beside me in the back.

"I'm asking Kliukvina to help you," he said, calling her by her family name as if she were a man. "She can do anything you need—translate, show you where to send your cables, be your secretary. You can see she speaks German. She worked in Vienna as a fur expert."

"And here?"

"Here! She's one of our top officials in the fur industry. We're giving her time off to be available to you. But don't worry about her. She'll be drawing the same salary as a fur specialist."

I glanced at her sidewise. Her mannish suit, her heavy low-heeled shoes, and her formidable body seemed to explain why Adamovich called her by her family name. I learned later she had a husband in Moscow.

Adamovich was still talking. "Kliukvina and you will both be guests in my house—"

"I already moved in," she interrupted and then turned to me. "We expected you for weeks. What took you so long?"

I shrugged my shoulders. "Bureaucracy."

Tonya pulled a cigarette out of her pack. "Everybody here wants to know what you look like, what you wear, and especially your politics."

I murmured something unintelligible and rolled the window down to see and experience this town I had traveled nearly eleven thousand miles to reach.

Yakutsk, like every Siberian town, was a city of wood, but unlike many of the drab towns along the river, its log cabins were brightened with painted shutters. Construction was going on everywhere. Rows of new two-story apartment houses of yellow pine with green or orange shutters were creating a new skyline. I could smell the freshly sawed wood.

Reindeer as well as oxen and horses were on the dirt road, pulling flat carts with wooden wheels. Copper-skinned Yakuts with Eskimo eyes, riding bareback, reined their small horses out of the mountains of dust kicked up by our Soviet Ford.

We drove a mile into town and stopped at a long fence about ten feet high with a sign on the gate in Cyrillic letters: Proletarian Street 20. Adamovich leaped out to open the gate and waved us into a dirt courtyard where six houses of fresh yellow wood stood walled in like the Kremlin courtyards Russians had built for centuries to resist invaders.

Adamovich pointed proudly to the house closest to the entrance gate. "Mine," he said.

I followed him into a four-room cottage, clean and bright and airy. Three doors led off the kitchen, where a belly-shaped Holland stove was burning with wood and coal. One door led to a small bedroom, another to the laundry and pantry, the third to the living room, and beyond it the master bedroom, where Adamovich dropped my gear.

He vaulted across the room to a punching bag attached to the wall and pummeled it with staccato punches. Then, despite his girth, he swung himself on two rings hanging from the ceiling, and finally, breathing heavily, he charged across the bedroom to a handsome desk at the window and brushed aside some papers.

Still heaving, he said, "You're to have my desk all the time you're in Yakutsk."

"This isn't right," I protested. "I'm putting you out of your own house. I'll find somewhere else to stay."

"Ridiculous. I have plenty of places to sleep. No more talk. It's yours. I'm going to my office now and I'll be back for dinner." He hit the punching bag with a right-and-left jab and departed.

I looked at the narrow brass bed, wondering how someone as fat as Adamovich could share it with his wife. It was covered with a rabbit-skin comforter as soft and white as ermine. A tapestry with a medieval hunting scene hung above the bed and near it a wall telephone with a handle to rouse the local operator.

On the opposite wall was a map of the USSR. We were only a few hundred miles from the North Pacific and, beyond the Pacific, the tip of Alaska. America. Home.

Stacked below the map was a bookcase filled with books in Russian, German, and English, and a shelf with a small phonograph, painted orange, a pile of phonograph records, and a black Fed—a Soviet camera built like a Leica.

Still marveling at what all this luxury must cost in Yakutsk, I began hanging my clothes on a nail when I heard heavy footsteps. Tonya entered without knocking and folded her arms as she watched me. Her face seemed grim, her body formidable. All she needed, I thought, was a uniform.

"Rutochka," she said. I was startled to hear her use the Russian endearment for my name. Maybe I had misjudged her.

"I wonder if you know what a big job you have here."

I stopped unpacking and waited for her to go on.

"This is a political world, and you, as a foreign correspondent from a big American paper, you have to understand that world. Are you a member of our party?"

"No, I'm not."

"What party, may I ask, are you? Are you—?"

I interrupted. "Tonya, I don't mean to offend you, but I'm sick of this question. I'll answer it now, and I hope we never discuss it again. I don't belong to any political party. Is that clear?"

Her voice became hostile. "Then you're not politically educated."

"*You* decide that."

"Here, every child knows why he was born, why he lives. Do you?"

I wet my lips and resumed unpacking.

"What is your father?" she demanded.

"What do you mean—what is my father?"

"I'm sure he's a *bourjuy* [a bourgeois]. If you came from a working-class family, you would know why you were born."

I'd had enough. Angrily, I walked to the desk, lifted my typewriter out of its case, and rolled in a blank page with a carbon.

"You don't answer." Her voice was a whip. "I'm not good enough for you to answer me?"

She stalked out of the room.

The first lesson for a journalist, I told myself, ought to be "Don't make enemies the first day."

Through the window I watched a young woman hurrying into the courtyard carrying four aluminum pots hinged to each other. Soon the smell of food brought me into the kitchen. I found the young woman heating the pots on the stove.

"I'm Nadya," she said in Russian. "I clean the house for Tovarishch Adamovich."

"Hello, Nadya. I'm Ruth."

"I know who you are," she laughed. "You're the first American I ever saw and I can't believe you look like everybody else except what you're wearing. It's my real pleasure to meet you."

I liked her instantly, especially after the encounter with Tonya Kliukvina. She looked about twenty. A string of blue beads around her neck set off her blue eyes and pink cheeks.

"You're the housekeeper?"

Most of the housekeepers I had met were ancient women with gnarled hands and bad teeth, wearing kerchiefs on their heads and old-fashioned skirts. Nadya wore a wispy peasant blouse, through which I could see her white camisole, and a flowered skirt that swirled around her calves. Somehow I knew she would never ask if I knew why I was born.

"My friends scold me," she confided. "They say I should be studying to be a wireless operator or a meteorologist. They say I'm lazy. But I like the job. Tovarishch Adamovich is almost never home, and when his wife and his two kids go south on vacation—they're there now—I have the whole house to myself."

"So it's not hard work then?"

"Easy," she said, conspiratorially. "Easier than anybody knows." She stirred her pots on the stove. "Dinner's good tonight. That's what the chef told me."

"Chef? You mean Adamovich has his own chef?"

"No," she tossed her head back and laughed. "It's the chef in the communal dining room. I go there to get our food."

"Hello, hello, hello," Adamovich called out before he entered the kitchen. "Ah, so you've met our little Nadya. I've brought Galishev home for dinner. Let's eat. Call Kliukvina. I'm hungry as a bear."

"So how do you like my house?" Adamovich asked as we seated ourselves at the square table in the living-dining room. "Real *kultura*, isn't it?"

"Real *kultura*," I agreed.

Culture! It was the new goal, the Soviet promise of a higher and better life.

I looked up at the electric lamp throwing a warm circle of light around us. The house was electrified, though I discovered, when I typed my first dispatch that evening, that the electricity was shut off at midnight. Late nights I worked with a kerosene lamp.

True, the house had *kultura*, but to wash my hands and face before dinner, I bent over a pretty little pink-and-white porcelain sink which drained into a slop pail in the kitchen. Next to the sink was a barrel with water from the Lena River. And the indoor privy, which Adamovich jocularly called the cabinet for thought was in the hall next to my room.

"Something to drink." Adamovich poured vodka into large glasses. I watched him and Galishev and Tonya swallow it in a gulp. Try as I would, I couldn't force the vodka down my mouth. It tasted like kerosene on fire.

Dinner was a banquet. Nadya entered with a tray of hors d'oeuvres of Swiss cheese, cold cuts, and Kamchatka crabmeat. We had hardly finished these delicacies when she returned with bowls of borsch made of sorrel, then breaded meat swimming in sauce, and finally (or so I thought), *kissel*, blackberries heated in boiled water and mixed in a potato paste.

I was ready to burst every seam when she appeared again with a tray of tea with crackers and jelly, chocolates filled with nuts, and hard candies.

"They're for export; they earn us hard currency," Adamovich said, explaining the English labels on all the wrappers.

"Can anyone buy them in Yakutsk?"

"No, they're not yet for the masses."

Soon the courtyard neighbors dropped in and then Adamovich's office staff. I was trying to sort them out when the editor of the *Polar Bolshevik*, one of Yakutsk's six newspapers, came, accompanied by two blond, well-dressed secretaries.

The editor, middle-aged with light hair turning gray and wearing heavy glasses, approached me. "I'm interested," he said in Russian, "in any insights you can give me into your President Roosevelt and your big depression. And some day I would love to see your newspaper, if you would send me a copy."

"I'll show you one right now."

I hurried to the bedroom, dug into my bag, and brought out a Sunday *New York Herald Tribune*.

His hands trembled as if he were weighing gold. "May I take it with me tonight? I'll bring it back tomorrow. I'll be very careful."

"Keep it. I have more copies."

"You mean it?" He turned the pages carefully. "It's so big. What do you read first?"

"I read every story about Hitler, Stalin, and now the trials in Moscow."

"I read about that too," he said softly.

I looked around the room and then, in a low voice, asked, "How do you cover the Moscow trials in the *Polar Bolshevik?*"

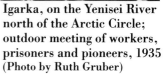

Igarka, on the Yenisei River
north of the Arctic Circle;
outdoor meeting of workers,
prisoners and pioneers, 1935
(Photo by Ruth Gruber)

Crossing the Arctic Ocean in
1935; Gruber aboard SS
Anadyr, the first commercial
ship in history to open the
Northeast passage from
Vladivostok to Murmansk

Author standing on wing of
Junkers flying boat en route
to Yakutsk, 1936

The white flying boat in
which Gruber flew down the
Lena River, 1936
(Photo by Ruth Gruber)

Native Yakuts at the entrance to the
Park of Culture and Rest in Yakutsk
(Photo by Ruth Gruber)

Yakutsk street scene
(Photo by Ruth Gruber)

A primitive reindeer-skin and birchbark
tent; in the background, one of the
modern, ready-cut wooden houses
(Photo by Ruth Gruber)

Yakutsk family outside their "yurt" in a collective farm in the Yakutia Republic
(Photo by Ruth Gruber)

Yakut babies in birchbark cradles, like the one given to Ruth
by Marfa Mikhailovna, a 104-year-old Yakut woman
(Photo by Ruth Gruber)

"I print what I get from Moscow."

He moved away with the *Herald Tribune* under his arm.

"Rutochka, take something." Nadya came toward me with her tray of vodka and crackers. I took a small glass and held it in my hand. I watched her as she moved cautiously toward Tonya.

"*Bozhe moi* [My God]," Tonya shouted loud enough to wake anyone in the courtyard. "Look at this glass. It's filthy. Take it back and wash it."

Nadya fled to the kitchen. The guests stopped talking and watched me. I wanted to hurry after Nadya and comfort her or confront Tonya with some biting remark. Instead I took a sip of vodka and felt it run its kerosene course down my throat.

"Listen, everybody." Adamovich, the man of power, the affable host, broke the tension. "I have some new records."

He bounded into the bedroom and brought out the small orange phonograph, set a record on the turntable, cranked the machine, and bowed to me, "In honor of our American guest."

The high voices of three little pigs filled the living room, singing "Who's afraid of the big bad wolf, the big bad wolf, the big bad wolf? Who's afraid of . . . "

Where was I? Was this really Yakutsk?

"Can you sing it for us?" Adamovich asked.

"I only know the opening lines."

"*Du must singen*, Rutochka," Tonya commanded in German. Soon the other guests were clamoring, "Sing, sing."

"You'll have to help me," I said.

They began clapping their hands and singing, "Who's afraid of ze big bad volf, ze big bad volf . . . "

"Everybody on the floor," Adamovich called out, as he put a British dance record on the phonograph. He and Galishev danced with the blond secretaries. Tonya danced with the editor of the *Polar Bolshevik*, a foot shorter than she. Nadya placed her fingers daintily around the waist of an officer, and I danced with Adamovich's handsome young deputy, Izofovich.

"We dance fox-trot or waltz?" Izofovich asked me in English. "I just begin now to learn."

"It's a fox-trot," I said.

He held me so close the buttons of his white naval uniform pressed against my chest.

"Maybe you teach me," he said.

I looked up at his face and laughed. "You don't need any lessons."

He smiled broadly, and never asked me if I knew why I was born.

35

"Tonya," I said at breakfast a few days after I flew in, "I'd like to interview some Trotzkyists."

"I never heard the word," she said.

"With the trials going on right now in Moscow, you never heard the word 'Trotzkyist'?" I spoke quietly. "Next you'll tell me there are no political prisoners in Yakutsk."

"There are some, but you won't find them very interesting."

"Then please telephone the head of the NKVD and tell him I want to interview him." The NKVD was the Russian acronym for the People's Commissariat of Internal Affairs. It was the name given in 1934 when the much-feared GPU was reorganized. Later it would be called the KGB.

Tonya bolted out of her chair. "Are all Americans as crazy as you? I can't call Tovarishch Carosin—"

So his name was Carosin. I committed it to memory.

She put her face close to mine. "I won't do it."

"Tonya," I looked into her light gray eyes, "you're supposed to be my interpreter, not my censor."

"Well . . . uh, well—" She drew back. "The head of the secret police is probably the busiest man in Yakutsk."

"If there are so few prisoners in Yakutsk, why is he so busy?"

She pumped the handle on the wall telephone. "I'll try," she mumbled through clenched teeth, "but I don't guarantee anything."

She spoke briefly into the phone, then turned to me, shaking her head in wonder. "His secretary asks when you want to come."

"I can come immediately."

She spoke again, listened, and hung up.

"Comrade Carosin will be happy to see you in an hour."

I dressed hurriedly, put fresh film in my camera, and raced to the door.

"I'll go with you." She stood at the door.

"It won't be necessary, Tonya. I'm sure the head of the secret police speaks not only Russian but German and English."

"What if you get lost?"

"Then I'll find my way back to Proletarian Street."

I opened the notebook. "But I would appreciate your drawing a map to his office."

Cheerfully I sloshed through the mud streets and gutters, the heels of my shoes clattering on the wooden planks.

The hot Siberian sun beat down on me as I sauntered past greengrocer shops, a movie theater, a school, a beauty shop, slow-moving Yakuts, Sibiryaks (Russians born in Siberia), and Russians who looked like bureaucrats carrying leather briefcases. On the steps of a crumbling church, two old women with kerchiefs crossed themselves. Plaques on log cabins told me that famous revolutionaries had lived here. Yakutsk, the City of the Future, a metropolis of twenty-five-thousand, had the soul of an old city of exile.

Maxim Gorky had called Yakutia the land of death and chains. And I was on my way to interview the man who kept the prisoners in chains. I was not afraid of meeting Carosin. My fear was that I might not be skilled enough to see through him if he lied or if he tried to manipulate me.

A plain wooden building said not NKVD but "Zags." Zags was the bureau that registered the city's births, deaths, marriages, and divorces. An elderly guard told me the NKVD was one flight up. How clever, I thought. The secret police have only to run downstairs to get your vital statistics.

I climbed a narrow stairway. A milk-faced boy in uniform greeted me.

"We're expecting you," he said in Russian, and showed me into a large room with a few hard chairs against a wall and a desk at the far corner. The morning sun threw shadows on the floor to emphasize the emptiness of the room. Was this where prisoners were interrogated?

André Petrovich Carosin came around the desk, crossed the room, took my hand, and, with the manners of a general at a society ball, bowed and told me he was very happy to make my acquaintance. He spoke in German.

His head was shaved smooth as a Ping-Pong ball, his face was tanned, and though he was at least fifty—an old man to me—his body was taut and lithe. In the khaki uniform of the secret police, with a burgundy red collar and a gold stripe and star on his arm, he could have stepped out of a Cecil B. De Mille movie, glass eye and all.

He led the way to the front of his tidy desk where he helped me to a comfortable chair. Then, sitting behind the desk, he reached into the upper drawer and brought out a huge bar of chocolate. I was sure he would never have taken such an approach with a male correspondent. Nonetheless, I broke off a piece and nibbled it. It was delicious, but I was not ready to be ensnared. I came right to the point.

"Look, Comrade Carosin, everybody knows you have political prisoners in Yakutsk. I've promised the *Herald Tribune* a story on them. But when I ask people where the Trotzkyists are, they pretend they've never heard the word."

Carosin chuckled.

"Of course we have Trotzkyists here," he said. "One of them runs the bookshop. We even have criminals and thieves."

"What do you do about rehabilitating them?"

"Our whole policy of rehabilitation is founded on work. Work. Work. Work. This is a country of workers." He lit a long cigarette from a silver case and exhaled smoke through his nose. "Our exiles, just like free citizens, must work. We don't have prisons here as they do in capitalist countries. We don't have guards or jailers, the way they did under the Czar. We give our exiles freedom."

"Did I hear you say 'freedom'?"

"Does that surprise you? Our political exiles are free to live anywhere they choose—in the province to which we send them, of course."

"And you call that freedom?"

"But they are free. Free to do any kind of work they like, or for which they're suited, until their period of exile is over. They live just like local free citizens, and they're paid the same wages we pay local help."

"What happens if they try to escape?"

"It's hard to escape from Siberia."

He blew three interlocking rings of smoke into the air.

"You asked about rehabilitation," he went on. "In capitalist countries the police do everything to make their criminals know they're outcasts. Here we do everything to make them intelligent people. We want to help them reform, and we do it by giving them work. No prisons. No segregation for political prisoners."

I jotted down his words with a question mark beside them.

"And criminals? You don't segregate them either?"

"Have more chocolate. Yes, we do segregate them but also not in prison. They're in a labor colony. If you'd like to see a labor colony, nothing would please me more than to escort you there some day."

"I'd like that very much."

"Good. I'll call you in a few days."

With a fatherly gesture, the head of the Yakutsk NKVD put the rest of the chocolate bar into my hand.

I left his office and made my way to the bookstore. In the window was a sign in Russian: *Kniga-Tsenter*, Center for Books. I caught the reflection of a young woman in an American white cotton dress and white shoes with high heels trying to look nonchalant.

Inside the shop, a tall, stooped man approached me. Books were stacked against all the walls, but there were no customers.

"I'd like to speak to you, if I may," I said in Russian.

He glanced swiftly around the empty shop.

"I know who you are," he said in fluent English, but so softly I had to strain to hear. "I read about you in the newspaper. It's unbelievable. Almost no one—no foreigners, not even Russians—can get to Yakutsk. And you—a mere woman!"

I let his words pass.

"When I read about you," he said, "I told myself someday I would find you and talk to you. It's very important, yes, very important that I talk to you. It's fate. Destiny brought you to me."

He spoke breathlessly, as though this were his last day on earth. "I'm going to tell you what you must do. You must see the true side of life here, not only the official side."

"I want that."

"But not here. Can you come to my apartment this evening? I live right over the store."

"I'll come."

"Be very careful. It would go bad for me if the NKVD found out I was talking to you."

At eight at night, he waited at the door of the *Kniga-Tsenter*. The twilight Arctic cold was in my bones. I huddled inside my suede coat.

He looked up and down the street, then led me through the darkened shop into a storeroom musty with books and up a flight of rickety stairs. As a little girl in Brooklyn, I too had lived over the store.

"Now," he said still speaking in English, "I will show you how a prisoner of Stalin lives in Yakutsk."

We entered a loft lit by a candle in a green bottle. It cast an eerie circle of light on a bare table next to the window and on a thin young woman with an infant in her arms, her eyes wide with curiosity and fear. I smiled, hoping to put her at ease. She scurried to a dark corner of the room.

A cot stood in the center of the loft with its four legs plunked in tin cans of water. From stories my father had told me, I knew the cans of water were an old Russian trick to trap bedbugs.

I glanced around the loft to two large photos of Marx and Lenin pinned on the wall. "I love those men, especially Lenin," he said, as we drew chairs up to the table. "Lenin is really our beloved father and the founder of our Revolution. But Stalin—*ya nye mogu*—I cannot—" His body shook in revulsion. "Ivan the Terrible."

I was prepared to like him, fascinated as always by people who swim against the tide.

The candle lit up his scholarly face. He fit my notion of a political exile—cadaverously thin, eyes red and suspicious behind heavy glasses, his clothes threadbare.

I leaned forward, opening the large notebook in which I would take notes that could not incriminate him. On my lap was a two-inch notebook in which I would jot down, as illegibly as possible, details that might lengthen his exile in Yakutsk if they were discovered. Mostly I hid this tiny notebook among papers in the bottom of my purse; sometimes I tucked it into my bra.

"My name is Medved," he said. "Ask me some questions."

I decided to test Comrade Carosin. "Is it true that you're free to do whatever work you're suited for?"

"Whoever told you that is lying. They pick the work. They gave me this job because I speak six languages."

He spoke bitterly. "I'm a historian of India. If they let me do my own work, I'd be in the library doing research. Instead, all day I work in the store. I can only do my own research here at night, with no electricity. So I do nothing. Another comrade here is a historian of China; he too can do nothing."

Somewhere in the back of the loft, I heard Medved's wife rocking in a chair.

"I was told," I said, "that political prisoners are not put into prisons, that they're sent into exile as soon as they're sentenced."

"Another lie. Political prisoners are put into prison and then exiled. I've been in different prisons almost every year since 1927. I was in prison for eight years. Then, in March 1935, I was exiled to Yakutsk for four years. We've been here over a year already."

"8 yrs prsn, 4 yrs exl," I scribbled in the tiny notebook.

"How many exiles would you say are now in Yakutsk?" I asked.

"They won't tell you. There are at least three hundred and fifty in this godforsaken city, but thousands, some of us think tens of thousands, are prisoners all over the Yakutia Republic."

"10s of thsnds prsnrs," I noted with horror.

"There's terrible sickness here. Eighty percent of the people are sick." He stopped. "They'll tell you it's only forty or fifty percent. Look around you. The Yakuts have tuberculosis, rheumatism, trachoma. Why? Because there isn't enough to eat. How can a poor worker who earns seven rubles a day eat himself and give his family food? Bread alone costs three rubles a kilo." A ruble was twenty cents. A little meat would be more than a month's pay.

"Prisoners were better off under the Czar," he went on, "than we are now. They were allowed to teach. Revolutionaries taught others to become revolutionaries."

He put a new candle in the bottle. "We are not allowed to teach. We're given our orders by the NKVD. They tell us," he said, his voice imitating Carosin's, ". . . you have to register every ten days at our office. You can work, live where you like, we'll pay you salaries even. But you're not free to teach . . ." He took off his heavy glasses and cleaned them with a handkerchief. "Do you understand what not teaching means to a revolutionary?"

"I can imagine."

"No one can imagine who hasn't lived this life. I'm thirty-seven years old. I look like fifty or sixty, don't I?"

He looked like a character in a Daumier painting.

"I was a soldier in the Great War. And I was in the Bolshevik party. Oh, I was a loyal party member. A Bolshevik with honors. I was a scholar of Hindustani at the Institute in Leningrad. That was until 1927, when Stalin and Trotzky split. The way Stalin began to run the country was inhuman. It was murder. He didn't think of the people anymore. He thought only of Stalin."

Back of us, the baby whimpered. I sensed that Comrade Medved's wife was silencing the infant with her breast.

"I decided to join the opposition," he said. "I believed with Trotzky that you can't build socialism in one country. I gave up my work at the Institute. I took a job as an ordinary laborer in a factory, so that I could do underground work against Stalin. I had a mimeograph machine."

"Tool of the Revolution," I murmured.

"Correct. I printed leaflets telling the workers in the factory the truth. I worked up a real proletarian base, a mass following. We committed sabotage."

"What kind of sabotage?"

"We entered factories and we wrecked machines. We caused a death or two by doing it."

He straightened his back. "It was the only way we could let the workers know that the opposition to Stalin was powerful."

"Did you ever regret that you killed?" I asked.

"Of course not. Then they found some leaflets on me, so they arrested me. They interrogated me days and nights. They tortured me. They didn't know I killed. And they never found the mimeograph machine. Oh, we were too smart for them."

In the candlelight his face changed again, growing softer. "I had many books, rare, wonderful books. But when my wife heard that I was arrested, she nearly went out of her mind. So she threw all my books into the fire."

"I had to," his wife cried from across the room.

"I don't blame you," he said. "You know I don't blame you."

She sobbed. "You weren't home when they came after I burned the books. They searched every corner. They chopped up wood from the floor. They kept asking, 'Where did he hide the leaflets, where is the underground material?' They kept threatening they would put me in jail, torture me."

"I know, my dearest. You were trying to protect me. I know it."

Her sobs filled the loft. The baby cried with her.

Medved walked toward them. *"Moya milenkaya* [My darling]," he comforted her. "Please don't cry."

Once again I felt drawn to him. How many times a day, I wondered, did they reenact this scene. You burned my books. . . . I had to . . . they would have put me in jail.

"She wasn't arrested," he said across the loft. "She could have stayed in Leningrad. But they allow wives to come along, if they want to. She's still free. She can leave any time she wants."

My throat felt dry. I was an intruder in their misery. They were locked in time, dwelling forever in the apartment in Leningrad where she had burned his books.

I walked slowly back to Adamovich's house, trudging carefully on the planked mud streets. The last glimmers of the subarctic sun lit my way.

36

There is a delicacy in the relationship between an interviewer and an interviewee.

I expected the straight party line on Yakutsk when I went to interview the secretary of the regional Communist party. I went angry with myself. I had still not captured the essence of this town in Siberia. The Medveds were one face of Yakutsk. But I needed to understand more about life in this Soviet republic.

"Adamovich," I had said at dinner the previous evening, "I'd like to meet the political boss of Yakutsk. What's the procedure?"

"Pavel Matvevich Pevsnak is the top boss, and he rarely gives interviews. But after all, this is his first opportunity to talk to a foreign journalist. I'll call him."

Adamovich cranked up the wall telephone. "Pavel Matvevich? This is Ilya Andreevich. The *Amerikanskaya zhurnalistka* wants an interview with you. What? Yes. No, I think she's an objective journalist. Yes, it's a capitalist paper. You'll give her an interview? Good. When? Tomorrow morning at ten. Thanks very much."

"He's a good man," Nadya, who had been listening, said. "People like him. Some of us like him so much we call him the little Stalin."

Not a recommendation to everyone, I thought.

Pevsnak's office was in one of the few stucco buildings in town. It had been the Governor's Mansion under the Czar.

He seemed small and slender sitting behind his desk at the end of the conference table. He was about thirty, with blond hair combed neatly back, his pale face framed in heavy brown-rimmed glasses. He wore an embroidered Russian shirt hanging over his trousers.

I had already learned that most Russian leaders expected journalists to give them written questions. I handed him my list.

Pevsnak copied each of my questions on his own long pad and changed the order. "What is Yakutia's main problem," he began in Russian-accented English. "It is transportation. We are opening a whole empire. How are we opening it? By boats, airplanes, and highways. Let me show you."

He walked to a map of the Yakutia Republic hanging on the wall.

"The rivers of Yakutia are our blood arteries. We have caravans and fleets on all the rivers that are navigable in the summer. Ocean-going ships bring goods from Europe and the Orient to Tixie Bay, a new port and polar station on the Arctic Ocean. From Tixie Bay, riverboats and barges reload and bring the goods up the Lena to Yakutsk. We are also building a railroad and a highway from Irkutsk to Ust-kut, where I understand you have been."

"Who is building the road and railroad? Prisoners?"

"Prison labor and free labor."

"Both under the NKVD?"

"Of course."

He returned to his desk chair. "A second question—the economics of Yakutia. We are the richest republic in the Soviet Union. We have the best quality of furs and gold in the world. We have rich coal mines and even richer gold mines. We have fine cattle, horses, reindeer, long-haired polar dogs. Listen to these figures."

He read off a list of statistics which I copied automatically. He suddenly stopped. "Will you have some *Butterbrod* and tea?"

He pressed a bell and soon a Yakut woman brought us a tray with tea and biscuits. He downed a long sip of tea.

"You want to know how I came to Yakutsk. I was born in Zabodndy Oblast, Matislav, in White Russia, of poor parents. My father was a salesman, my mother a dressmaker. I studied very well. When I was fifteen, I met a Social Democrat who gave me books to read. I began to learn the difference between rich and poor. At seventeen, I joined the Communist party. At twenty-one, I had held different leading positions and had lived all over European Russia. Six years ago I came out here as a worker for the party and then was elected secretary of the regional committee.

"How much longer will I be here? I have no idea. I may remain for years, I may be commandeered to another republic, or I may be called back to Moscow. I must keep myself in readiness, like a soldier in battle. I must go wherever the party sends me. Meanwhile I have one of the best jobs in the world—to raise Yakutia up to the level of all our great Soviet Socialist republics."

Once again he was studying the list of questions. "So you want to know what we're doing for the Yakuts? Before, the Yakut people believed everything the shamans—their witch doctors—told them. Not any more. Soon the shamans will be ancient history."

"But the shamans," I interrupted, "have been so much part of the Yakut's life."

His mouth formed a half-smile.

"That's why we're getting rid of them," he said. "We're even putting some of them in prison if we think they're dangerous." He stopped, sipped more tea, and went on. "Before, among the Yakuts, there was less than one percent literacy. Now it's sixty percent. All Yakut children must go to school. They go to boarding schools while their parents hunt. Soon we will have one hundred percent literacy."

"How soon?"

"In a few years. Maybe five. You want to know about their

health? The government has given ten million rubles to liquidate trachoma and tuberculosis. We'll do that in four years."

"That's impossible."

I had seen too many dying TB patients in my brother Harry's office.

Pevsnak raised himself in his chair. "We are used to making the impossible possible," he said as if he were reading a slogan on a wall.

"Do I believe there will be a war?" he was reading his list again. "Yes, I believe it is coming soon. But I tell you this—the enemy will not enter Yakutia easily. Our borders are strongly guarded on all sides. War with Japan or Germany, maybe. War with the United States? It's not economically sound for Americans to want war with us. I don't think we will fight each other."

He seemed pleased with his prognostication and called for more *Butterbrod* and tea.

"Now, this was your last question and it's mine also," he said. "Yes, we have a lot of Trotzkyists and Zinovievists. It's no secret. The whole world knows about the sabotage and the terrorism and about the trials in Moscow. What people don't know is what we're doing for the exiles. Before, the jailers themselves were criminals and drunkards who beat the prisoners. Now the Soviet officials who work with them have ideas, intelligence, enthusiasm, and speak with kindness. We are making the impossible possible."

"Thank you," I said, closing my notebook.

I didn't believe him, but it would be forty years before the full truth of the gulag would become known.

Still I had learned that Pevsnak, the little Stalin, of this old-new Empire, could be instantly "commandeered to another republic"— a bureaucrat as insecure in his job as I was in mine.

37

The cable from the family shook in my hand. ALL WELL WHEN ARE YOU COMING HOME?

I owed it to the *Herald Tribune* and to Stefansson to stay on. Stef was working for the United States War Department on a confidential report encompassing the entire Arctic world.

"Every fact you can bring back is important for our government," Stef had said. "We don't know a single person who has been allowed into any part of that whole region. If war comes, the Arctic can become the crossroads of the world."

Stef was not asking me to spy for him or our army. What he wanted was what I wanted of myself as a journalist, to see and feel, taste and experience, and try to capture it all in words.

There were the native Yakuts I wanted to visit in their reindeer-skin tents and huts called "yurts." There were the gold miners dredging up precious metals in the Aldan Goldfields. And mostly there were the slave labor camps for criminals and political enemies.

In Moscow, the trials of the founders of the Revolution were being covered by seasoned correspondents like Walter Duranty of the *New York Times* and Ralph Barnes of the *Herald Tribune*. If the prisoners are found guilty, I told myself, they could be exiled to Yakutsk.

I cabled home. NEED TWO MORE MONTHS LOVE RUTH

Two days later I was in a Soviet Ford with Carosin and his chauffeur, both in NKVD khaki uniforms with maroon shoulder boards. We were on our way to the Labor Colony for Criminal Workers in the village of Kilmantsie. Starting a fresh page in my notebook, I wrote, "visiting my first slave labor camp."

An hour and a half out of Yakutsk, we entered a huge courtyard and stopped in front of a helter-skelter camp of log cabins, work-shops, dormitories, and in the distance, green fields. I saw men and boys at work repairing trucks and tractors. There seemed to be no guards.

A youngish man bounded out of the first cottage. Carosin intro-duced him; "Please meet Comrade Maïs, the director. He and I will go inside and talk, and you are free to go anywhere you like."

The smell of fresh bread drew me into a small log building partitioned into a bakery and kitchen. "Come in, come in," a chef in a white hat beckoned. As I entered, three men stopped cooking and lined up behind each other, speaking in Russian.

"I speak first." The chef waved his wooden soup ladle in the air. "I worked in a communal restaurant and I stole twelve hundred rubles for wodka. That's what ruined my life. I tell you, madam, I'm through with wodka for life."

A short man in a black smock spoke next, hardly pausing for breath. "*Yah* [I am] Ivan Ivanovich. I went with some comrades to prospect for gold in the Aldan Goldfields. They said I stole white flour and especially butter, and gave me ten years in this colony. I'm innocent, madam. You must help me."

He moved aside to let a tall man with a white beard bow to me in Czarist style. "I am a priest, your grace. I too am innocent. A woman neighbor in Yakutsk, a Yakut, told the NKVD that I was

poisoning the brains of the children with anti-Communist slop, and
I got five years. It's a lie. She was a thief. Madam, I am innocent.
You must help us. They will listen to you."

I guessed they had been primed to talk to me. But why? Was this
another game Carosin was playing with the American journalist?

"It may not help," I said. "But I will talk to Carosin and the
director."

He kissed my hand. "God will hear your voice."

I walked through the labor camp, ill at ease, like a visitor in a
classroom knowing the children must have been drilled before-
hand. On the grounds of the camp, some of the men told me they
were serving time for smuggling, others for robbery, still others for
speculating in hard currency. They sounded like the petty criminals
I had once interviewed in a prison in Pennsylvania. Here was none
of the tragedy that doomed the lives of the Trotzkyists and Zinovievists.

I felt restless. I was spending valuable hours among common
thieves when I wanted to talk to political prisoners. What was
Carosin trying to prove to me?

Back in Maïs's house, I found Carosin sitting in a rocker, bouncing a fat baby on his lap and singing a children's song. I asked Maïs
about Ivan Ivanovich and the priest.

He dug into his desk and opened a heavy folder.

"See for yourself." He placed the files in front of me. "Ivan
Ivanovich, who told you he's here because he stole flour and butter,
speaks like butter itself. But he was caught speculating in dollars.
And here's the priest's file. He was turned in not by a Yakut woman
but by his own parish for stealing fifteen thousand rubles."

Reports can be doctored, I thought, but I was an idiot to think I
could help.

Carosin, still cradling the baby, was watching me through his
good eye as if he were reading my mind. "I know you're wondering
why I brought you here. It's to show you how we rehabilitate our
prisoners. You saw them working in the daylight. If we could stay

till night you would see them educating themselves. They play chess, read books, write for the wall newspaper."

"It's like a school all right," Maïs added. "Next week fifty prisoners here will be released, and they all have jobs waiting for them in Yakutsk."

I nodded. The wily Carosin had taken me to his favorite Potemkin jail.

Adamovich's radio sat in a place of honor in front of him at the dining table. The Military Collegium of the Supreme Court of the USSR was expected to give its verdict. The 1936 trials in Moscow were ending. Sixteen men and women who had helped overthrow the Czar and launch the Revolution would learn their fate.

Friends of Adamovich had come to share the excitement of the verdict. There was no music, no laughter. Tonya and Nadya took turns serving us hot borsch and boiled potatoes.

Adamovich addressed us like a prosecutor cajoling the jury. "Death is the only thing these traitors deserve."

The man I knew as a jovial bureaucrat with a ready smile looked hard and pitiless. "We should send Stalin a cable begging him not to allow his great pity to save these dastardly enemies of the people. If they live, they'll go on plotting to kill all our leaders. They'll even try to kill Stalin. Let's cable him." Adamovich spoke through clenched teeth. "Let's tell him we believe he must have these traitors shot."

"No, no, Tovarishch Adamovich," pleaded a middle-aged woman sitting next to me. "We must send him a telegram not to shoot them. It will be a scandal in the eyes of the world."

A young woman waved her finger in the older woman's face. "If anyone lays a finger on our Stalin, I myself will go out and kill him. They are murderers, these men on trial. All of us who are wives and mothers"—her face was turning purple—"all of us will tear these butchers limb from limb."

The room was silent as she turned to me. "I don't believe in God, but if I did, Stalin would be my God. He has given us everything—

our clothes, our education, our health. He has made us a happy, joyful people, and these murderers want to destroy him. They want to make us slaves again like under the Czar."

I looked at the grim faces around the table. Were people all over the USSR also sitting at their radios, waiting? Was all of the Soviet Union one big Yakutsk?

Adamovich looked at his wristwatch, then jumped up. "Silence. The news."

Tonya and Nadya stood frozen at the door holding their trays. I clasped my hands under the tablecloth until I could feel them losing blood. The commentator's voice came through the air, jubilant.

"The court has decided. All the prisoners are guilty."

Tonya's tray crashed to the floor. "Hallelujah," she screamed. Adamovich overturned his chair.

Some of the guests vaulted into the air, some slapped each other on the back, some danced around the room kissing everyone—even me.

I pictured Walter Duranty and Ralph Barnes in Moscow pounding their typewriters, rushing to cable the news to New York. Whatever they suspected, few knew that the accused had been tortured, their families threatened if they did not confess. No one knew how many millions Stalin would eventually put to death.

"Nadya," Adamovich's voice rang out, "bring in the vodka."

38

Mid-September and the long Arctic summer days were coming to a close. I suggested to Tonya that we visit the Regional Museum to see its works of art.

On the second floor of the museum, I stopped in my tracks.

Standing at the head of the stairs was a lifesize model of a radiant young Yakut woman. A crimson caftan enriched with beaver covered her slender figure. Rows of silver necklaces encircled her neck, filigree earrings pierced her ears, silver chains cascaded down her bosom and her back, and delicate silver bracelets rode up her arms and around her ankles.

"She's gorgeous," I breathed.

"You have such bourgeois taste." Tonya tried to move away.

"Come on, Tonya. Admit she's beautiful. She could be in *Vogue*."

"Dresses and jewelry like that, they go with when women had no rights. The Revolution changed all that."

I was in no mood to argue. "Let's go to the market," I said.

"Don't you get enough to eat?"

"I've been here so long and I've never been there."

Inside the market, I was prepared for the wooden gates, the earthen floor, the stalls and vendors selling food and fresh flowers and cotton housedresses. But I was not prepared for the chaotic barrage of animal and human smells. Butchers with long knives chased chickens and chopped off their heads. Other butchers with even longer knives slaughtered pigs. Rivers of blood carpeted the ground. Horses brayed, reindeer chewed on straws of grass, dogs romped and whined, while families of Yakuts, Russians, Poles, Chinese, and Tatars sat in wooden carts with their wares. The Russians called this their black market. But it was capitalism, a market economy in a socialist society.

I suddenly had a mad craving for a tomato, spotted a wizened Yakut woman with a faded flower headscarf, squatting on the ground. On a low table before her were six red, round, succulent, mouth-watering, love-kindling tomatoes.

"How much?" I demanded.

"Two rubles each," she said.

With my penknife, I cut the tomato in four quarters with the precision of an engineer and the slowness of a masochist. I put a piece in my mouth, and immediately memories of tomatoes in Brooklyn welled up. Tonya watched me with her arms crossed. I handed her one of the quarters, a peace offering.

"Keep it." She pushed my hand away. Then, as if she had a second thought, she accepted my offering. I watched her broad Slavic chin drip with tomato juice. Flushed with victory, I bought the Yakut woman's whole stock. We were still munching tomatoes when we left the market, walked through town, and stopped in front of the fire station. It was a small wooden building with a tower that soared over all the low houses around it.

We entered to watch the Yakut fireman feed his horse. An antiquated engine stood in the center.

"Are there more fire stations in Yakutsk?" I asked. Could there be just one horse and engine for the whole town?

"This is it," he said. "Our planning people tell me that's all we need."

Tonya and I continued walking.

"You're writing about women," she said. "How about a visit to the bathhouse? It's ladies' day."

I detected an unfamiliar note in her voice. Had the tomatoes softened her?

Soon half-naked Amazons were flogging us with huge leaves in the dimly lit steam room. Three Russian women climbed up on the wet top shelves beside us.

"Of course, you're the American," one of the women said, though I hadn't uttered a word. "How do you like it in Yakutsk?"

"*Khorosho*." [It's good.]

"Are you married?" was her next question.

Tonya scoffed good-naturedly. "Can't you tell she isn't married?"

"How can she tell?" I asked.

"Anyone can tell from your body. Look at the rest of us. We're fat, but you're skinny."

"I'm far from skinny," I said, pinching the roll of unwanted flesh Nadya's meals had pumped around my midriff. "And a lot of married women in America are much skinnier than I am."

"Will you get married some day?" one of the women asked.

"I hope."

"Then maybe you'll be fat too, like us."

Still naked, the three Russian women followed us to the ice-cold shower and then to the locker room, where we began to dress. Sitting on their towels, they flung questions at me. "Is it true in America, if you want an abortion, they take the baby out of your body with a clothes hanger?"

"Abortions are illegal in America," I said. "If a doctor is caught, he can lose his license or go to jail. We're trying to change that so doctors can perform abortions legally."

"When it comes to abortions," she said, "I think we're more advanced than you. Here abortions are legal. It's our best birth control."

"Is it true," another of the women inquired, "that they hang black-skinned people with a rope from a tree?"

"There are lynchings, but only in certain places in the South. There are no lynchings in New York, where I live. And some day we hope the men who hang other men from trees will be tried and sent to jail."

I felt like three people: the American visitor trying to answer their questions honestly, the girl from Brooklyn searching for history, and the journalist imprinting this scene in my brain—sitting in a bathhouse in Siberia talking to naked women as if we were in the sixth floor women's lounge at NYU.

Tonya, now dressed in her floor-length leather coat and boots, stood up. "We have to go home. Adamovich is expecting us for dinner."

One of the naked women came toward me. "Are you ever afraid?"

"I know fear. But I don't let it get in my way."

"*Nichevo* [Never mind]. When you get married and have children, we hope you'll remember this night in Yakutsk."

Tonya telephoned for the horse and wagon that had brought us, and soon we were home regaling Adamovich with our holiday adventures.

Suddenly Nadya burst into the dining room. "Ilya Andreevich, there's a fire near here."

We raced into the courtyard and climbed the ladder to our roof. Red tongues of fire leapt into the sky.

"*Bozhe moi* [My God]." Tonya was breathless. "It's the printing plant."

We dashed down to the street, instantly swallowed in a crowd of people rushing, shouting, weeping. We ran toward the printing plant. Dozens of men were breaking the windows with hammers or their fists and tossing out sheets of type. Some of the lead had already melted. Yakuts, Chinese, old men, even children carried the heavy sheets and piled them in an open space in the center of town.

The flames were moving perilously close to the headquarters

of the Communist party. Pevsnak, the party leader, was on the street, snapping orders to a small army of men who set ladders against the building, climbed to the roof, and spread huge tarpaulins across it. Others dashed into the building and ran out with folders and documents in their arms. But where was the fire engine?

Next, the flames encircled a wooden warehouse stacked with pelts already tied and scheduled for the international fur market in Leningrad. Scores of women holding buckets and pots and pans were tossing water at the warehouse.

The crackling and hissing of the wood became a grisly backdrop for the anguished cries of the people. The one-story wooden houses and log cabins, in close proximity, were igniting each other.

At last, the horse-drawn fire engine came clanging down the road. The Yakut fireman looked like a Roman gladiator, his head protected by a copper helmet. He was standing up, whipping the terrified horse.

He stopped at the printing plant, jumped to the ground, and blew a tiny whistle. "Young men, help." His yell was louder than his whistle. "Help. Help."

A dozen young Russian and Yakut men helped him turn the hose on the flames. I ran toward them. "Let me help. I can do that too," I cried.

"Not you," a man shouted. "You can get hurt. Move, girl, move."

I stood angry and helpless. Within minutes, the water in the engine gave out. The fireman blew his little whistle again. "Everybody, bring water," he wailed. "Men and women, bring water from the Lena."

So now they need me, I thought, racing toward the river and filling pots with water.

But the city was in chaos. People were running helter-skelter with bedding under their arms and bundles of clothes tied to chairs. Pigs romped and groaned and evaded old women who were trying to lasso them.

The fire was moving in a new direction, away from our house. I caught sight of Adamovich helping a Yakut militiawoman direct the traffic of horses and reindeer and open Fords. He took a moment to talk to me. "We have these terrible fires all the time. Tomorrow we'll be counting how many people have lost their homes." He motioned to a car to move on.

"Can I help you?" I asked a trembling old woman.

"Yes, please. Come with me." While we ran, she said, "Last year I lost everything in the fire. The only clothes I had were on my back."

We dashed into a courtyard, entered her cottage, pulled up her tablecloth, and filled it with the few trinkets she cherished.

"We must go now," I said. She looked longingly at her home. With one arm I clutched her samovar and with the other helped her as we ran out to the street. The flames had already reached her courtyard. They were leaping to the sky, lighting up the city.

Yakutsk, the City of the Future, working toward a better world with one antiquated fire engine, was burning.

39

Victor Galishev, the Arctic pilot, helped me climb into his seaplane. I was awkward, weighed down with heavy leather boots and a cotton-padded black raincoat. Two men climbed up after me, and the cabin door was shut. Even in the semidarkness, the two men looked like middle-aged twins in brown leather coats bulging around their waists. I soon learned they were officials in the gold industry.

I was happy and relaxed. It was early afternoon, and I was on my way at last to the Aldan Goldfields.

Two weeks earlier, I had sent a query in cablese to George Cornish at the *Herald Tribune*: THOUSANDS FLYING TO ALDAN BIGGEST SOVIET GOLDRUSH WOULDU LIKE STORY? GRUBER

SOUNDS FIRSTRATE. DO IT, Cornish cabled back.

But I needed permission from the Gold Trust in Moscow. The magic words "Permission granted" had finally arrived this morning.

After three hours of flying over a calm highway of water, we came down to refuel at Churan. The river village looked like Chekhov's pictures of old Siberia—dismal, isolated, desolate.

A gaggle of little boys materialized out of the desolation, barefoot, their noses running, their pants open, brandishing axes as if they were warriors. A solitary seaplane, camouflaged in khaki and green, swooped overhead and landed near us. I was reminded again—as if I could ever forget—that Russia was preparing for war.

"Ready to leave this island paradise?" Galishev grinned mischievously.

"What are we waiting for?" I ran toward the plane.

A ceiling of black clouds pressed down on us. Heavy rain beat against the walls. I could feel Galishev fighting to hold the little craft steady until, at 6:30, we came down in the Aldan River and landed at Tommot. After Churan, Tommot, even in the freezing rain, looked like civilization.

From the plane door, I saw a frontier town of yellow buildings and a yellow highway that stretched into the horizon. Soon a motorboat pulled up to take us to Okulun, a nearby river town, where we were to spend the night.

"Welcome, welcome." A tall man, elegant in a long rubber coat and high rubber boots, helped me out of the launch.

"Kupryanov." Galishev embraced him. "Ruth, meet Alexander Semyonovich Kupryanov, the head of the whole Gold Trust here."

"We are honored by your visit." Kupryanov bowed and then stood erect, proud of his splendid figure and his high position. He had blond hair growing thin, blue eyes, and a mouthful of gold teeth.

A woman who looked as if she had once been a great beauty held out her right hand. "And I am Olga Nikolayevna, his wife." She was still attractive, though overweight. Her straight blond hair straggled over her ears, she had a cigarette in her left hand, and of course the obligatory gold teeth, which had never seemed as luminous as here in the heart of the goldfields.

Pulling my eyes away from their dazzling teeth, I managed to say in Russian, "I'm happy to meet you both."

"Ah, so we can talk Russian," Kupryanov smiled. "I was worried we would not have a language together. I speak Turkestan, Afghanistan, and Kazakstan, but not one European language."

Olga Nikolayevna exploded with laughter. "It's the first time in my life that I hear he speaks Afghanistan."

They each took an arm and rushed me out of the rain to a bright new hotel with a Russian sign that said "House of Culture and Rest."

In the banquet room with a table piled high with food, Kupryanov drew a chair for me and seated himself at my side. Olga Nikolayevna sat facing us, her eyes darting from her husband to me.

"Good dinner? Yes?" he asked.

"Good dinner," I said, welcoming the hot tea with jelly. I asked Kupryanov what kind of people were flocking here in this new gold rush.

"All kinds," he said. "Pioneers. Geologists. Adventurers. Even former criminals, racketeers, gangsters. But of course no speculators. If we catch them, we put them right into prison."

"And do you have political exiles—like in Yakutsk?"

"No," he said blandly.

"No exiles at all?" In Yakutsk I had heard that hundreds of prisoners had died at forced labor in these gold mines.

"We have thieves," he said, "who've been sentenced to five or ten years exile. In 1933 we had two thousand criminals sent here to work the mines. But not any more," he added quickly. "Only about three hundred criminals are left. Some remained after their sentences were served and became many of our best workers."

"Women criminals too?"

I saw Olga narrow her eyes. "If you mean prostitutes, no."

"But I've heard prostitutes were sent to areas being opened—"

She puffed on her cigarette and nodded. "In 1933 they sent seven hundred prostitutes to take care of the men who were building the Baltic White Sea Canal. But no prostitutes were sent here."

Kupryanov laughed. "It's true no prostitutes were sent here, but we don't know how pure everybody is. All types of people flock wherever there's gold."

Olga said meaningfully, "I know quite a few who are not so pure."

He shot a disapproving glance at her and then leaned toward me. "We're making life here *kultura*. Maybe more *kultura* than in the central cities. Tomorrow you'll be able to see everything, the schools, the state farm, the geological institute, the—"

"I'd like to go down in the mines," I interrupted.

"Of course. That's the next day. You're going to stay with us in our house in Nezametny. You're our guest."

Olga stood up. "That Alexander Semyonovich. He never knows when to stop talking." She glared at him. "You've charmed her enough."

Two days later, I was in the goldfields, dressed in a miner's raincoat several sizes too big, a miner's cap, heavy cotton gloves, and leather boots. I felt like a refugee from a Barnum and Bailey act, with a tin candleholder in my hand.

I followed Michael Balakhnin, the thirty-three-year-old shift boss, through a cavernous wet darkness lit only by the miners' candles, stumbling on planks, balancing myself to keep from sliding into puddles of water, bumping into pit-props of wood that sheltered us from the falling debris.

We descended deeper and deeper into the earth, down tall shafts into narrow pits and tunnels where men were chopping away at wet walls with picks and axes, and shoveling their treasures into wheelbarrows.

In the gold rushes in California and Alaska, I thought, men dreamed of becoming instant millionaires. Did they have the same dreams here, I asked Balakhnin.

"They can become very, very rich," he said.

"In a socialist society?"

"The government gives big rewards to anybody who discovers precious metals. But most work from idealism. Our newspapers give them a lot of publicity, especially when they create innovations to increase production. They receive higher wages, longer vacations, and lots of time in rest homes."

"But they get the same advantages when they go to Igarka or Yakutsk," I said. "What makes a gold rush different?" I brushed away the icy brown water dripping on my face and into my notebook.

"It's the word *gold*," he said. "Gold! That's why we now have forty thousand living here. A year ago, we surpassed America; now we want to surpass the South African Rand who produced 400 million dollars' worth of gold last year. We want to become first in the world."

He took my hand. "Let me help you. We're going down into a deep pit. I want you to meet the best worker we have, Simon Vassilyevich Vassilyev. He earns as much as three thousand rubles for twenty-two days of work."

Our candles lit up Simon's face. In the underground shadows his teeth looked like nuggets carved by an expert. "In each pit," Simon explained, "we work as a brigade, with one master. That's me. We even have women masters. I'll show you."

He led us to a pit where two husky women with red headkerchiefs and high boots were working with picks and shovels. They had pink cheeks and welcoming smiles.

"They're two of our best workers," Simon said. "But they have no time to talk." The two women laughed and continued axing away.

We climbed back to the surface. Pulling off the heavy boots, I asked Balakhnin about accidents and miners' diseases.

"We have very few diseases and only one accident, and that was over a year ago," he said, drawing a picture so rosy that I thanked him, left the mine, and prowled through Nezametny. It was the center of the goldfields, lying in a valley with new wooden houses and gardens climbing up both slopes of a mountain. A stream of yellow water, washed down from the hydraulic dredges, hurtled through the town as though to boast of its importance.

Women of all ages were panning in the yellow stream with kitchen pots. Old men and children home from school were digging up the sand and dirt in front of their houses. And, punctuating gold's dominance, a junk heap rose in the very middle of town, on the site where once a dredge had excavated and emptied the earth of gold.

I entered one of the many gold-stores, *Zoloto-skupka*, where people exchanged the gold they had found outside the mines. The shelves were filled with perfumes, cognac, wine, Russian dolls, gold jewelry, silver knives, furs, pure silk from Japan, cloth from England—all the luxuries that gold could buy.

"Gold, gold, gold," I scribbled in my notebook, sitting on a bench outside the gold-store. "I see it being washed, I hear it flowing into troughs, I feel it taking shape until the very air I breathe seems saturated with gold dust. I wonder if Lenin's prophecy will come true—that when communism really comes, gold will be obsolete, used only for toilets and gold teeth."

40

Back in Yakutsk, Sofya Petrovna Sidorova came toward me putting her hand out to mine. "Welcome to our women's conference." She was in her thirties, sturdy, with short, straight black hair and a motherly smile. It was six in the evening and the assembly hall was dimly lit and cold.

"This conference," she said in Russian as she led Tonya and me to chairs near the dais, "is very important for us Yakut women. We used to be less than nothing. Many of us were sold as soon as we were born."

I scrawled her words in my notebook.

"Sold when you were born? Were you slaves?" I smelled a feature story on Yakut women for the *Herald Tribune*.

"It was not slavery," Sofya said. "It was economics. We were sold to families or older men, and we began to work as soon as we could walk. Girls never learned to read. Now every woman here can read and write."

She stretched her strong hands out as if she wanted to make me part of the hundred young Yakut women who were talking, shaking hands, kissing each other's cheeks with the excitement of a woman's convention almost anywhere in the world.

But this was no ordinary woman's convention. These young women were members of an Arctic tribe so long isolated that few Russians and fewer foreigners had ever seen them.

Thousands of miles from Moscow, they were dressed not in reindeer skin and beads but in dark wool skirts, crisp white blouses, and *torbasie*, fur boots. A few wore their black hair in tightly woven braids down their backs. But most had "Siberian fox-trot" haircuts, which suited their serene Asiatic faces far better than mine.

"The future is waiting for us," Sofya said proudly. "We have risen up in our republic. We even have two Yakut women in the Central Executive Committee of the Communist party. I am one of them."

"What decisions do you make?" I asked.

Sofya thought for a few minutes. "Decisions on how to do even more for our women. Too many are still illiterate. The Revolution liberated women in Moscow, in Leningrad, in Odessa. But it took longer to reach us. Now, with education, we have jobs that women never dreamed about before."

I scanned the faces of the young women sitting on hard chairs holding earphones in their ears. I was already fashioning the lead for my story: "Of all the revolutionary changes in the Soviet Arctic, the changes in the lives of Yakut women must surely be among the most spectacular."

"Before the Revolution," Sofya continued, "we girls could not travel from village to village without permission from our husbands or our fathers. Now these delegates have come to Yakutsk without even a chaperone to—"

A hush fell over the hall. Pevsnak, the political boss, and Yefremov, the twenty-three-year-old Yakut secretary of the Komsomol [Young Communist League], took seats at the dais. They were the only men in this convention of Yakut women, but they took over the meeting with greetings from Comrade Stalin and other leaders and with exhortations "to build up our great republic."

"To our youth," Pevsnak shouted. "May they grow like flowers. Hurrah. Hurrah. Hurrah."

The meeting was over.

I shut my notebook in frustration. This was a woman's convention. Why hadn't any of the women spoken?

"Is this the whole conference?" I asked Sofya.

"Oh no. This was the opening session. The conference will go on for four more days when we will learn about each other's lives and how the government can help us. But those meetings will not be open."

"Then may I talk to the women now?"

"Of course." She beckoned a group to join us. "I will ask them to tell you what they do."

Quickly I reopened my notebook.

"I drive a tractor," one woman said in Yakut while Sofya translated into Russian. One by one, they spoke up. "I work in a factory." "I am a hunter." "I'm a shipbuilder." "I herd reindeer."

A round young woman with a strong voice moved close to me. "I do the kind of heavy work in a fur factory that only men did before. Do you know why we girls came here? To prove that we nonparty women, who work like men, are just as good workers as party members."

"You see," Sofya explained, "Stalin has taught us there are two kinds of Bolsheviks, the party ones and the nonparty ones. I am a party Bolshevik but all the girls at this convention are nonparty. They're politically conscious, but not politically active."

A woman with a thin face and a high brow accentuated by her fox-trot haircut, spoke next. "My name is Katerina Vassilyevna Vinokurova." She wore a man's white shirt, a red belt around her waist, and on her lapel a pin with the order of Stakhanov. Stakhanov was a miner whose output in the Donets coal mine had been so extraordinary that Stalin had made him a national hero.

"I am a hunter," Katerina said. "For six months in the winter I hunt fox and ermine and white rabbit. I just earned 2500 rubles

[$500]. In the summer, I am the director of the kindergarten in my kolkhoz, you know that's what we call a collective farm. I live in Temtor in the north. I'm twenty-nine and I have no husband."

"So you put career ahead of marriage?"

"What do you think? Of course. I want to better myself. I never went to school as a child. But five years ago I went to the adult school in the kolkhoz and now I read and write in Yakut. I'm nonparty but I believe in socialism."

"What has socialism done for women hunters?" I asked.

Her face broke into a smile, as if the naive American had finally asked the right question.

"One," she counted on her fingers like the teacher she was. "Socialism has made women equal with men. Two, women have a fuller life now. Three, socialism has improved the fur industry and women have gained from it so they can live a good life."

"And what problems do woman hunters have?"

"Problems?" She shrugged her shoulders. "The same problems every woman has. No different. But if you ask me what I would like to do I will tell you. I will hunt for two more years. Then I absolutely would like to study at the fur technical school and become a fur specialist. I want to give an example to other hunters. I want to teach them the Stakhanovite method through scientific hunting and breeding."

Sofya held up her hand. "Tovarishchi, wait a moment." She turned to me. "Ruth, why not come with us to the House of the Peasant, where some of us are staying? There are so many questions we would like to ask you."

Tonya, who never left my side, interrupted truculently. "It's too late."

"It's only seven o'clock, Tonya."

"I'm hungry," Tonya insisted, "and you must be starved."

"If you're hungry, please go home," I said. "Sonya will translate for me."

Tonya's stout body wilted. "If you stay, you know I must stay."

The three of us set out, Tonya on one side of me and Sofya on the other, followed by a small army of laughing and giggling young Yakut women. The Arctic sun washed gold on the wood and mud city.

"We were lucky to get rooms here," Sofya said as we entered the House of the Peasant, a rambling hotel in a large courtyard behind high gates. "Most of the rooms are for a convention of Stakhanovite hunters."

She led us into a reading room where half a dozen men, hunters dressed like American Indians in chino pants and colorful shirts, sat at tables leafing through books. "Some of them," Sofya whispered, "have just learned to read."

Within minutes the room overflowed as young women delegates and Stakhanovite hunters filled the hard chairs, sat on windowsills, and crowded behind each other in the doorway. Two male interpreters flanked us at a square head table, while portraits of the two ever-present father figures, Lenin at one end and Stalin at the other, hovered over us.

Sofya opened the gathering in Yakut and waited after each sentence for the interpreters to translate into Russian. "It is a great honor to welcome our first American visitor to this formal get-together. You are our guest. So we beg you to ask us the first questions. What would you like to know?"

I spoke in German, Tonya translated into Russian, and the two interpreters took turns translating into Yakut.

"I would like to get a picture of your lives," I said, "so that I can tell my countrymen something about your culture. For instance, Sofya Petrovna told me that before the Revolution girls were sold as soon as they were born. The Revolution is now nineteen years old. How has it changed your lives?"

The first one to stand up was an elderly-looking man, scarcely five feet tall, with a brown, oval face, small beady eyes, and a head shaved clean.

"I am an Evenkee," he said, "from the Ust-Yana District northeast of here. My name is Baramishkin, and I am fifty-three years old. Until I was eighteen, I worked as a hunter for kulaks, they're

293

the rich ones. Many of them are now serving in labor camps. I earned 150 rubles [$30] for a whole year."

He rested his hands on his bald head, as though he were addressing a tribal meeting. "Now I'm a member of a kolkhoz and our whole collective farm earns 990,000 rubles a year. Today I myself got 15,000 rubles from the Fur Trust in Yakutsk for my skins, and another 1,000 rubles from the kolkhoz. I earn more than an engineer. I work. Work makes us happy. Work gives us enough money for everything we want."

I hoped he would sit down. But he held the floor.

"About my own life," he said, removing his hands from his scalp and bending his body back and forth, "I had no education when I was a boy. Now I have seven children and they are all educated, two are even in the village council. Before, my children never saw an airplane. Now I ride to Yakutsk in an airplane. Before, I was a nomad; I rode to the tundra with the reindeer so they could feed on moss and lichens. We lived in a tent made of reindeer skin. Now I have two houses in the kolkhoz."

"And the mother of your children, what did she do while you were hunting?" I asked, trying to steer the conversation.

"She came with me on the hunt, of course. She sewed the skins of the tent, she set the tent up when we stopped in the tundra, she fixed the fireplace in the center of the floor, she took care of the cooking, she made the sleeping places, and when we started to move again, she rolled the tent up and put it on the reindeer sledge."

"Who do you think worked harder? You when you put out traps or your wife?"

"Women are supposed to work harder," he said. "That's what women were made for."

The Yakut women made no comment.

The hunter took his seat, obviously pleased with his story. Another man stood up. "I am a Yakut from the Bulun region. My name is Ilya Prokopovich Kaledesnikov, and I too am fifty-three years old."

294

He laughed at the coincidence, displaying a mouth of tobacco-stained teeth. A heavy black mustache rode across his lips.

"Three years ago, in 1933, I joined the kolkhoz," he said. "Before, in the old days the traders would sell us a pot in exchange for all the foxes that fit into it. Or they would sell us a shotgun; they would stand the gun up straight and then lay the skins of the fox or ermine or sable or squirrel in a pile. And when the skins reached the top of the gun, they said, 'That's how much the gun costs.' We'd have to give them more furs again for the bullets."

He waited for the translators to relay his story. Then, brushing his mustache with his fingers, he reminisced about his past. "Some years ago I married and had a son. But my wife died, and my son ran away. He became a *besprizornik* [a young vagabond]. I didn't see him for years. But just now in Bulun I met him again. Now he's a teacher."

A murmur of admiration swept through the room.

"Now I have a new wife, but no children. My wife is fifty years old, and she is my helper in everything. She cleans the white fox, she takes the fat and meat out of the ears and nose and the bones from the tail. She is very happy. She doesn't have to go on the hunt anymore. I go without her."

"Does she like being home alone?" I asked.

"She likes it better when I'm home." His body shook with laughter.

More men stood up with similar stories. Candles, placed on the reading room tables, lit up their faces.

"Won't the women talk?" I whispered to Sofya. "I'd like to hear their stories."

"They are shy," she said, "especially in front of the men. Perhaps you can talk to them after the men go."

"Then let them ask me questions now," I said.

A man in a bright orange shirt and suspenders holding up his chinos asked the first question. "What kind of government do you have in America?"

Briefly I explained our government and the Constitution.

"Is it a good constitution?" he asked.

"Yes. Many other countries have used it for their model."

He shook his head. "How can you have a good constitution when you have differences between the classes?"

Before I could answer, Tonya called out. "It's a bad constitution. Capitalism is so corrupt it wouldn't permit a good constitution."

"Please tell the people," I turned to the interpreter closest to me, "her words are not mine. Please tell them that my constitution guarantees life and liberty and everyone's right to happiness."

He translated, and I waited for the next question. But Tonya was not to be silenced. "How can you guarantee these things when you have exploitation, when you have unemployment and corruption?"

"Tonya, I must remind you, you are not my spokesman."

She raised her massive body from the chair. "We have no right to speak of political things. This isn't a political meeting. There is no political leader here."

The nonpolitical meeting ended abruptly.

41

A Yakut teenager named Natasha handed me a navy blue jumpsuit and giggled as I hoisted it up over my American plaid skirt and white jacket.

"Now you're a glider pilot." Natasha thrust a green leather pilot's cap on my head. "And you can even fly."

There were no mirrors in the camp, but a circle of young Yakuts, all in blue jumpsuits and green leather caps, trying to suppress their laughter, told me I looked more like a clown than a pilot.

Gregory, one of Adamovich's young Russian assistants, handsome in crisp navy whites, had driven me outside Yakutsk to a training camp for glider pilots and parachute jumpers. There was a sense of heightened adventure in the air.

Two dozen young people were spending their three weeks' vacation from their farms and factories and offices, learning to glide, jump from towers with parachutes, shoot rifles, attend classes on politics and on the war they knew was coming, click their heels, and salute each time an officer appeared. The youngest was seventeen, the oldest, twenty. They had all signed up with the *Osoa-*

viakhim, an acronym for the formidably named Society for the Promotion of the Development of the Airforce and Chemical Defense.

Nine army pup tents were guarded by trees as if we were in a combat zone. Wooden gliders seesawed over our heads. A khaki gas mask, the only one in the camp, and a bell and lantern hung like warning symbols on a watchtower.

"You know how a glider works?" Natasha challenged me as we walked toward a small, white wooden plane sitting on the ground. It looked like a toy model assembled by bright students.

"I have no idea," I said, aware I was incurring her disapproval.

"It's just like an airplane only it has no motor, so it has to be launched."

She reached for my hand and placed it around a tow rope attached to the glider. Her teenagers lined up behind me and grasped the rope.

"Pull," Natasha commanded. I sucked in my stomach and pulled.

"Harder, harder," she bellowed. I pulled until the rope cut into my palms. "Run," she cried. "Run. Run." Suddenly, with a sense of exhilaration, I felt the wind we had created hit my face. The tow rope, released by the pilot, slackened and dropped in our hands. Without a sound, the white plane rose on the wind and dipped and flowed and careened like a carefree child dancing on air.

"How do you feel?" asked Natasha.

"As if I could stretch my arms and fly."

"Good," she said without smiling.

I felt I had to add more. "It's like—like a special joy of living."

She frowned at me. "Some day we'll be landing behind enemy fields in these gliders. We'll carry machine guns and motorcycles and tents. We'll disrupt airports and railroads." She seemed intoxicated with danger and death. "We'll terrorize civilians, we'll demoralize troops. Would you call that 'joy of living'?"

I shook my head. Sure, they're raising the standard of living of these young people, I thought. They're teaching Yakut children how to keep their bodies clean, how to combat TB and trachoma, how to sit in chairs and eat with knives and forks and sleep in beds instead of on the floor.

My earlier visit to a Yakut boarding school flashed through my head.

"Paper can talk," a Russian teacher had said, startling her eight-year-old students.

"How can you talk with paper?" a little girl named Tayet-Khema had asked. "You talk with your tongue."

Tagrai, a feisty eight-year-old boy, scoffed. "Dogs use their tongues also to bark and to lick water. But dogs can't talk. Only man can talk."

"I will prove to you," said the teacher, "that paper can talk."

She sat at her desk. "I'm writing a letter to a friend near here. I am asking her to send me a pair of reindeer boots. This afternoon, dogsleds will carry my letter to my friend. Tomorrow evening the fur boots will arrive. This is how paper talks."

Now, looking at the exuberant faces of the young people watching the glider come in for a landing, I felt a knot of pain in my stomach. These Yakuts are the new generation, I thought. They know paper can talk. They may go on to become engineers and doctors and leaders of their people. They may not die from TB and measles and smallpox and the white man's diseases. But they may die from war. The war I had seen Hitler preparing in Germany.

A slim Yakut girl climbed a ladder and poised herself atop a high ledge. I thought I saw fear as she looked around before she opened her parachute. In seconds, she leaped, landed on the ground, untangled herself and stood up, her face radiant with victory.

She was followed by a boy who bit his lips and held his body rigid. Then he jumped and, once safe on the ground, waited proudly for his next turn up the ladder.

"Do you train only for war?" I asked Natasha.

"What kind of question is that? We use gliders and parachutes in the Arctic wherever airplanes can't land. When hunters or fishermen are caught on ice floes, we drop food and medicines to them until they can be picked up. Doctors parachute down and save lives. You call that training only for war?"

I was abashed.

It was evening in Yakutsk when, back from the training camp, Gregory and I walked to the Park of Culture and Rest.

On top of a white pavilion, two airplane models were attached to a half-globe that depicted the northern part of the world, as if it were the only part of the world that mattered. The toylike planes seemed poised to fly out to the east and the west. Below them, a red banner with white Russian letters exhorted, "Fly higher than all. Fly faster than all. Fly farther than all."

"Stop a minute," I said to Gregory, "I want to copy the words on that red banner, 'Fly higher than all.' "

"Do you always have to be a reporter?" he complained.

"That banner—it's like tom-toms beating for war."

"Come on." He took my arm and squeezed it against his side. "This is a night for dancing and singing."

"First the camp and now the banner. I keep thinking of Germany. Every day Hitler makes new and terrible laws. He marches across the Rhineland, and no one stops him."

Gregory looked down at me. "You have friends in Germany?"

"Many. Especially Jewish friends. They can't go to the university. They're thrown out of their jobs. Germans can't marry or sleep with anybody unless they are 'racially pure Aryans.' "

Gregory put his arm around my shoulder. "They're madmen. You're right, they should be stopped. But why are you ruining our evening?"

"Forgive me," I said, drawing away from him.

We were walking through the carefully manicured grounds of the park. Evergreen trees were festooned with paper lanterns and bunting. Yakut women strolled, graceful and erect, in white dresses, their bronze faces shining, their jet-black hair catching the last light in the sky. Some carried parasols like women on a summer day in New Orleans. Young men in white pants and white shirts who had exchanged their soft reindeer or heavy leather boots for dusty store shoes walked as if their shoes did not fit. Old men sat on benches peacefully smoking pipes and playing chess and checkers. Children ate American-style Eskimo pies.

"Gregory," I said suddenly. "The training camp this morning was preparing for war. Aren't you worried sometimes that you may become like the Germans? Goose-stepping down the streets? Herding people into internment camps?"

"We're too civilized for that."

"But that banner," I insisted. " 'Fly higher than all, Fly faster than all.' Is it telling your people to go out and conquer?"

"You're so far from Europe and Asia," he said. "You sit so nice and safe between your two oceans that you can afford to want peace. We would like peace too, but we have to be prepared. War may be right around the corner. We turned Napoleon back. We can turn Hitler and Hirohito back too."

"I see those young people this morning flying and jumping and—and dying."

He squeezed my arm. "Ruth, let's forget death and war for tonight."

We walked toward a small mound where a group of six Yakut dancers had formed a circle and begun a kind of slow fox-trot, swaying, one step forward left, one backward right. Soon about a hundred Yakut men and women, old and middle-aged and young, were stamping the ground, arms interlocked in a giant circle, singing as they danced. There were no drums, no musical instruments. They touched each other as they swayed.

A tall, elderly Yakut in Western clothes and steel-rimmed glasses, who looked like a college professor, walked toward me. "Ah, the American journalist. Can I help you?"

"What are they singing?"

"They're singing of their happiness," he said. "We call this dance *oi-yokhur*. It's our national Yakut dance, to show the cultural happiness of our people."

He pointed to a strong-faced man with a powerful body. "That man is the leader. He makes up the song, chants the words, and the others repeat what he says."

"What is he saying now?"

He listened for a few minutes. "He's singing of the glorification of industry and the building of socialist culture in Yakutsk."

"You mean this happy dance is a political exercise?"

He put his fingers to his lips and listened to the singers again.

The dance was growing faster as more Yakuts joined the circle. Despite the shuffling of feet and swaying of bodies, the people's faces seemed serious and taciturn, as passive as faces carved on a mountain.

"They're singing now," he said, "of how badly they lived in the olden days and how well they're beginning to live now. They're singing of how culture is growing, how industry is growing, how material goods are increasing."

"What if a leader decided to sing a song of how good the old ways were—?"

He laughed. "I once heard of a leader singing that kind of song here in the park. But the circle threw him out and took a new leader."

"Was he arrested?"

"No. When our people dance like this, they're free. There are no police around. They dance whenever they feel the mood. Sometimes they dance in the daytime, sometimes at night, chanting and dancing. Sometimes, in places like Olekma, not too far from here, they chant only two words all during the dance."

"And those two words?"

He reached for my notebook, flipped it open, and stopped at a page titled "YAKUT SHAMANS." He did not look surprised.

In Latin script, he wrote, "Ehiekej-chuckaj."

"And they mean . . . ?"

"Happiness."

"Did the Yakut shamans dance and sing like this when they cured people?"

He shot a swift glance at Gregory, who seemed absorbed in watching the dancers. "There are no shamans today," he said.

"But before . . . ?"

"You must realize I don't believe in shamanism. But I do believe that happiness in dancing and singing can cure diseases. Why do you ask? Are you interested in healing?"

"I'm interested in how shamans heal."

"Then ask me your questions."

"How did the shamans use dancing to relieve pain?"

"They danced to drive out the evil spirits that caused the pain of illness and disease. They danced when their souls traveled to other worlds, looking for power and the knowledge to heal. They danced to purify themselves before they could begin the healing."

I felt a rush of people behind us. The young men and women of the glider camp, still wearing their blue jumpsuits, had entered the park and now climbed the mound. The dancers smiled and extended their hands to welcome them into the circle.

Natasha spotted me, broke ranks, and ran to my side. "Join us," she cried. She pulled a red scarf off her neck, draped it over me, and, holding my right hand, raced back up the mound. A glider pilot put his hand out and drew me into the circle.

I danced, excited and exhilarated, one step forward left, one backward right. The red scarf billowed behind me as if it were a parachute lifting me in the air. As we whirled by, Gregory stood outside the circle, pouting.

Someone tapped my shoulder. It was the scholarly Yakut.

"I wish you good vision," he murmured. Before I could break out of the circle to thank him, he had vanished.

42

The days were growing short and cold. Soon I would have to return to America. I wanted one more interview. I had heard about a wise 104-year-old Yakut woman living in a Yakut kolkhoz.

"How do I get there?" I asked Kuzmin, the shy young Yakut chairman of the People's Commissariat for Health.

"I will drive you to Kallandarshvil myself," he said.

Early the next morning we sat in the rear of his open car. The sun, beating down on us, burnished his copper-gold skin. I looked out at the landscape of grassland dappled in sunlight. We were traveling through the northern steppes of the Mongolian Empire that Genghis Khan had conquered in the thirteenth century.

I could almost see the Mongolian tyrant, like a medieval Hitler, with *his* hordes of warriors, murdering thousands as he swept out of China across Asia into Europe.

Suddenly, startled out of my reverie, I was flung to the roof of the car. The chauffeur, undoubtedly a descendant of Genghis Khan, was hurtling us through dense fields of tall grass. He stopped abruptly inside the kolkhoz.

It seemed symbolic that my last interview in Siberia should be in a collective farm that combined new Russia with old Yakutia. Brand-new frame houses and weatherbeaten cabins lined the main mud street, and beyond the houses, fitting into the ancient landscape of steppes and far horizons, were reindeer tents and native yurts, caked with mud and dung and latticed with struts of wood.

I was delighted when two Yakut women in white cotton housedresses, white head-kerchiefs and high boots, carrying their babies, stepped out of a yurt followed by three Yakut men in Russian shirts. I promised I would send them copies of the photos I took, and later, from New York, I did.

The director hurried toward us. "Tovarishch Kuzmin," he cried, "why didn't you prepare us that you were coming?"

Kuzmin patted him on the shoulder. "Don't worry, Federov. I wanted the American journalist to see how things are when we're not prepared."

No doubt, a planned spontaneous meeting. I was prepared to play the game with them.

"She wants to talk to some of your women," Kuzmin explained my visit.

"You don't want to hear about our boarding school with eighty children and our dairy with windows and six hundred cows who give a thousand liters of milk a year, and next year we—?"

"No, thank you. I would like to meet Marfa Mikhailovna."

He led the way to a yellow frame house.

"Please come in," a beautifully preserved woman with an Eskimo-like face said graciously. She wore dangling gold earrings, a gay calico-printed dress, a kerchief around her head, and reindeer boots trimmed with white fur. But her eyes were clouded. I did not need to ask. She had the curse of the Yakuts. Trachoma.

She sat on a hard chair in her grandson's house with the self-confidence of a matriarch. "I am the mother of twenty children," she said proudly. Kuzmin translated her words from Yakut. She spoke no Russian.

"Twenty children," I gasped.

305

She bent toward me, trying to decipher my face. "We gave birth like cattle, right on the mud floor, sometimes with moss for bedding. Nobody counted, nobody knows how many women died at childbirth, nobody knows how many of our babies died."

"Twenty children," I repeated. The picture of this beautiful matriarch in labor on a mud floor made me shudder.

"It was a hard life," she rubbed her eyes. "I was an orphan. I didn't have to be sold; my uncle took me to his house. I worked for him without pay, though he was a rich man, and he married me off very young. My husband was a poor boy who had to work three years for my uncle. That was the price men had to pay to buy a wife."

She scrutinized me again through her clouded eyes. "You have children?" Her dangling gold earrings caught the sun peeking through her window.

"No. I'm not married, Marfa Mikhailovna, and I have no children."

"You sick?" she asked. "You can't have children?"

"I'm not sick. I'm sure I can have children—some day."

I glanced around the two-room house with its kitchen-dining room and single bedroom. We were sitting on straight chairs in a circle, a table with a white cloth was behind us, a one-page Yakut newspaper was tacked to the wall. The wood floor was spotless.

Suddenly I was back in our kitchen-dining room in Brooklyn. "Nu," I could hear Mama prodding. "So when are you going to settle down? Nearly twenty-five. You want to be an old maid?" Had I traveled more than eleven thousand miles to find another Jewish mother?

In her culture, a family and children were the sum of her life, as they were in Mama's culture. For both of them, I was wasting the best years of my life.

"If I had children, Marfa Mikhailovna," I tried to explain myself, "I would be home nursing them, bathing them. I wouldn't be in your house today." I wanted her to feel the warmth I felt toward her. "I would never have met you."

306

"Don't have twenty children," she said, "but don't wait too long."

She rubbed her eyes again. "Come closer."

I moved my chair beside her and looked into her opaque eyes. Blindness, I had read somewhere, was so common among the Yakuts that often of the five to ten people living in a yurt only one could see.

Kuzmin saw my concern. "Trachoma is a bacteria, and a whole family can infect each other."

Marfa closed her eyes. I wondered if she was dozing off.

"It comes from filth," Kuzmin went on. "In my health department, we're trying to teach people to keep their bodies and their houses clean, to bathe, to change their underwear at least every month."

"Every month!" I exclaimed.

"What does he say?" Marfa was not asleep.

Kuzmin good-naturedly translated into Yakut for her and back into Russian for me.

"Underwear!" she repeated. Her body rocked with laughter. "Who talks of underwear? We wore pants made of leather and six or seven dresses on top of each other. We didn't take them off sometimes for six months. We smelled like bad fish."

She rose from her chair. She was heavy and rounded, yet she seemed to glide on her reindeer boots as if she were moving soundlessly through a forest. She made her way to the table, cut a thick slice of black bread, and returned to her chair. "Eat it. I baked it myself." She squinted her eyes, trying to watch me.

I smelled its sweet aroma and bit into it. "It's delicious."

"I knew you would like it. Before, I ate food made from birchbark. Now I eat bread. That's why I live so long."

"And your children? Do they also live long?"

Tears rolled out of her eyes.

"All of them are dead. Only their children are alive."

Unable to talk, I reached for her hand. Her brown skin was thin and almost transparent, her knuckles gnarled like the rings on an old oak tree. She had been born in 1832. She had lived through a hundred years of Russian history. She seemed to embody the whole cycle of life, bearing twenty children, feeding them, nurturing them, healing them when they were sick, then burying them all.

"Marfa Mikhailovna." I finally trusted my voice again. "When your children got sick, who helped you? Was it a shaman?"

"Oh yes," she leaned toward me again.

Federov and Kuzmin looked uneasily at each other and then at Marfa. In the new order, shamans, like priests and rabbis, were enemies, opiates for the people.

"We believed in the shamans," Marfa said, as Kuzmin continued to translate. "Years ago when the missionaries came, they told us the shamans were no good. The missionaries would come around and baptize us with vodka and tell us that now we were good Christians. We let them baptize us every time they came. We had fun fooling them."

She smiled as if the memory of those days still delighted her. "When we went out hunting and fishing, we didn't pray to the Christian God, we prayed to the spirits of our ancestors like the shaman told us. And when we got sick, the shaman beat his drum and we had secret songs and secret dances and that's how we got better."

Federov seemed alarmed that I was writing her words down. "You know, of course, the shamans were nothing but magicians. Isn't that so, Marfa?"

"Of course," she said. "I got very little good from them. And now I know that the shamans told us only lies."

Federov breathed relief.

A smile played on Marfa's lips. I sensed she was still having fun fooling the new missionaries, even without vodka.

She rose again from her chair, glided to the second room, and returned carrying something that looked like a small Viking boat.

It was a cradle—an ingenious cradle—made of birchbark carved to fit a baby's body. It had thin leather straps to tie it to a reindeer's antlers when the family traveled, and reindeer-bone bars hung from the sides to rock the baby when they pitched their tent. Under the baby's bottom was a soft smooth ledge of birchbark with a hole, and under the hole a wooden pan with a sluice leading out to a birchbark potty!

"It has its own irrigation system," I laughed, thinking Yakut babies would never need diapers.

"You like it?" Marfa asked.

"It's a wonderful piece of engineering."

"It's for you."

"Oh no, no. Really, I can't accept it."

Kuzmin whispered to me in Russian, "You would humiliate her if you don't take it. If a guest admires something, it must be given to him."

"Then let me pay for it."

"That would not be *kultura*."

I grasped her warm hand again. "I will cherish this cradle all my life and if I ever have children—"

The sly smile spread across her lips again. "Who knows?" she said, as I kissed her 104-year-old cheek.

It was time to go home.

I opened the duffel bag and began to pack.

First came the notebooks, dated and indexed by subject matter. They were the timetable of my life. They would keep memories fresh, memories of people speaking in their own voices, of experiences I hoped I would never forget.

Next came the film to be developed in New York, and finally the clothes I would need to get home. I had already given the rest to Nadya, who pranced through the house on Cuban heels and American dresses in sheer ecstasy.

I hugged Nadya, shook hands with Tonya and Adamovich, took off with Galishev, flying back to Irkutsk, and from there to Europe. At Le Havre, I boarded the SS *Normandie*, grateful for the respite and the calm that water gave me.

Pacing the deck, I asked myself the old questions: What had the experiences in Germany and the Arctic meant for me? Had they given me new depth, new understanding of people, new faith in myself? Had they made me a better human being?

No, they had not made me a better human being. I still had all my limitations and faults. But they *had* given me new understanding and a little more faith in myself. I was bringing home the thoughts and emotions and sensibilities I had taken with me, but now they were sharpened and intensified.

Someday I hoped I would marry and have children. But not yet. I wanted to go on traveling, exploring, searching for history, trying to capture in words and film this world on the brink of chaos.

"Think with your heart," Edward Steichen, the great photographer, once advised me. "Take pictures with your heart."

I was trying to live by his advice. To write with my heart. To think and speak with my heart. To be adventurous, to be an activist, to be a rebel, to be compassionate and, most of all, to be a *mensch*—a decent human being. Only then would I be ready to become a mother.

"In the beginning was the Word." I loved words. I loved writing and speaking with a passion, and for the rest of my life, I would go on doing both and never ask for special treatment as a woman. But I would always see as a woman, feel as a woman, and write as a woman.

Sixteen years later, after covering wars and bringing a thousand refugees to America, I would use the Yakut cradle that my 104-year-old friend, Marfa Mikhailovna, had given me.

Index

Acknowledgments

Many people have helped in the writing of this book, among them Peggy Brooks, Dr. Irving and Fannie Gruber, Dr. Alice Ginott-Cohn, Henny Haas, Nina Kogan, Kathaleen and Dan Levin, Edna Lonstein, Luisa Herz Leopold, Aïda Lovell, the late Peggy Mann, Celia Michaels, Dr. David Michaels, Sylvia Miller, Rabbi Judah Nadich, Barbara Seaman, Dr. Samuel and Betty Sobel, Dava and Art Sobel, Dr. Penelope Russianoff, Helene B. Weintraub, my agent Sherry Arden, my editor Pat Kossman, and my good friend Susan Shapiro and her writer's workshop. To all those who helped, I give thanks for their wise suggestions and for sharing their time and memories.